I0729576

ART

RULES

ART ——— RULES

HOW GREAT ARTISTS THINK, CREATE AND WORK

CASSIE PACKARD

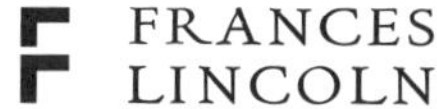
FRANCES LINCOLN

CONTENTS

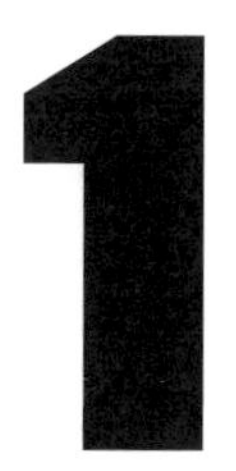

THINK LIKE AN ARTIST

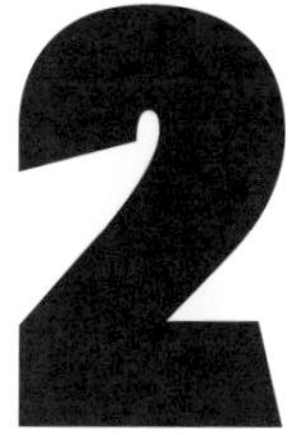

MAKE LIKE AN ARTIST

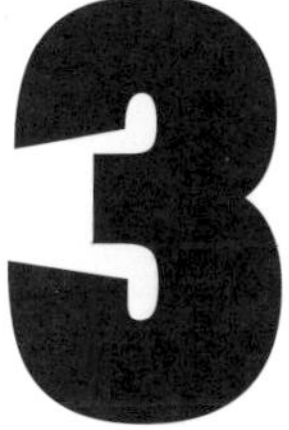

WORK LIKE AN ARTIST

INTRODUCTION

I am not a visual artist. But as an art historian and art writer living in perpetual dialogue with artists' works and writings - and, increasingly, in direct conversation with artists themselves, at all points in their careers - I am fortunate enough to have a window onto a diversity of artists' practices: the many ways in which artists approach, think through and wrestle with the problem, privilege and necessity of creating art. Whether through a spirited written credo or singular artwork, a repeated action or the long arc of a lifetime of work, artists generously offer up frameworks for - and pose questions about - making and being. This book is premised on the belief that those frameworks and questions merit our attention and even have the capacity to change our lives.

The artists whose disparate (and sometimes directly conflicting) stances and strategies appear in dialogue in this book hail from the eighteenth century to the bleeding edge of the present day. They are associated with movements ranging from Suprematism and Die Brücke to Neo-Concretism and process art, and media as varied as painting, textiles, sculpture, video, photography and performance. I have separated the examples that comprise this book - which can be read in any direction or manner you please - into three sections. The first is devoted to the ways in which artists think about art: how they conceive of its function or nature, how they approach being an artist and how they integrate art into their lives. The second section is focused on the process of making, from locating initial inspiration to executing and completing a work. The final portion of the book is oriented towards professional practice and spans maintaining a studio, seeking out mentorship, managing roadblocks and determining what a successful practice means to you.

The book's title, *Art Rules*, is something of a provocation. There are so many ways to make art and be an artist beyond the parameters of these pages, including the immeasurable possibilities that have yet to be discovered. And no artist can be encapsulated in a single work, a quote or a couple of paragraphs; the threads of artists' practices that I have chosen to pull out and hold up for examination are invariably part of a much larger picture.

It is my hope that this book will act as an invitation or entry point, not only to various ways of thinking and working as an artist, but also to more sustained engagement with the artists whose work or ideas excite you.

Cassie Packard

THINK
LIKE AN ARTIST

ON THE FOLLY & OCCASIONAL WISDOM OF GIVING ARTISTS ADVICE

AT SOME POINT MOST ARTISTS ENCOUNTER OTHER PEOPLE'S NOTIONS OF HOW TO MAKE ART OR BE AN ARTIST, WHICH MANIFEST IN EVERYTHING FROM TECHNICAL RECOMMENDATIONS TO SPIRITUAL GUIDANCE TO LECTURES ON ART HISTORY. HERE, ARTISTS CONTEMPLATE THEIR RELATIONSHIPS WITH ADVICE, RULES AND CONVENTION.

ADVICE SHOULDN'T COME FROM OTHER PEOPLE

Your own vision is the one that matters.

When asked as part of an interview series by the Louisiana Museum of Modern Art in Denmark what advice she would give to young artists, Japanese installation artist, sculptor, painter, performance artist and fashion designer **Yayoi Kusama** was adamant in her response. 'I believe that advice shouldn't come from other people but that each person should gain a direction for oneself,' she declared. 'My wish for you is to explore yourself and find a marvellous view,' she added.

Kusama, who has resided at a Tokyo psychiatric hospital for the better part of her illustrious seven-decade art career, has consistently marched to the beat of her own drum, producing work that reflects experiences and visions that are uniquely her own. At the age of ten, Kusama began to contend with hallucinations in which the world around her dissolved into polka dots, unsettling yet generative episodes that suggested interconnection among all things. The artist would go on to visually explore the obliterative effects of this endless field of dots, grappling with the personal obsessions and private neuroses that the allover pattern engaged as she tapped into the infinitude that it made accessible.

The artist's distinct vision has served as a driving force in media-spanning work across the subsequent decades: from the intricate 'Infinity Nets', an ongoing series of paintings begun in 1958, to *Kusama's Self-Obliteration*, a 1968 experimental film in which she painted polka dots on her environment, to the 'Infinity Mirror Rooms', immersive, reflective installations that she has been producing since 1965.

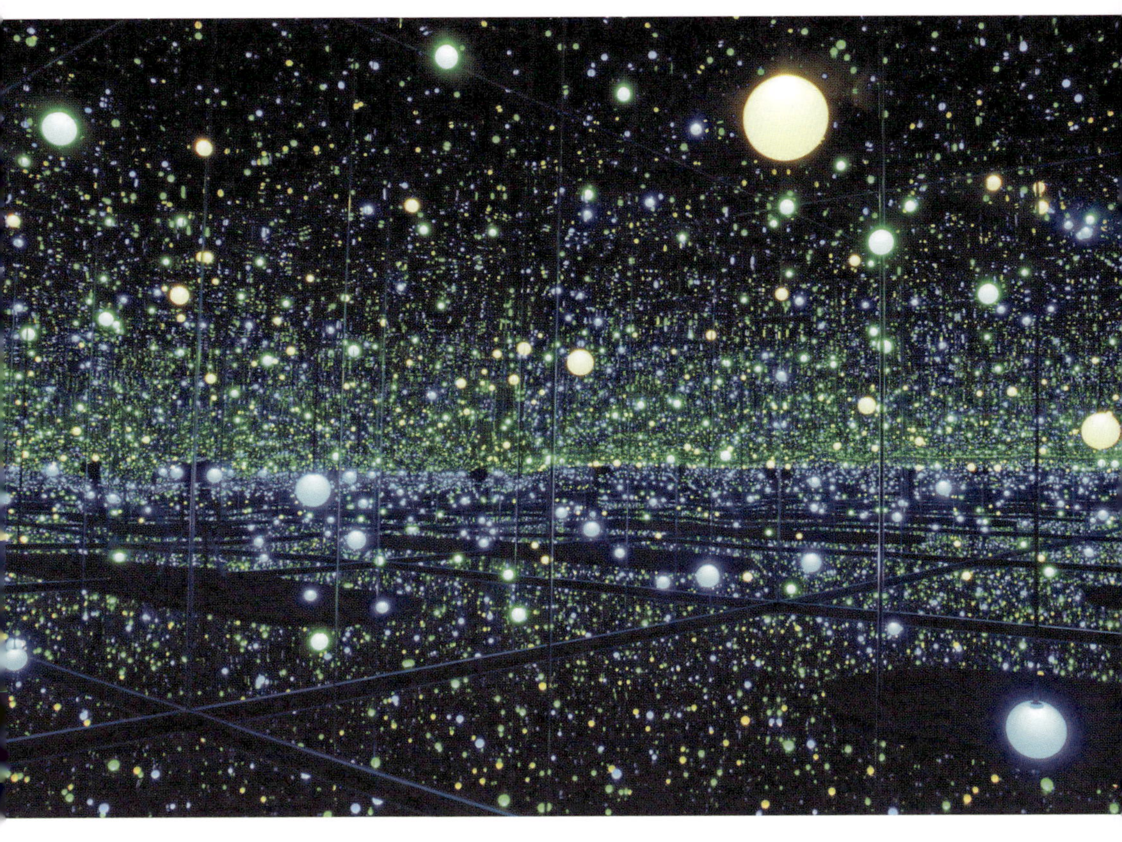

Yayoi Kusama, Gleaming Lights of the Souls, 2008. Mixed media, 415 x 415 x 287.4 cm (163⅜ x 163⅜ x 113⅛ in).

'I HAVE A FLOOD OF IDEAS IN MY MIND. I JUST FOLLOW MY VISION.'

YAYOI KUSAMA

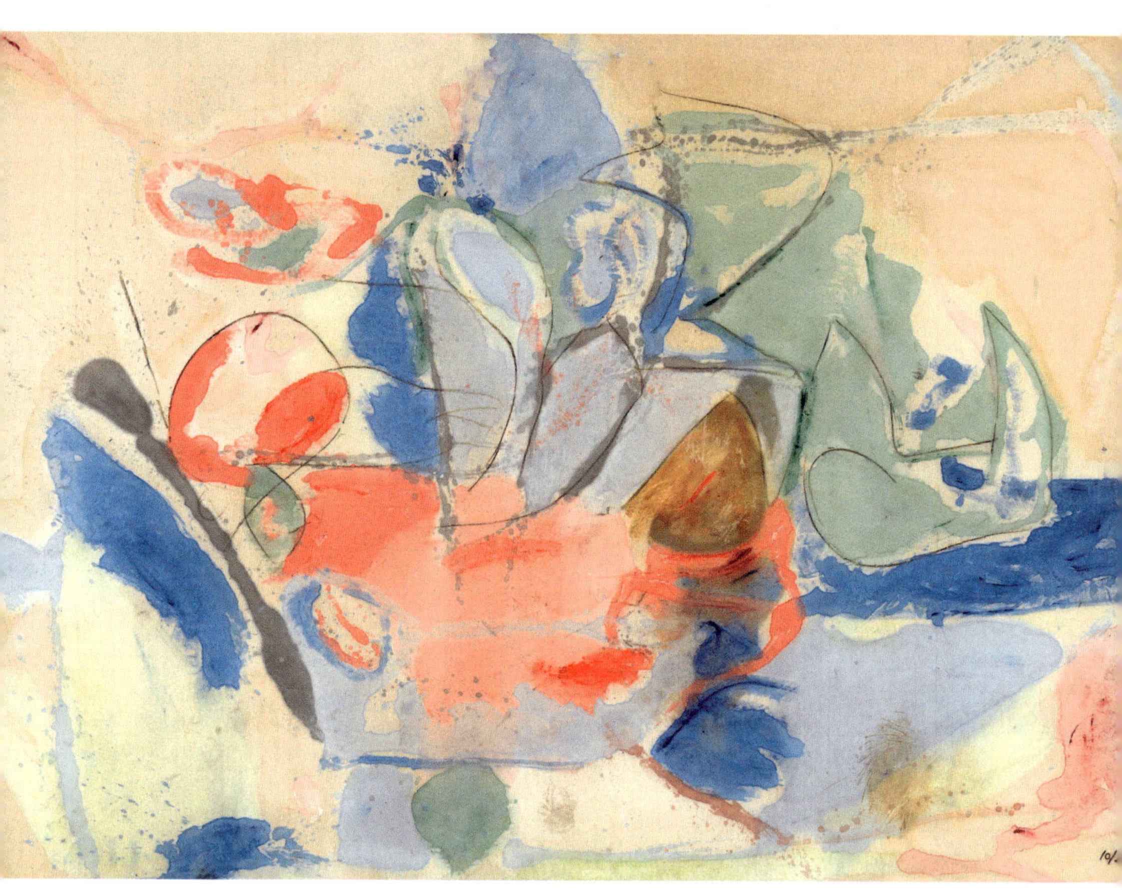

Helen Frankenthaler, Mountains and Sea, 1952. Oil and charcoal on unsized, unprimed canvas, 219.4 x 297.8 cm (86⅜ x 117¼ in).

GO AGAINST THE RULES OR IGNORE THE RULES

Bypass artistic convention and 'rules' in order to innovate.

In 1952, when she was just 23 years old, second-generation New York School painter **Helen Frankenthaler** pioneered her 'soak-stain' technique in an effort to unify figure and ground. Experimenting in her studio, the artist thinned oil paint with turpentine until the paint resembled watercolour in its consistency. She proceeded to pour the liquid onto unprimed canvas laid on the floor, abandoning the easel as Jackson Pollock – whose ink works on paper moved her when she encountered them in 1951 – had done in the late 1940s. Operating at the nexus of control and chance, Frankenthaler tilted the canvas, boldly letting the colour pool, seep and bloom into its own forms for an unprecedented and highly evocative visual effect. A decade later, with some additional experimentation, she adapted her method to acrylic paint.

Mountains and Sea (1952), a watery abstraction of intermittently charcoal-limned pink, blue and green forms that drew inspiration from the Nova Scotian landscape, is widely viewed as Frankenthaler's first soak-stain painting. Its outsize influence on painters Kenneth Noland and Morris Louis – who admiringly described Frankenthaler as 'a bridge between Pollock and what was possible' – was critical to the development of Colour Field painting, a non-gestural form of abstract painting characterized by saturated expanses.

'There are no rules,' Frankenthaler advised in 1994. 'That is one thing I say about every medium, every picture… that is how art is born, that is how breakthroughs happen. Go against the rules or ignore the rules, that's what invention is all about.'

LOOK TO OTHER MINDS

Engagement with other artists' practices can enrich your own.

French Neoclassical artist **Jean-Auguste-Dominique Ingres** - a history painter and portraitist who studied under Jacques-Louis David, won the Prix de Rome on his second attempt and received numerous significant commissions (and scathing criticisms) - proffered many a maxim, some of which were taken up by the modern artists who admired him, including Impressionists, Cubists and even Surrealists. In addition to underscoring the importance of drawing and the essential function of line, Ingres argued for the necessity of engaging with the art and thinking of others. 'He who is not willing to ask the contribution of any mind other than his own will soon find himself reduced to the most miserable of all imitations, which is to say the imitation of his own works,' Ingres cautioned.

Though it was largely the distortion of his line - the daring exactitude with which he readily sacrificed realism at the altar of beauty, as when he painted extra vertebrae into the impossibly elegant back of the figure in *La Grande Odalisque* (1814) - that inspired the modernists that succeeded him, Ingres came out of a classical tradition (characterized by its own distortions). He rigorously studied the work of the Old Masters, including Italian and Northern Renaissance painters, and the art of antiquity, especially painting on ancient Greek vases. During his professorship at École des Beaux-Arts, Ingres likewise encouraged his students to see as much art - albeit in his preferred genres - as possible. When he took his students to the Louvre, he said: 'Do you think that in ordering you to copy [great paintings] I want to turn you into copyists? No, I want you to get the juice of the plant.'

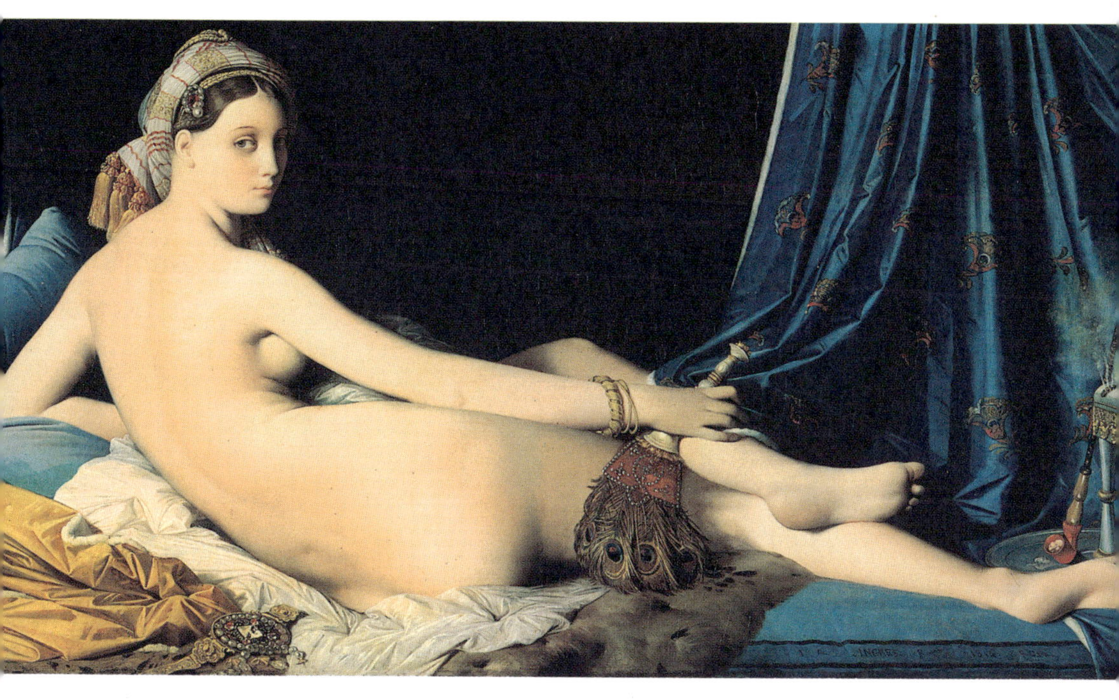

Jean-Auguste-Dominique Ingres, La Grande Odalisque, 1814. Oil on canvas, 91 x 162 cm (35⅞ x 63¾ in).

REFUSE GRATUITOUS ADVICE

Artists – even young ones – shouldn't be told what to do.

In his resoundingly quiet still lifes, twentieth-century Italian artist **Giorgio Morandi** highlighted the abstract and architectonic beauty of small everyday objects. Working in a precise, measured and famously slow fashion, the artist arranged bottles, vases, cups, pitchers, jugs and candlesticks in his studio. After studying and sketching the objects, he painted them in a subdued palette, void of any extraneous details, against neutral backdrops. As he poetically parsed the trappings of domestic life, Morandi invited the viewer to contemplate the formal beauty under the surface of the everyday.

While Italian art cycled through Futurism, the Metaphysical school and the Novecento movement, each with which Morandi experimented, the Bologna-based artist continued to produce his distinctive still lifes, honing his approach across more than four decades. When Edouard Roditi asked him whether he would advise younger artists to work in an abstract or figurative mode, Morandi responded: 'When I was young, I never felt the need to ask anyone for advice of that kind... Younger painters of today who really deserve this appellation as well as our attention would refuse, quite properly, to accept any gratuitous advice of the kind that you seem to suggest. I respect the freedom of the individual and especially of the artist, so that I would not be of much use as a guide or instructor, nor have I ever wanted to be one.' (Morandi did in fact teach etching – and elementary school drawing – but viewed the instruction as purely technical.)

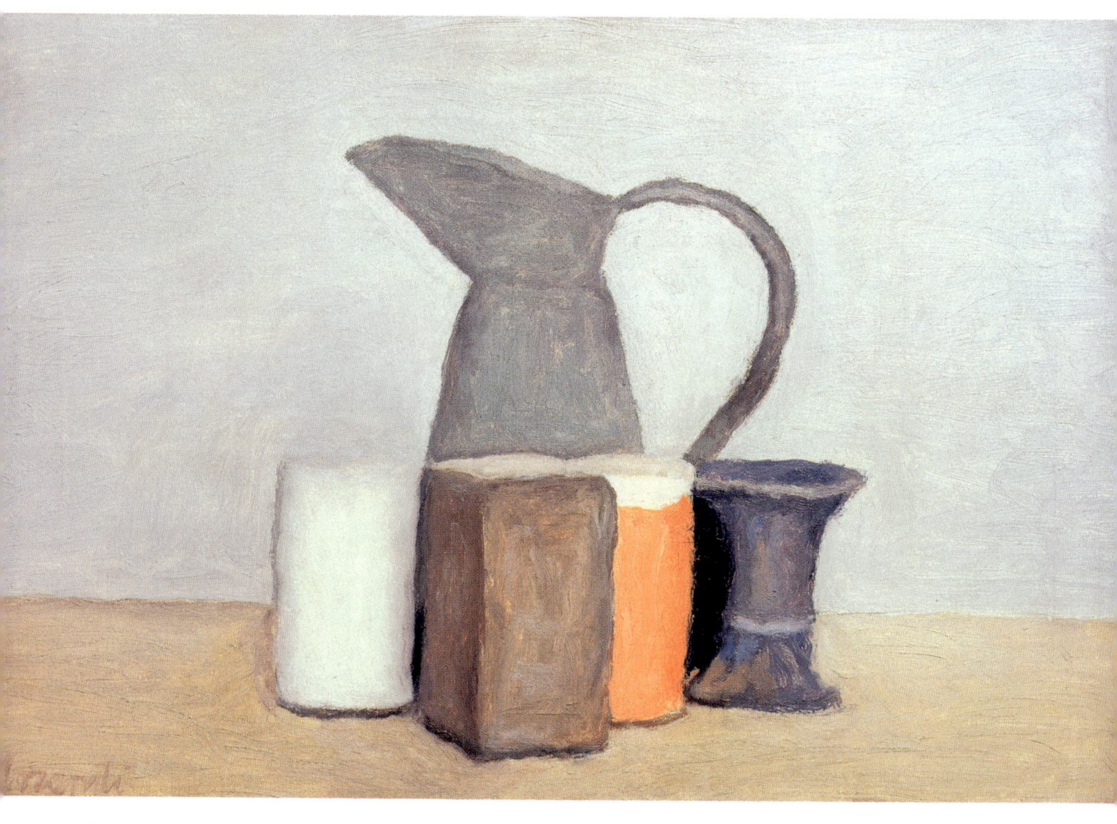

Giorgio Morandi, Still Life (Natura Morta), 1960. Oil on canvas, 30 x 45cm (11¾ x 17¾ in).

ON THE NATURE OF ART & CREATIVITY

WHAT IS ART AND WHY DO ARTISTS MAKE IT? THE ANSWERS TO THESE DECEPTIVELY SIMPLE QUESTIONS ARE BOUNDLESS. CONSTITUTING THE TIP OF THE ICEBERG, THESE PAGES CHARACTERIZE ART AND CREATIVITY AS VARIOUSLY CATHARTIC, RISKY, TRANSFORMATIVE, ORDINARY, MOBILE AND MORE.

ART EXPRESSES THE BIG EMOTIONS

Convey feeling with religious zeal.

When it came to his luminous fusions of colour and form - stacks of floating rectangles of pure hue, often painted on a large scale - **Mark Rothko** had grand affective aspirations. In response to being characterized as an abstract artist with predominantly formalist concerns, the New York School painter declared in 1956: 'I'm not interested in relationships of color or form or anything else. I'm interested only in expressing basic human emotions - tragedy, ecstasy, doom, and so on.' The artist was confident he had tapped into these 'basic' big emotions due to the regularity with which people broke down in front of his work. 'The people who weep before my pictures are having the same religious experience I had when I painted them,' he added.

Rothko's ability to access such intense and even sublime emotional registers in his work landed him a commission to create a series of paintings for a new interfaith chapel in Houston, Texas in 1964. Over the next three years, the artist worked slowly and privately to produce 14 murals: three triptychs and five single paintings, the largest of which was 4.5 metres (15 feet) wide. Rothko's palette darkened as early as 1957, and in 1958 he began to paint open shapes that resembled portals in lieu of his hallmark rectangles. These stylistic shifts - and the contemplative mood they provoked, and the discourses of emptiness and infinitude with which they engaged - came to a head in the velvety, dark, modulated paintings that overtook the grey stucco walls of the Texas sanctuary. Sadly, Rothko didn't live to see the completion of the Rothko Chapel, which was designed by Philip Johnson, Howard Barnstone and Eugene Aubry; the artist died in 1970, one year before the building opened.

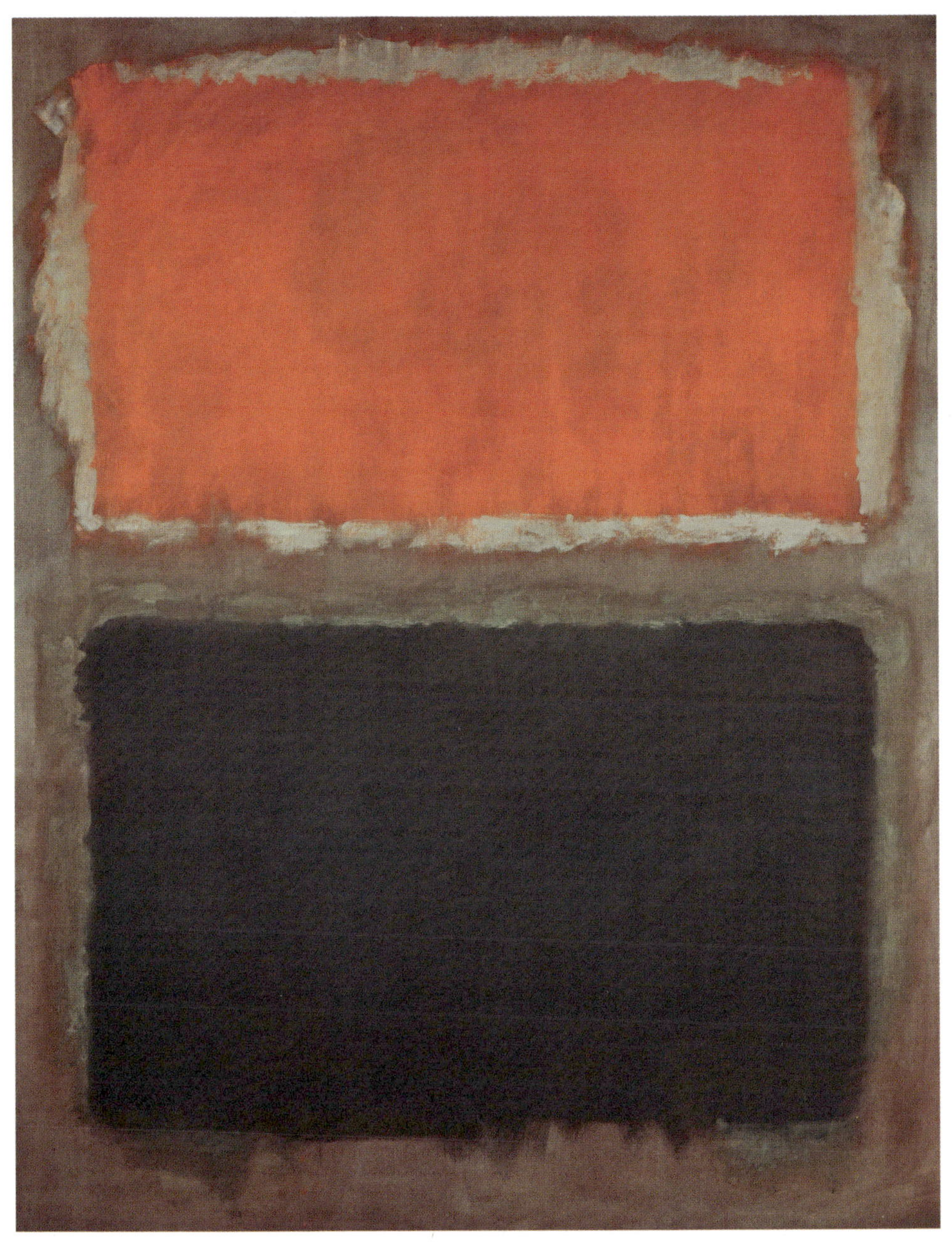

Mark Rothko, Black and Dark Red on Red, 1958. Oil on canvas, 233 x 176 cm (91¾ x 69¼ in).

ART TAKES MAINTENANCE

View art as ongoing, everyday work – and ongoing, everyday work as art.

'After the revolution, who's going to pick up the garbage on Monday morning?' asked New York-based artist **Mierle Laderman Ukeles** in her 'Manifesto for Maintenance Art 1969!'. As Ukeles, a feminist, enumerated some of the menial upkeep that she regularly performed as an artist, woman, mother and wife, she pointed out that 'maintenance ideas, maintenance activities, and maintenance materials' were integral to process art, a subset of the conceptual art that was flourishing at the time. Her manifesto proposed the reframing of paradigmatic acts of maintenance, such as cleaning, as high art.

Less than a decade later, Ukeles joined New York City's Department of Sanitation (DSNY) as its inaugural artist-in-residence after sending a letter of request referencing her recent photographic collaboration with 300 maintenance workers at the Whitney Museum of American Art. For her first project with DSNY, 'Touch Sanitation Performance' (1979–80), the artist shook the hands of 8,500 sanitation workers across New York City. Documented in photographs, videos, maps and writings, Ukeles' radical gesture underscored the importance of the labour of these workers as well as viewers' implication in that labour, while pushing the bounds of process art and systems art.

'IN THESE ART INSTITUTIONS, I'D TAKE OVER THE PERSONA OF THE MAINTENANCE WORKER, WHO IS SUPPOSED TO BE UNSEEN, AND CLEANS BEHIND THE SCENES, AFTER HOURS. OR THE GUARD, WHO KEEPS THE KEYS SILENTLY. I WAS TRYING TO BRING MAINTENANCE OUT IN PUBLIC.'
MIERLE LADERMAN UKELES

ART TRANSFORMS

Shape-shifting art can offer a transformative experience.

The same year that the Brazilian Neo-Concrete movement, a poetic and participatory take on geometric abstraction, cemented around an artistic manifesto penned in Rio de Janeiro, one of its leading members, **Lygia Clark**, embarked upon her 'Bichos' series. From 1959 into the 1960s, Clark, who had recently forayed into sculpture from painting, made about 70 'Bichos', or 'Critters' (alternatively translated as 'Creatures', 'Beasts' and 'Animals'). The Bichos had no fixed form. Composed of geometric metal planes connected by visible hinges, they invited the viewer to manipulate them by hand. In moving the Bichos' components into new shapes, the participant animated the sculpture, thus completing it.

'I always thought it was fabulous to have given something of my art for someone to express themselves,' Clark wrote to fellow Neo-Concrete artist Hélio Oiticica in 1968. Increasingly driven by an interest in the healing potential of objects that fostered interaction, Clark was passionate about changing the way people experienced art. Her 'Bichos' were not only endlessly transforming; they were transformative.

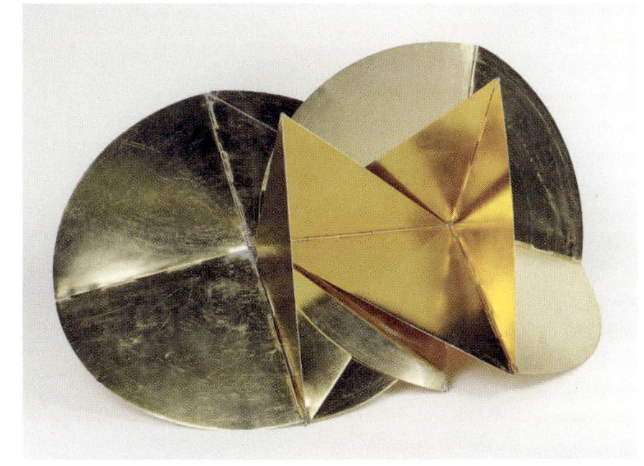

Lygia Clark, Bicho (máquina), 1962. Gilded metal with hinges, variable dimensions.

CREATIVITY INVOLVES RISK-TAKING

Trust your own capabilities and leap.

In an article published by *Fast Company* in 2000, artist and activist **Faith Ringgold** likened creativity to early experiences of play, emphasizing the place of risk-taking in exploratory gambols on the playground and in the studio alike. 'The great enemy of creativity is fear,' Ringgold asserted. She explained that, to the contrary, 'Creativity has a lot to do with a willingness to take risks. Think about how children play. They run around the playground, they trip, they fall, they get up and run some more. They believe everything will be all right. They feel capable; they let go.'

Born in 1930 amid the cultural flourishing of the Harlem Renaissance, Ringgold was rejected from New York's City College's art programme on the basis of her gender but found a loophole of sorts by studying in their arts education programme, which was open to women. In 1963, she embarked upon her 'American People' series, a cycle of clear-eyed paintings adumbrating race relations in the US amid the civil rights struggles of the period. These daring political paintings culminated in a blood-spattered mural of violent interracial upheaval titled *Die* (1967).

In 1983, Ringgold took another, different risk when she began a series of narrative quilts. Made (often in collaboration with her mother) at a time when such textiles were typically dismissed by art institutions due to associations with the feminine, craft, domestic labour and, in this case, African American tradition, Ringgold's quilts were inscribed with original stories that were rooted in a Black feminine perspective. Today, these quilts, some of which served as inspiration for children's books, are among her most important works.

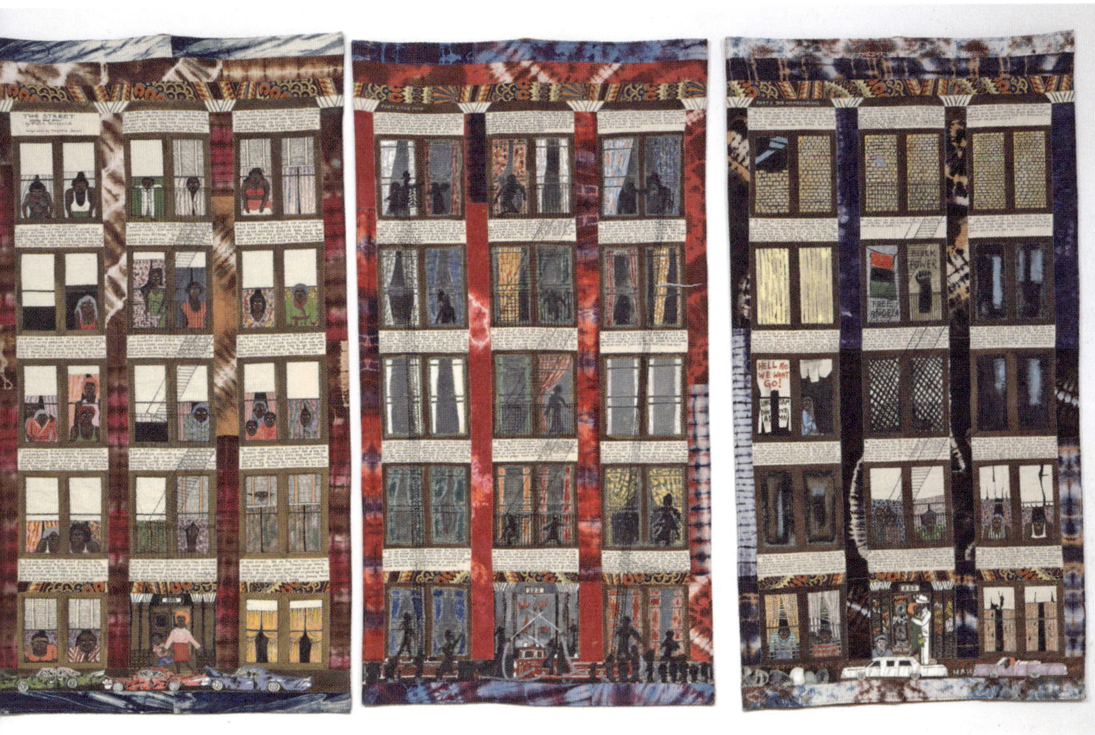

Faith Ringgold, Street Story Quilt, 1985. Acrylic, ink marker, dyed fabric and sequins on canvas, sewn to quilted fabric, 228.6 x 365.8 cm (90 x 144 in).

ART TAKES ITS FORM FROM LIFE ITSELF

The day-to-day can be a subject, a medium or a set.

A fascination with, and even an allegiance to, the quotidian was a driving force behind **Claes Oldenburg**'s beloved public sculptures: monumental Pop renderings, for some time made in collaboration with his wife Coosje van Bruggen, that radically scale up ordinary and non-precious objects ranging from clothes pegs (Philadelphia) to ice cream cones (Cologne) to shuttlecocks (Kansas City). Oldenburg's enduring impulse to use everyday life as artistic material is present in some of his earliest sculptural endeavours. In 1960, the artist produced an installation that recreated his neighbourhood in New York City's Lower East Side with replica signage and detritus fabricated from scavenged cardboard, newspaper and sacking. The next year, he opened an ersatz storefront out of which he sold sculptures - crudely constructed from plaster, chicken wire and paint - that masqueraded as basic commodities, like underwear and cigarettes, or comestibles, like hamburgers and pies.

On the occasion of an exhibition at New York's Martha Jackson Gallery that year, Oldenburg penned 'I Am For...', a meanderingly poetic and somewhat tongue-in-cheek statement on the artistic possibilities posed by everyday life, a notion integral to Pop Art and Happenings. 'I am for an art that is political-erotical-mystical, that does something other than sit on its ass in a museum,' wrote Oldenburg, adding shortly thereafter: 'I am for all art that takes its form from the lines of life itself, that twists and extends and accumulates and spits and drips, and is heavy and coarse and blunt and sweet and stupid as life itself.'

Claes Oldenburg, Clothespin, 1976. Cor-Ten steel, with stainless steel 'spring' on concrete base, 14 x 3.73 x 1.37 m (45 ft x 12 ft 3 in x 4 ft 6 in).

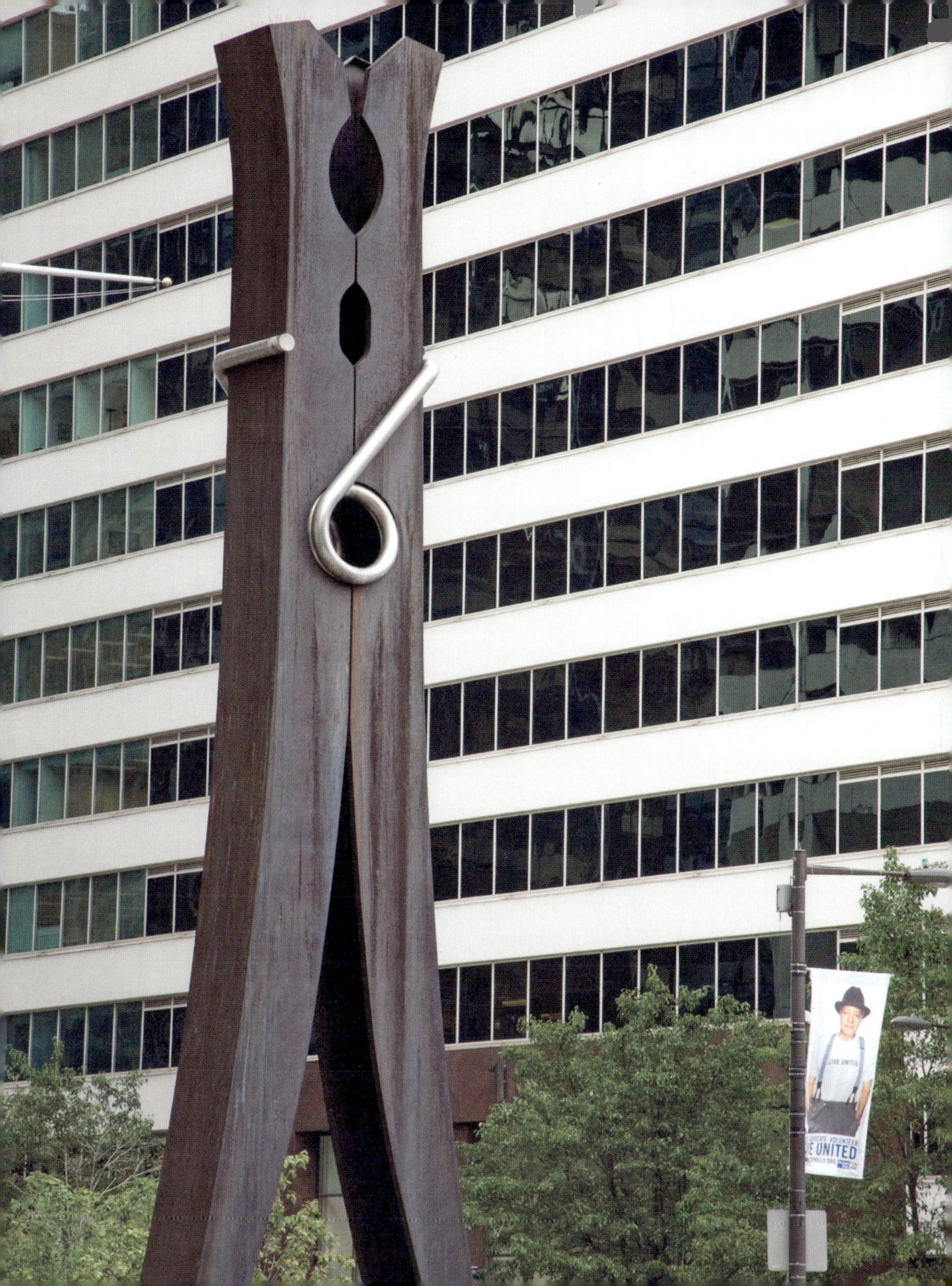
LIVE UNITED

CREATION HAPPENS IN DIALOGUE

Nurture a spirit of collaboration.

Collaging video, theatre, dance, performance art, drawing and sound, often with repetitive or mirrored elements, **Joan Jonas** creates mesmerizing multimedia pieces that frame 'the real' as something fragmented or unfixed. Interior or psychological space and the exterior landscape become fully interpolated in the world of the artist's work.

To make artworks with so many components, Jonas calls upon a long, varied and decidedly non-hieratic list of collaborators, including, as art historian Pamela M. Lee has enumerated, 'musicians, artists, dancers, performers, poets and storytellers' - as well as the artist's canine companions, who often play key roles in her videos. The long-term relationships that Jonas has nurtured with many of her repeat collaborators - perhaps most prominently with the composer and pianist Jason Moran, with whom she has collaborated for 18 years - are integral to the magic of her work.

'Art is about communication,' Jonas advised in an interview with the Louisiana Museum of Modern Art in Denmark. 'Art is a dialogue with art, a dialogue with other artists, a dialogue with the past, with the future, and it's an important dialogue to have.'

'THIS HAS BEEN MY LONGEST COLLABORATION WITH A COMPOSER AND MUSICIAN, AND HAS INSPIRED MY MOVEMENT AND SOUND-MAKING IN A MORE DYNAMIC WAY . . . WHILE PLAYING THE SAME MUSIC WE'VE BASICALLY DECIDED UPON FOR THE PERFORMANCE, HE EMBELLISHES AND INVENTS DIFFERENT WAYS OF PLAYING IT EACH TIME. THIS ANIMATES ME.'

JOAN JONAS

ART STALKS INTO THE WORLD LIKE A NEW MONSTER

Your creation might take on a life of its own.

German-born British artist **Frank Auerbach** makes emotive, gestural paintings - figurative cityscapes and portraits - so thickly layered that they approach other categories of artistic creation: sculpture, relief, palimpsest. The artist might paint directly atop an existing painting, leaving a heavy impasto, or alternatively scrape off layers of paint to render, for the umpteenth time, the same subject a little differently, modulating his approach.

Though he often revisits subjects repeatedly - painting, for example, a number of pictures of his friend Leon Kossoff or longtime lover Estella West - Auerbach has underscored that his subject matter is present to serve or 'feed' the art, rather than the other way around. 'What I'm trying to make is a stonking, independent, coherent image that has never been seen before,' said Auerbach. His subjects, he explained, are 'not there for their own sake; they're not there for sentimental reasons; they're there to feed this new, independent image that one's trying to make, that stalks into the world like a new monster'.

'I THINK ALL GOOD PAINTING LOOKS AS THOUGH THE PAINTING HAS ESCAPED FROM THE THICKET OF PREPARED POSITIONS AND HAS ENTERED SOME SORT OF FREEDOM WHERE IT EXISTS ON ITS OWN, AND BY ITS OWN LAWS, AND INEXPLICABLY HAS GOT FREE OF ALL POSSIBLE EXPLANATIONS.'

FRANK AUERBACH

ART IS A MATTER OF FRAMING
Shift the focus with a new context.

'That's right, that's what art is, *we*'re the art!' cheered a participant in **Lorraine O'Grady**'s intervention into the African American Day Parade in Harlem, titled *Art Is...* (1983). O'Grady, a cultural critic and conceptual artist working across performance, photomontage, video and text, has long centred Black and female subjectivity in her work. In 1980 she blazed onto the scene with the performance persona 'Mlle Bourgeoise Noire' (Miss Black Middle-Class), who made her debut at the avant-garde Black art space Just Above Midtown. Donning a debutante gown sewn from 180 pairs of white gloves, Mlle Bourgeoise Noire called attention to issues of race, class and gender in the domain of contemporary art as she demanded radical new frameworks for artmaking.

O'Grady's somewhat Duchampian decision to enter a float into the African American Day Parade as an artwork was spurred by a social worker acquaintance's assertion that 'avant-garde art doesn't have anything to do with Black people'. In the September 1983 parade, O'Grady – in the guise of Mlle Bourgeoise Noire – rode a float topped with a colossal, gilded picture frame that fluidly captured the surrounding scene; a group of 15 performers accompanying her carried smaller gold frames out to audience members. O'Grady's intervention turned the event and its attendees into art, a simultaneously joyful and critical gesture that posited an active spectator while bringing Black representation into the frequently white-coded space of avant-garde art. Emblazoned with *Art Is...*, the float left art's meaning open-ended while making space for new definitions and under-represented perspectives.

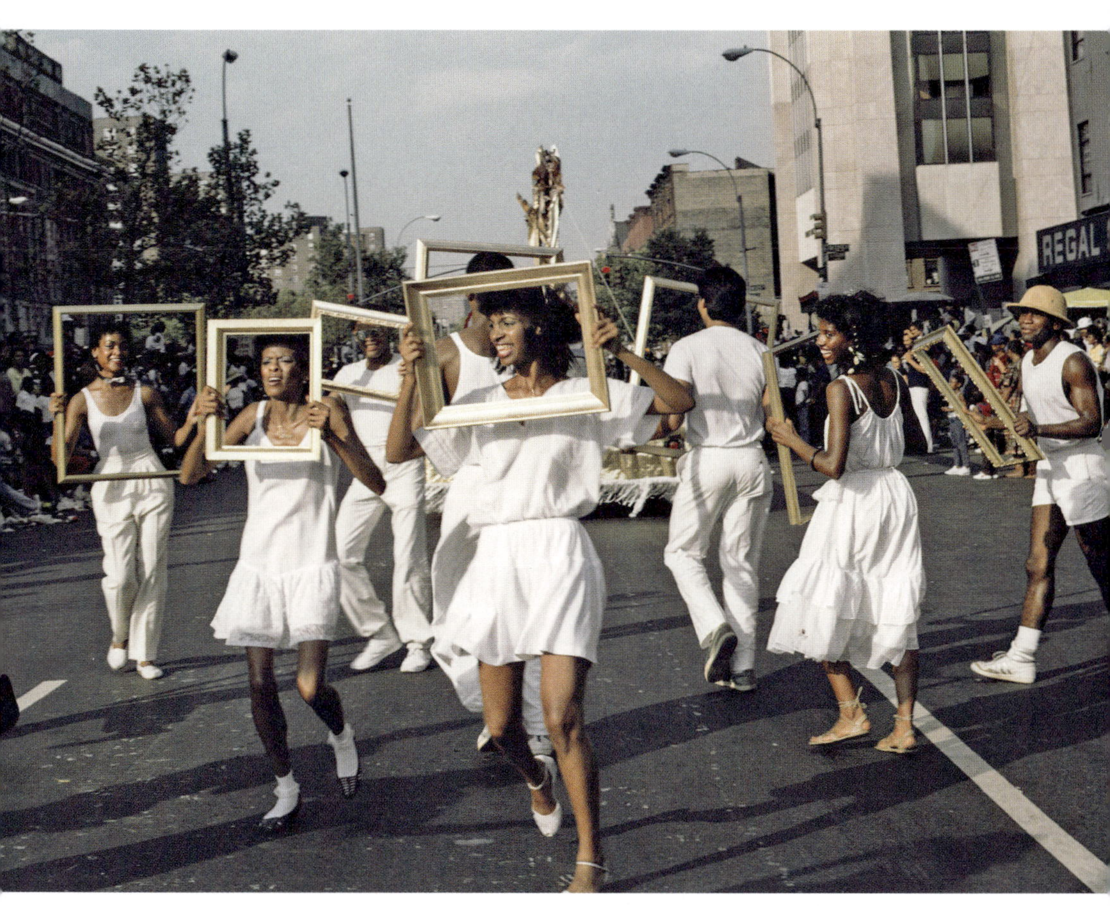

Lorraine O'Grady, Art Is . . . (Troupe Front), 1983/2009. C-print in 40 parts, 40.64 x 50.8 cm (16 x 20 in).

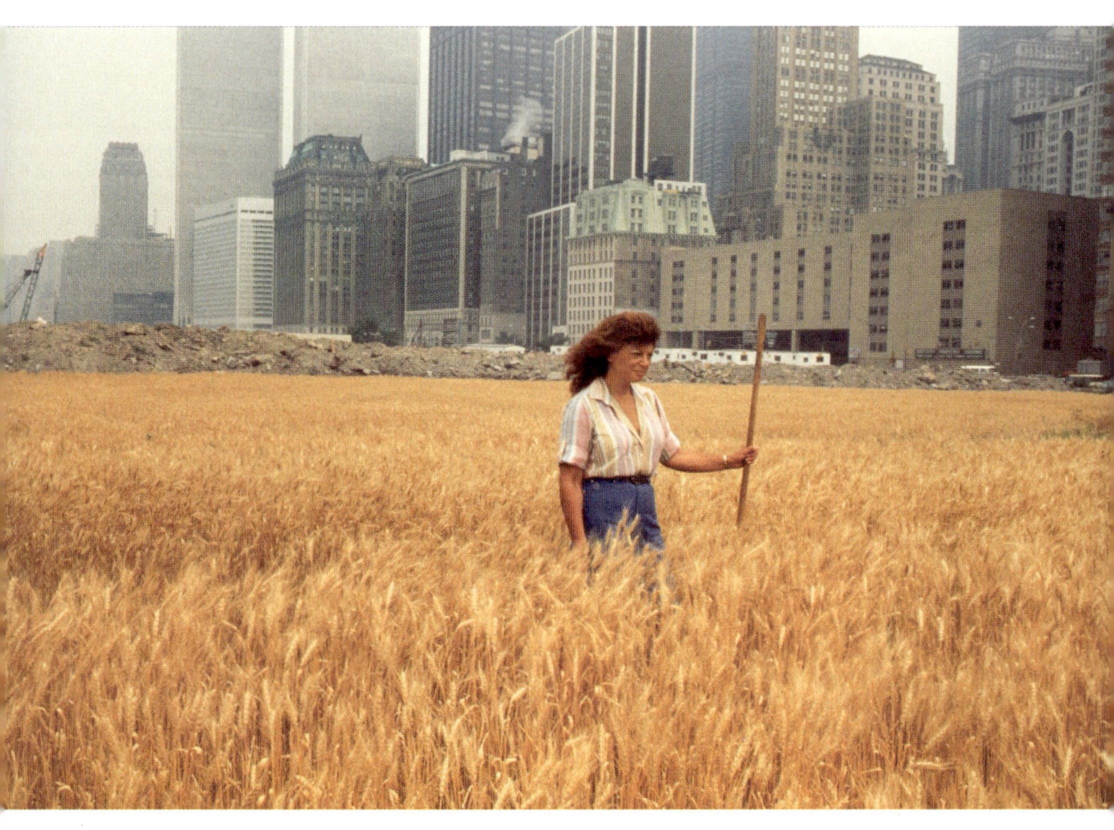

Wheatfield - A Confrontation: Battery Park Landfill, Downtown Manhattan - With Agnes Denes Standing in the Field, 1982.

ART OFFERS SOLUTIONS

Through your work, proffer visions of a different — better — world, and how we might get there.

Hungarian-born American artist **Agnes Denes**, who emerged in the 1960s amid the male-dominated Land Art movement, has spent the last half-century producing ecologically minded art with an activist bent. Often integrating knowledge from other disciplines, the eco-feminist artist works across earthworks, drawing, sculpture and performance to call for change in how we treat, relate to and engage with the natural world.

In her most famous work, *Wheatfield - A Confrontation* (1982), Denes planted a wheatfield on 2 acres of landfill located near Wall Street in a bid for New York City, and the world, to reconsider its priorities, putting care for people and stewardship of the planet over the reckless pursuit of capital (the latter of which was signified by the nearby Financial District). The seeds of the project spread across the globe when wheat harvested from the field was delivered to a spate of international cities via the group exhibition 'The International Art Show for the End of World Hunger', which travelled throughout the United States, Europe and South America from 1987 to 1990.

'Wanting to change the world morphed into a unique artistic output of a lifetime of creation, and the visualization of invisible processes, such as math, logic, thinking processes, and so on,' Denes said of her oeuvre in her 2019 address to the Graduate School of Design at Harvard University. 'This process of re-evaluation and visualization became a process of offering humanity benign solutions to some of its problems.'

ON WHAT IT MEANS TO BE AN ARTIST

UNDER THE MALLEABLE AND EXPANSIVE SIGN OF ARTIST, INDIVIDUALS MIGHT DIRECT THEIR EFFORTS TOWARDS BUILDING A FANTASTIC NEW WORLD OR SHEDDING MUCH-NEEDED LIGHT ON THE ONE THEY'RE IN; TOWARDS EXPRESSING THE ZEITGEIST OR ATTEMPTING TO REDEFINE IT.

LET GO OF WHETHER YOU'RE AN ARTIST

Instead, focus on bringing what you want to see into the world.

Jeffrey Gibson, a queer multidisciplinary artist of Choctaw and Cherokee descent with an itinerant upbringing, began to box with a physical trainer in an effort to process and acknowledge some of his frustration around issues of 'race, class and entitlement' in the art world. In 2010, this experience gave rise to the first work in an ongoing series of densely decorated, neon-bright punch bags, which are adorned with intricate glass and plastic beading as well as metal cones, artificial sinew, crystals and nylon fringe.

Nodding to the fluidity and dimensionality of the artist's identity as they problematize the institutional tendency to silo Indigenous art, these hanging pieces draw inspiration from a wealth of sources including pow-wow regalia, rave aesthetics, Op Art, punk DIY culture and geometric abstraction. Gibson sources his materials from diverse locales – acquiring jingle cones from China, for example, and beads from the Czech Republic or India – and collaborates with Native American artisans on adorning the repurposed punching bags. Often, he incorporates all-caps text into his designs: snippets of poems, lyrics and, increasingly, his own writing.

'When I began working with the punching bags, it was at a period when I was questioning whether I really wanted to be an artist,' Gibson told Emily Zimmerman in an interview for *BOMB*. 'What I came to was that I needed to let go of whether I was an artist or not, and I needed to pursue the things that I want to see existing in the world that don't exist.'

Jeffrey Gibson, What We Want, What We Need, 2014. Found punching bag, glass beads, artificial sinew, copper jingles, nylon fringe and steel chain, 180 x 35.6 x 35.6 cm (71 x 14 x 14 in).

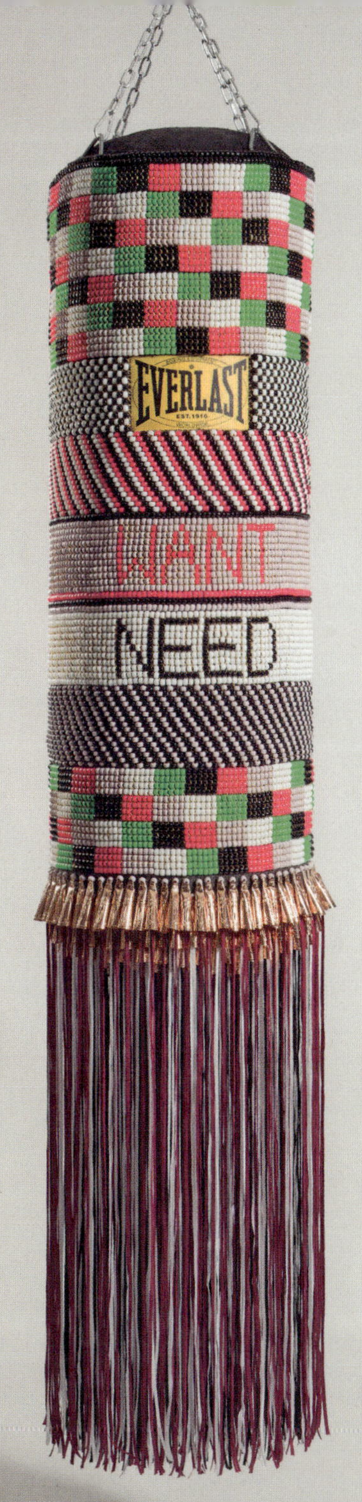
EVERLAST
WANT
NEED

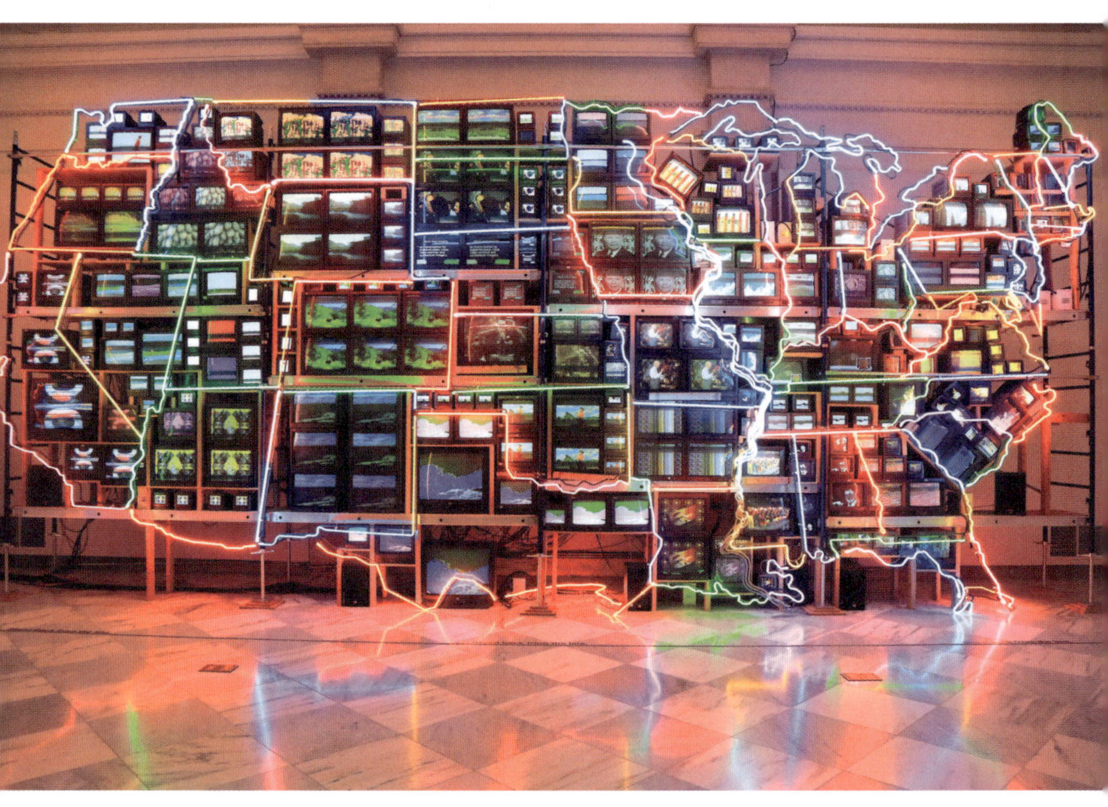

Nam June Paik, Electronic Superhighway: Continental U.S., Alaska, Hawaii, 1995. Fifty-one channel video installation (including one closed-circuit television feed), custom electronics, neon lighting, steel and wood; colour, sound, approx. 4.57 x 12.2 x 1.2 m (15 x 40 x 4 ft).

ARTISTS CHANGE THE RULES OF THE GAME

New technologies invite new ways of thinking and working.

Korean American video art trailblazer **Nam June Paik**, who famously coined the term 'electronic superhighway' in 1974, was remarkably prescient in his understanding of how new media would reconstitute our understanding of the world and reconfigure how we live, connect and interrelate. Paik, who asserted in 1965 that the cathode ray tube would come to usurp the canvas and 'artists will work with capacitors, resistors and semiconductors as they today work with brushes', maintained a zeal for experimentation and innovation throughout his career.

Paik didn't just push the envelope, he tore it wide open, with an output that ranged from prepared televisions like *Magnet TV* (1965), in which a magnet affixed to a television set distorted and abstracted the images onscreen, to *TV Buddha* (1974), a closed-circuit video installation featuring a Buddha statuette watching itself on television, to *Electronic Superhighway: Continental U.S., Alaska, Hawaii* (1995), a massive sculptural map of the United States made from 335 television monitors outlined with neon lighting. (Monitors in each 'state' displayed video associated with that locale; fitness classes played in 'California'.)

Ruminating on how artists might redress that nagging feeling that there is nothing new under the sun, Paik said in 1992: 'I bet there are still many openings and loopholes in art history... which are being overlooked right now by millions of young people who complain that everything has already been done, so that they cannot do new breakthroughs. However, the history of the world says that we don't win the games, but we change the rules of the games.'

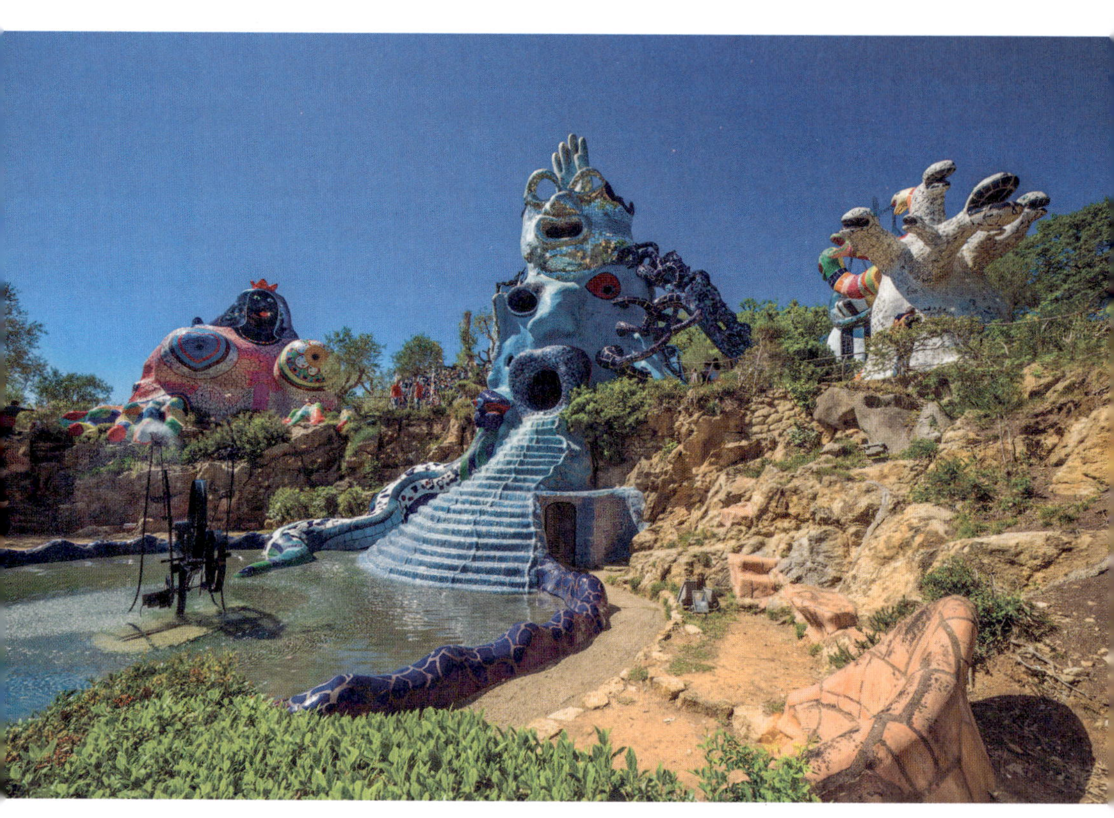

Niki de Saint Phalle, The Tarot Garden, Tuscany, Italy.

ARTISTS GO ALL OUT

Commit to your outrageously big visions.

Niki de Saint Phalle was not one for subtlety. The French American artist's 'shooting paintings', in which she fired a rifle at found object assemblages or canvases affixed with bags of paint, put her on the map in 1961. Five years later, she invited visitors to Stockholm's Moderna Museet to enter a colossal fertility figure – part of the artist's series of psychedelically hued, joyfully zaftig 'Nana' ('women') sculptures – through its ample vaginal canal. 'I always admired people who went all out,' Saint Phalle said, a sentiment very much in-keeping with her own oeuvre.

After encountering Catalan modernist Antoni Gaudí's Park Güell in Barcelona in 1955, and subsequently Sacro Bosco in Bomarzo, Italy, and Palais Idéal in Hauterives, France, Saint Phalle dreamed up her own public sculpture park, a fantastical and liberatory 'garden of joy' with colossal structures that would prove her ability to work on an epic scale. The artist decided to overtake and transform a 14-acre former quarry in Tuscany with a group of 22 wildly colourful, marvellously playful monuments, one for each of the Major Arcana of the Tarot, made from materials including concrete, polyester, mosaics and ceramics.

In 1998, after nearly 30 years of construction – seven of which the artist spent living in the mirrored interior of one of the structures, a sphinx – the Tarot Garden opened to the public, boasting monuments up to 15 metres (50 feet) high. Saint Phalle was savvy at getting her big visions realized; one-third of the substantial cost of the multimillion-dollar endeavour was fundraised through sales of an eponymous perfume.

ARTISTS SUMMARIZE

Strive to capture the feeling or essence of the moment.

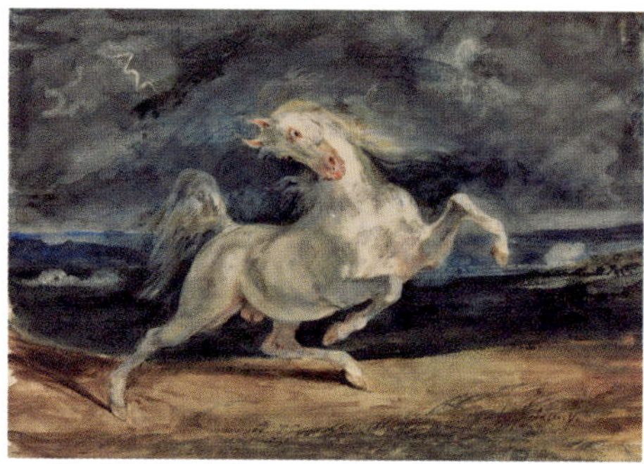

Contemplating the distinctions between various art forms in his journal in 1854, **Ferdinand Victor Eugène Delacroix** zeroed in on 'the effect that can be produced by the rough sketch of an idea'. The French Romantic painter argued that, while in music and literature a certain roughness or lack of finish can prove detrimental to quality, in visual art (particularly painting), 'a fine indication, or a sketch infused with great feeling, can be equal in expression to the most finished production'.

Though Delacroix's paintings sobered slightly in execution and took a classical turn in subject matter as Romanticism fell out of fashion, many of his most enduring works are characterized by a sketchy facture, uninhibited brushstrokes and turbulent surfaces. Made at a time when the artist was creating visual studies of horses, the watercolour *Horse Frightened by Lightning* (*c.*1825-9) takes as its subject a rearing horse in the background of a painting by Sawrey Gilpin. A rare sketch shared by Delacroix in his lifetime, it is precisely the roughness of the work's rendering that allows it to powerfully capture the intensity of the storm and the extent of the animal's alarm.

Eugène Delacroix, Horse Frightened by Lightning, *c.*1825-9.
Watercolour, 23.5 x 32 cm (9¼ x 12⅝ in).

ARTISTS DO NOT RETIRE; THEY SIMPLY DIE

Being an artist is more than a career: it is a framework for approaching the world.

The late spousal artist duo **Christo and Jeanne-Claude** are celebrated for their decades-spanning practice of producing temporary environmental installations on a grand scale, often through wrapping buildings in large quantities of fabric. With this simple yet ambitious intervention, the pair have transformed buildings, monuments, parks and coastlines into unfamiliar forms, breathing new life into public space.

Christo and Jeanne-Claude, whose projects were always free to the public, constantly sold preparatory sketches and models to fund their work independently. Evincing the extent to which their artistic vision was knitted into the fabric of their lives, their home predominantly consisted of a buyers' reception area, a framing and shipping centre, and of course, a studio. In *The Gates*, a 2007 documentary devoted to the pair's installation of 7,503 saffron-coloured fabric panels in New York's Central Park, a journalist asks Jeanne-Claude whether she will retire. Jeanne-Claude retorts: 'Artists do not retire; they simply die.' 'It's not a profession, it's existence, you know?' added Christo in a later interview with *The Talks*. 'You exist through art.'

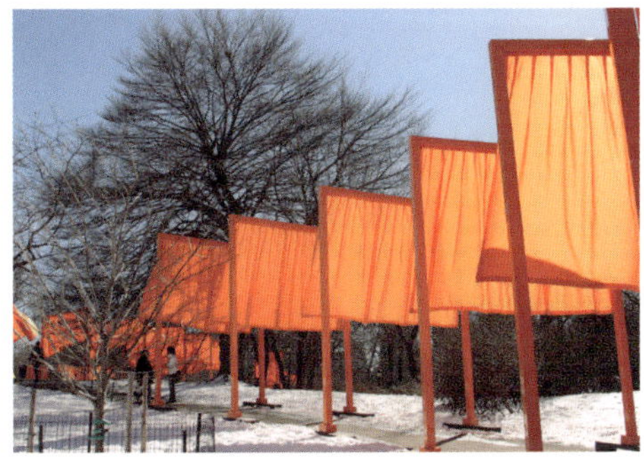

Christo and Jeanne-Claude, The Gates, Central Park, New York City, 1979–2005. Fabric panels, variable dimensions.

ARTISTS DEPICT UNVARNISHED REALITY

Portray the real, even when it's unflattering.

The mid-nineteenth-century French art world, with its penchant for grand Neoclassical history paintings, exoticizing fantasy scenes and bucolic idylls, was not prepared for the paintings that **Gustave Courbet** debuted at the 1850–51 Paris Salon. Produced on the heels of the February Revolution in France and the publication of Karl Marx's *Communist Manifesto*, *The Stone Breakers* (1849–50) was a frank depiction of two workers – one old, one young – performing back-breaking labour. (The painting was unfortunately destroyed in a bombing in World War II.) A second painting, *A Burial at Ornans* (1849–50), was an anti-heroic image of a provincial funeral; a motley crew of working-class mourners – men, women and children – and members of an unidealized clergy surrounded a freshly dug grave in a country landscape.

Critics recoiled. Courbet had depicted everyday people and everyday life, declaring both to be a worthy subject of fine art; in the case of *A Burial at Ornans*, he did so on an epic scale (3 x 5 metres/10 x 16 feet) typically reserved for history painting. Exemplifying

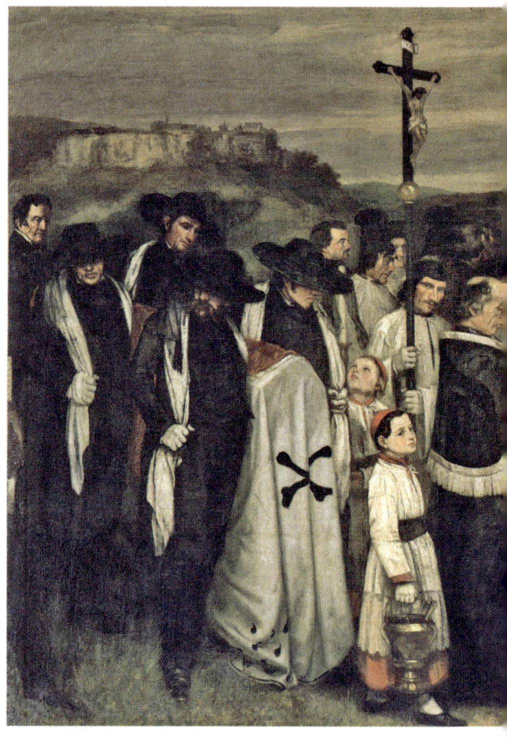

Courbet's belief that art should stem from lived experience and the flavour of the times, both paintings exhibited in the Salon were inspired by events in the artist's own life. Courbet had seen two men labouring by the road near the French town of Ornans, where he grew up, and later invited the men to model for him in his studio, giving rise to *The Stone Breakers*; *A Burial at Ornans* was based on his own father's funeral and portrayed the people who attended it. 'Painting is an essentially concrete art and can only consist in the representation of real and existing things,' the artist wrote in 1861.

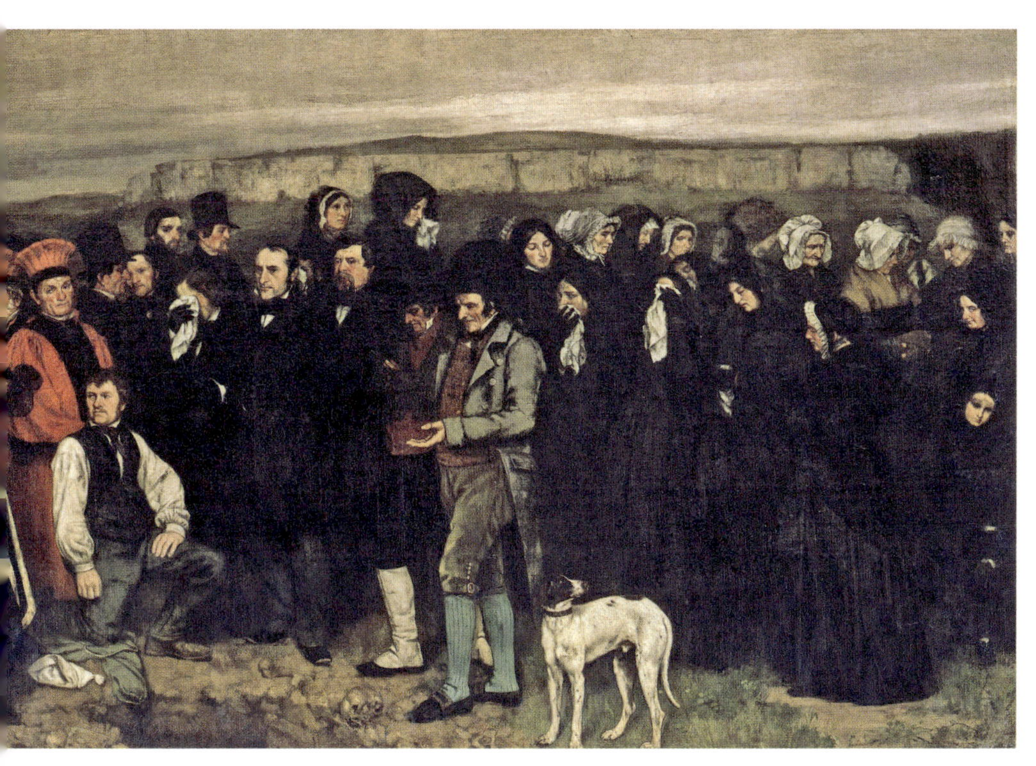

Gustave Courbet, A Burial at Ornans, 1849–50. Oil on canvas, 3 x 5 m (10 x 16 ft).

BE BRAVE ENOUGH TO TELL YOUR STORY

Representation matters.

Kia LaBeija, known mononymously as **Kia**, did not see her story represented in art and media as a child. 'When I was a girl I promised myself that I would be brave enough to tell my story,' she said in a 2018 *Artforum* interview. 'I understood the power of representation, and I wanted to make sure that the lives of children born with HIV could not be reduced to one sentence in a report about "mother-to-child transmission".'

Kia, a photographer, performance artist, activist and former Overall Mother of the House of LaBeija, was born HIV-positive; her mother, a lifelong AIDS activist, died from complications from the disease when the artist was 14 years old. As a queer woman of colour – and member of the ballroom scene – living with HIV and mourning her mother, Kia did not fit neatly into prevailing narratives of the AIDS epidemic that centred cisgender white gay men and were solely tragic in tone. She decided to depict something different.

Kia was 24 years old when she embarked upon '24', a series of staged photographic self-portraits addressing the complicated reality of living with HIV, beginning with a photo of the artist in her childhood bedroom, *In My Room* (2014). *Eleven* (2015), taken 11 years after her mother's death, is a glamorous shot of Kia in a cardinal red prom dress, her expression deadpan, getting her blood drawn to check her CD4 count at a routine doctor's appointment; *Mourning Sickness* (2014) depicts the dolled-up artist lying on her side on the bathroom floor, a reference to the stomach pain she experienced as a side-effect of antiretroviral therapy. These vulnerable and specific images brought her own experience into the picture.

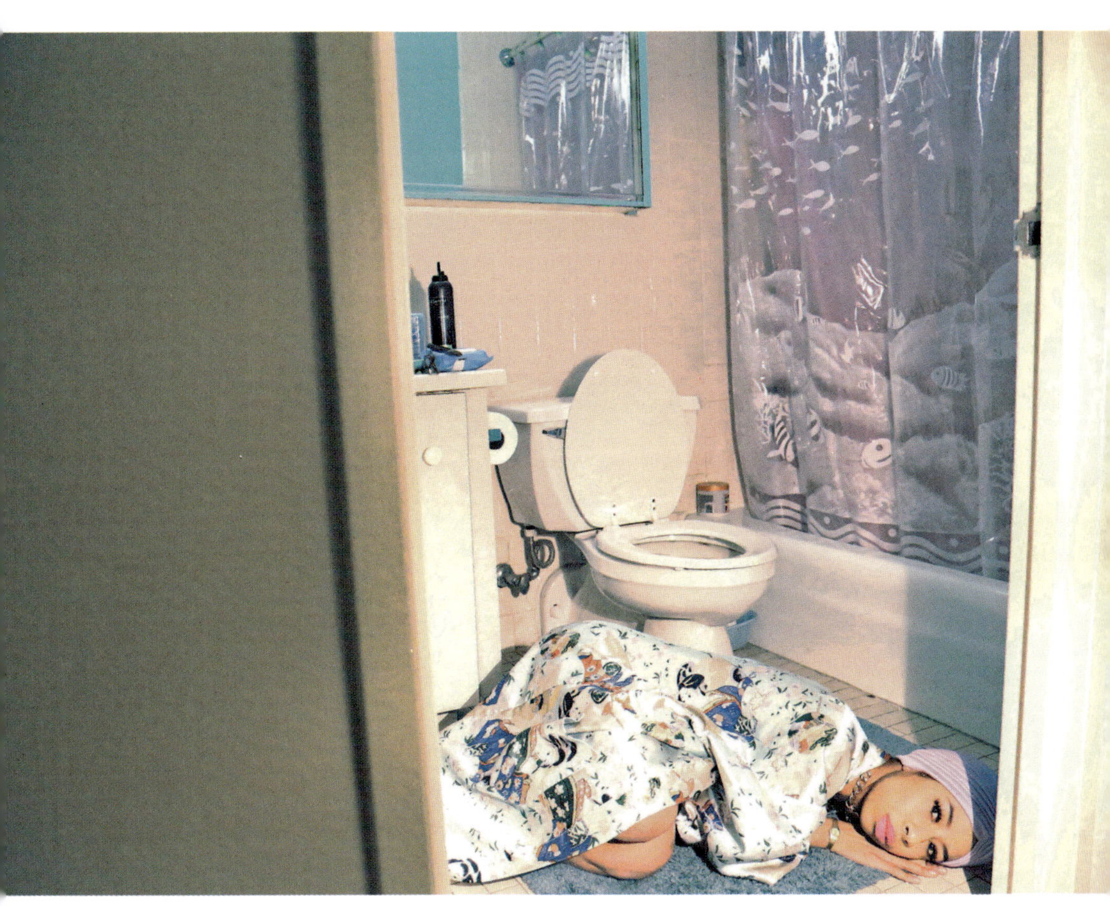

Kia LaBeija, Mourning Sickness, 2014. From series 24. Digital photograph, edition of 3, 24 x 20 cm (9½ x 7⅞ in).

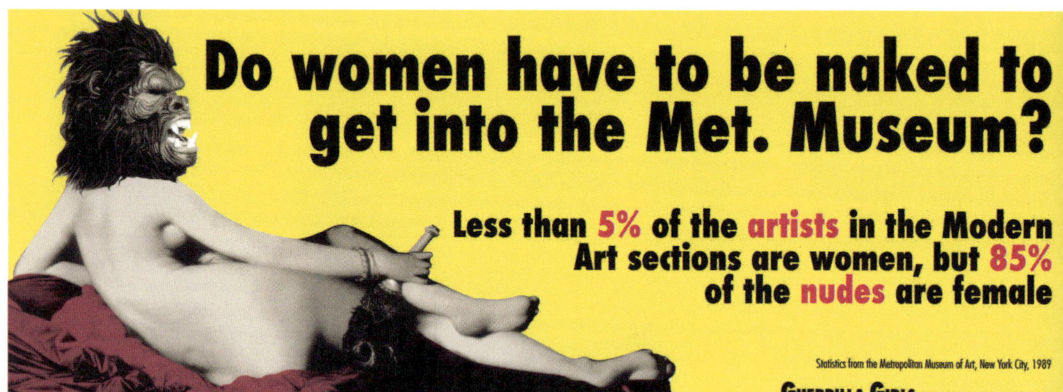

Guerrilla Girls, Do women have to be naked to get into the Met. Museum?, 1989. Screenprint on paper, image: 28 x 71 cm (11 x 28 in), support: 36.1 x 79.1 x 3 cm (14¼ x 31⅛ x 1⅛ in).

ARTISTS TAKE A STAND

Find your own crazy, creative way to be a feminist and an activist.

In 1984, the Museum of Modern Art in New York mounted an international survey of recent painting and sculpture by 169 artists, just 13 of whom were women. In response to the show's lack of gender parity, a group of women artists banded together to form the **Guerrilla Girls**. Sporting gorilla masks and using pseudonyms belonging to famous women forebears, such as Frida Kahlo and Hannah Höch, the feminist collective's anonymous members - who self-described as 'visual artists and culture jammers in the world of art, film and politics' - devoted themselves to exposing gender inequality and racial inequality in the art world.

Via populist art forms such as posters, stickers and protest actions, the Guerrilla Girls shared their frustrations, often incorporating statistics derived from a combination of their own research and publicly available data. After walking through the Metropolitan Museum of Art in New York in 1989, they determined that less than 5 per cent of the artists included in the Modern Art wing were women, while 85 per cent of the nudes on view were female. The bright yellow poster presenting their findings (alongside an image of Jean-Auguste-Dominique Ingres's nude Odalisque with a gorilla head) travelled around New York City as a bus advertisement until the Metro Transit Authority refused to renew the ad due to its provocative imagery.

A shifting group with an invitation-only membership, the Guerrilla Girls have kept at it for nearly four decades, completing more than 100 street projects in locales as far-flung as New York City, Mexico City, London, Istanbul and Shanghai. Though their project has elicited its fair share of controversy, their ongoing calls for change resonate to this day.

MAKE ART FOR YOUR TIME

Choose forms and media that express the spirit of your historical moment.

Visionary German multidisciplinary artist **Oskar Schlemmer**, who headed the stagecraft workshop at the Bauhaus school from 1923 to 1929, thought that theatre was uniquely poised to serve as 'the image of our time'. Schlemmer envisioned a new distinctly German form of theatre that would be emblematic of the post-World War I period, which he viewed as defined by abstraction and mechanization.

Schlemmer's 'The Triadic Ballet' ('Das triadisches Ballett'), which premiered in Stuttgart in September 1922 before travelling more widely in Europe, manifested the artist's vision for an art of the times as it radically broke with the pre-established norms of dance. Eschewing plot or narrative, which were the gold standards of dance at the time, this mathematical manifesto performance consisted of three acts distinguished by their differently coloured backdrops and moods: a yellow burlesque, a ceremonial pink and an enigmatic black.

The three dancers donned elaborate geometric costumes designed by Schlemmer based on spheres, cones and cylinders; these bulky get-ups turned the performers' bodies into abstract shapes and changed the way they moved through space, endowing them with the appearance of mechanization and an air of futurity. Writing in 1926, Schlemmer characterized his interest in making art rooted in technology, organization and precision as a 'repudiation of Chaos and a longing to find the form appropriate to our times'. Unfortunately, chaos was on the horizon, and in 1937 Schlemmer was among the artists included in the Nazi-organized Degenerate Art exhibition.

Oskar Schlemmer, Figurines in Space: Study for the Triadic Ballet, *c.*1924. Gouache, ink, and cut-and-pasted gelatin silver prints on black paper, 57.5 x 37.1 cm (22⅝ x 14 ⅝ in).

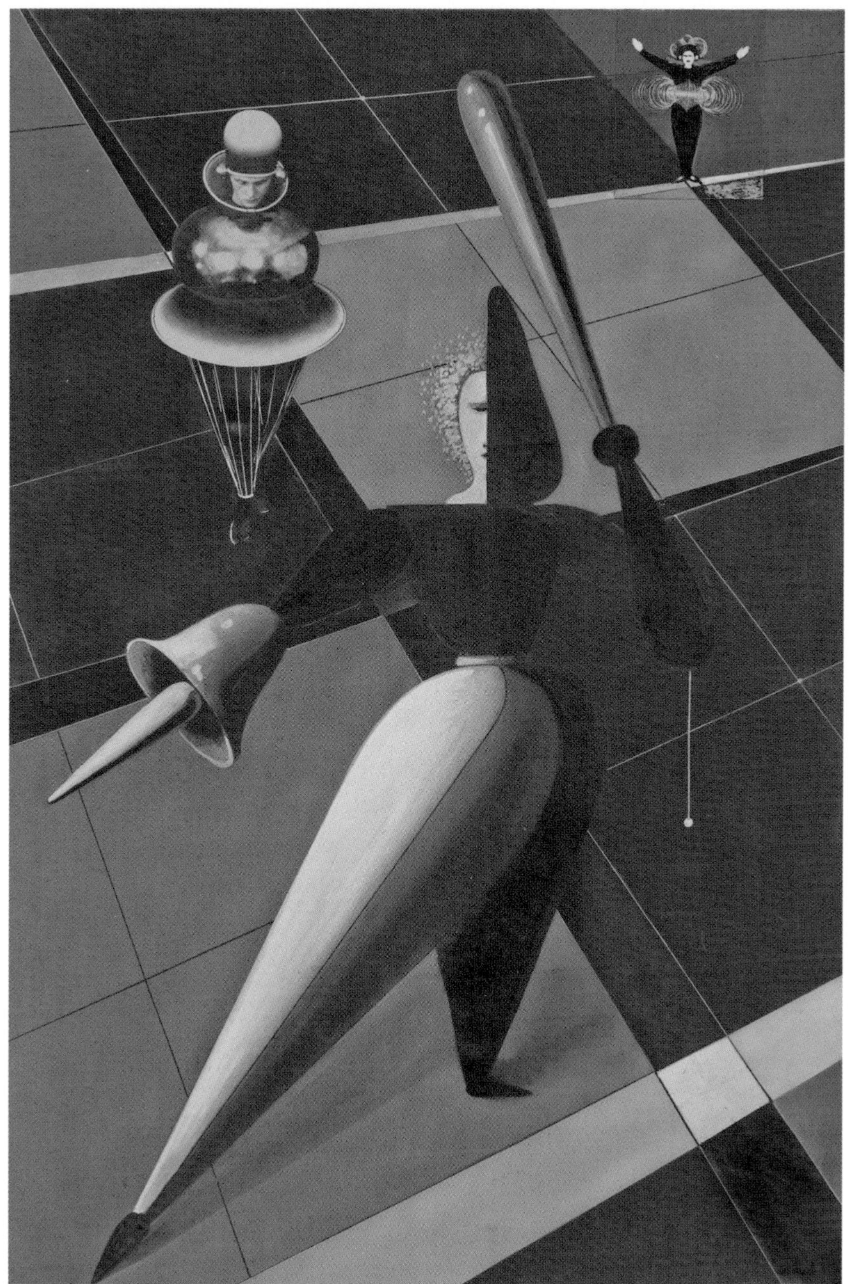

ON LOOKING & LEARNING

AS MUCH AS BEING AN ARTIST IS ABOUT THE ACT OF MAKING, IT IS ALSO ABOUT CULTIVATING A SPIRIT OF INQUIRY, SEEKING OUT ART AND BEAUTY AROUND YOU, AND CRAFTING A LENS OF YOUR OWN.

SEEING TAKES COURAGE
Part of the work of artmaking is the work of seeing.

French modernist **Henri Matisse** established himself as both a formidable colourist, as seen in his Fauvist paintings, and an impressive draughtsman, as exemplified by his line drawings. From the late 1940s through the remainder of his days, the artist gracefully unified colour and line in his cut-out paper collages, which he created from his wheelchair following surgery for stomach cancer.

After his studio assistants painted paper with colourful gouache, Matisse proceeded to shape the paper with scissors; the artist and his assistants then pinned and unpinned the forms in various arrangements over the course of weeks until the collage was finalized. Sometimes, as with his 'Blue Nudes', a series of collages from 1952 depicting a cobalt nude female figure in different poses, Matisse would pause to draw furiously, to see how the parts of a body came together and might be remade in paper. These elegantly distilled cut-outs necessitated a deep understanding of form as well as a rejection of conventional ideas around how form should look and operate.

A year after making the 'Blue Nudes', Matisse penned the essay 'Looking at Life with the Eyes of a Child', which was published in 1954 in *Art News and Review*. Matisse suggested that the act of seeing clearly was tantamount to creation itself. 'Creation begins with vision,' he wrote. 'To see is itself a creative operation, which requires effort. Everything we see in our daily life is more or less distorted by acquired habits... The effort needed to see things without distortion demands a kind of courage; and this courage is essential to the artist, who has to look at everything as though he were seeing it for the first time.'

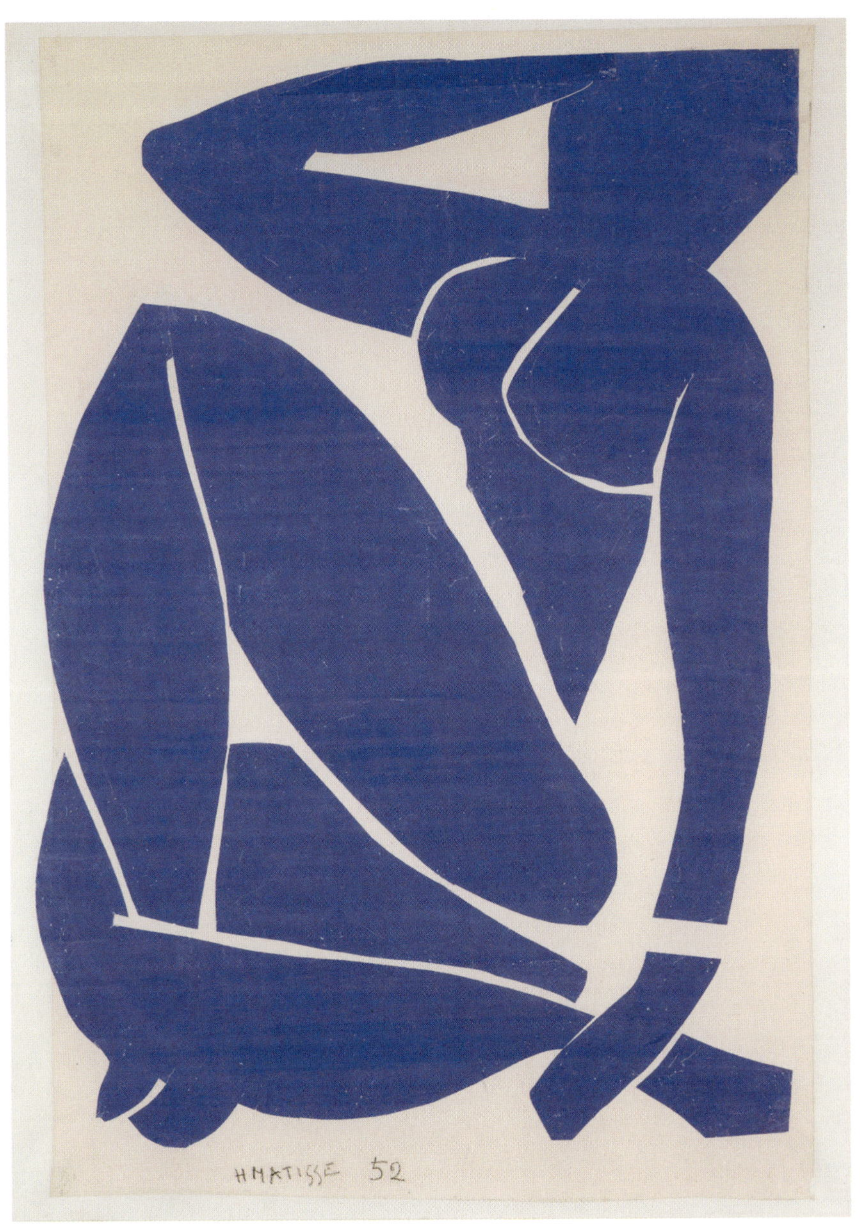

Henri Matisse, Blue Nude III, 1952. Gouache on paper, cut and pasted on white paper, 116.2 x 88.9 cm (45¾ x 35 in).

OBSERVE YOUR IMMEDIATE SURROUNDINGS

Your world is beautiful if you look at it.

English Pop artist **David Hockney** has said that 'everything comes from nature', a sentiment echoed by many, though certainly not all, visual artists. However, in contrast to those who might be inclined to deem their own home or town to be too familiar a subject matter when considering the broad category of the natural world, Hockney views these near and dear sites as a wellspring of inspiration to which he is particularly attuned.

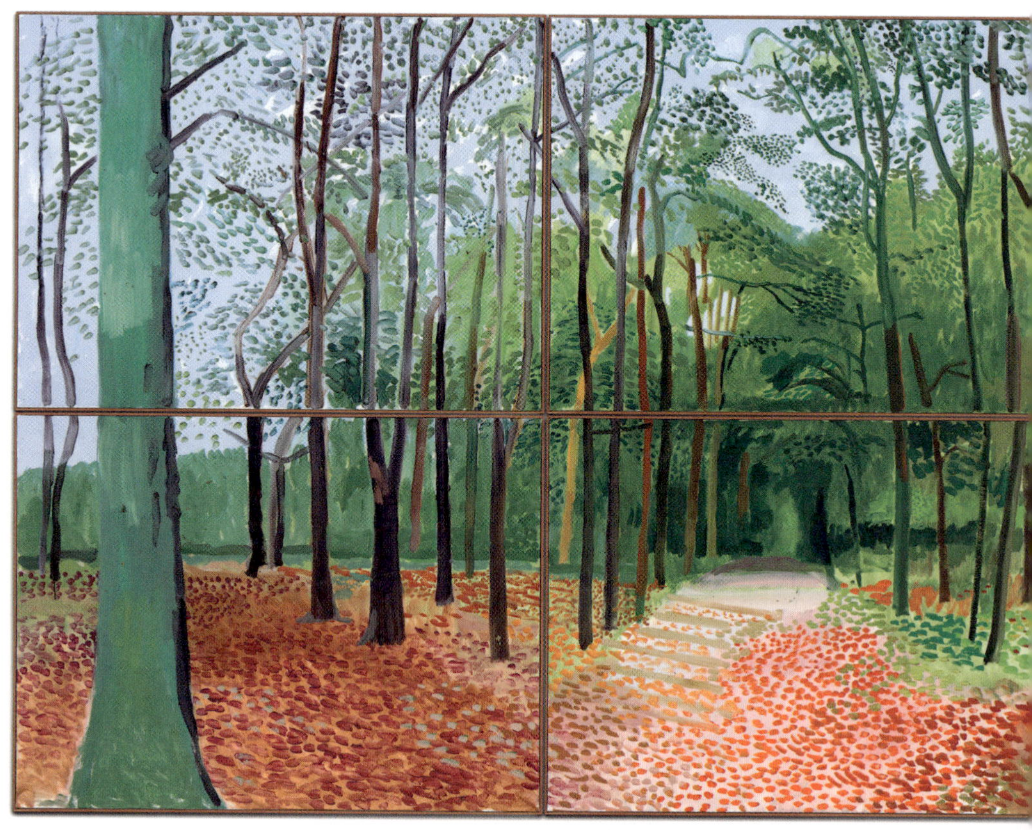

Working observationally in means as varied as painting, drawing, photography and video, Hockney - who is equally celebrated for his portraiture - depicts his environment with clarity and nuance, often using compression and layering to capture various seasonal, temporal and perspectival shifts in the space of a single composition. Among the artist's most celebrated subjects are his quaint country house and environs in Normandy, the woods by his childhood home in East Yorkshire and the eternally blue skies and even bluer pools of Los Angeles. By witnessing and contemplating these places over time, by fully immersing himself in them and inhabiting them, Hockney is uniquely positioned to ascertain their idiosyncrasies and access something of their essence.

In a 2019 interview at his home in Normandy, Hockney told Marc-Christoph Wagner: 'The world is very, very beautiful if you look at it. But most people don't look very much. They scan the ground in front of them so they can walk, but they don't really look at things incredibly well, with intensity. I do, and I've always known that.'

David Hockney, Woldgate Woods, 24, 25 & 26 October 2006. Oil on 6 canvases 91.4 x 121.9 cm each (36 x 48 in), 182.9 x 365.8 cm overall (72 x 144 in).

ART SCHOOL ISN'T A REQUIREMENT

Make the study of art part of your everyday life.

Neo-Expressionist painter **Jean-Michel Basquiat**, a leading figure in the East Village's vibrant artistic counterculture in the 1980s, is celebrated for his high-octane, seemingly improvisational work characterized by a unique iconography of scrawled lists, skulls, boxers, three-pointed crowns and diagrams. Throughout his life, which was tragically cut short at the age of 27, the artist was a staunch autodidact. Born into a middle-class family in Brooklyn, Basquiat grew up with a love of cartoons, comic books, anatomical drawings and Alfred Hitchcock films. From a young age, he went to art museums with his mother; when he was six years old, he became a junior member of the Brooklyn Museum.

After dropping out of high school at the age of 17, Basquiat began painting graffiti, often containing cryptic phrases, on New York City's downtown buildings and subway cars. Alongside the artist Al Diaz, Basquiat tagged his creations with 'SAMO©', an abbreviation for 'Same Old Shit'. Basquiat first received art world recognition in 1980 when he was featured in The Times Square Show, a group exhibition of work by downtown artists including Keith Haring and Nan Goldin. He began making work not only on the street but also on the canvas, and by 1982 he had gallery representation and a cult following. As Basquiat developed his craft, he regularly visited New York City's major museums with a sketchbook in hand, often accompanied by his friend, the visual artist and musician Fred Braithwaite. 'I never went to art school,' Basquiat said. 'I failed the art courses that I did take in school. I just looked at a lot of things. And that's how I learnt about art, by looking at it.'

Jean-Michel Basquiat, Maid from Olympia, 1982. Acrylic, paper and crayon on canvas, 122.5 x 76 cm (48¼ x 29⅞ in).

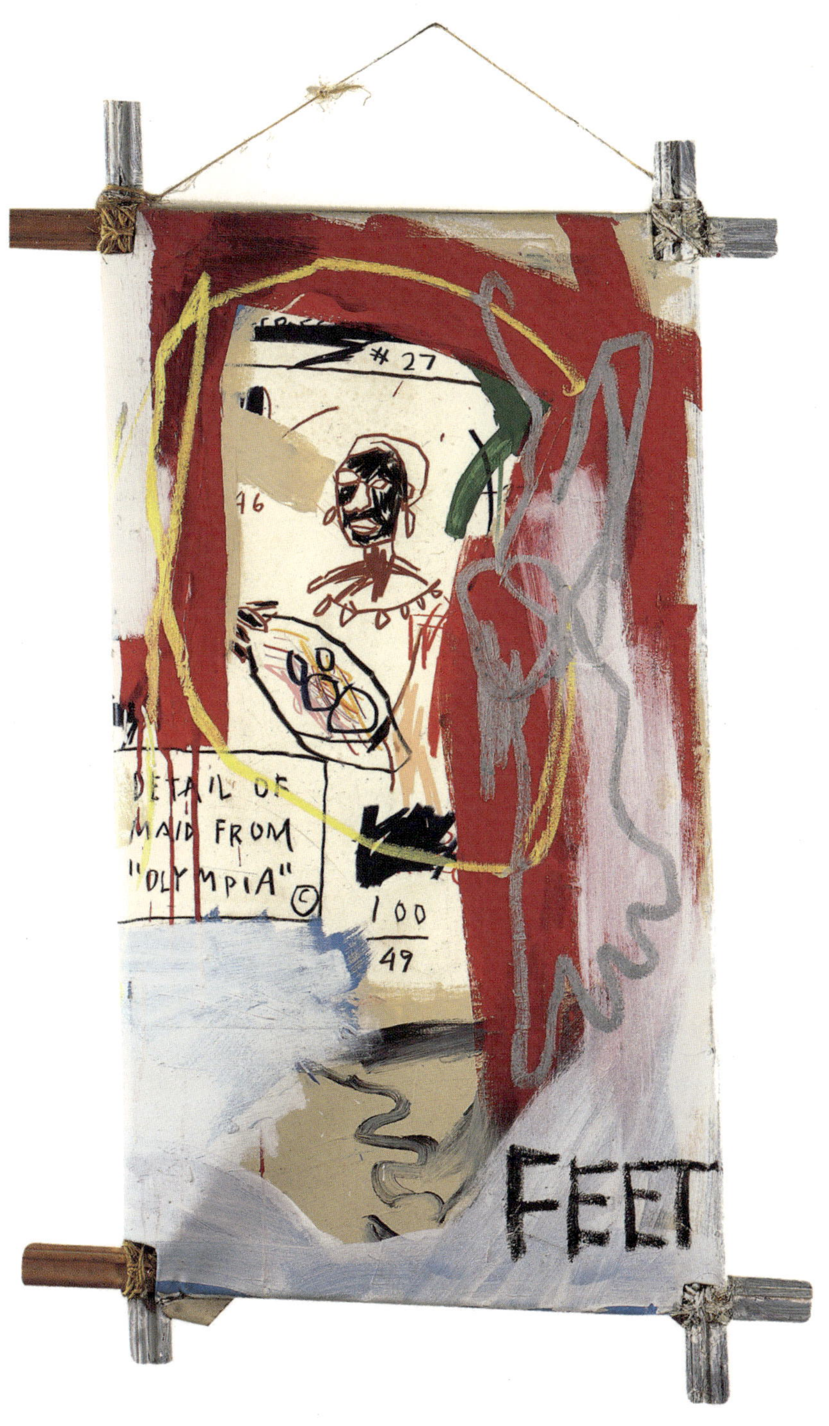

27
76
DETAIL OF
MAID FROM
"OLYMPIA"
100
49
FEET

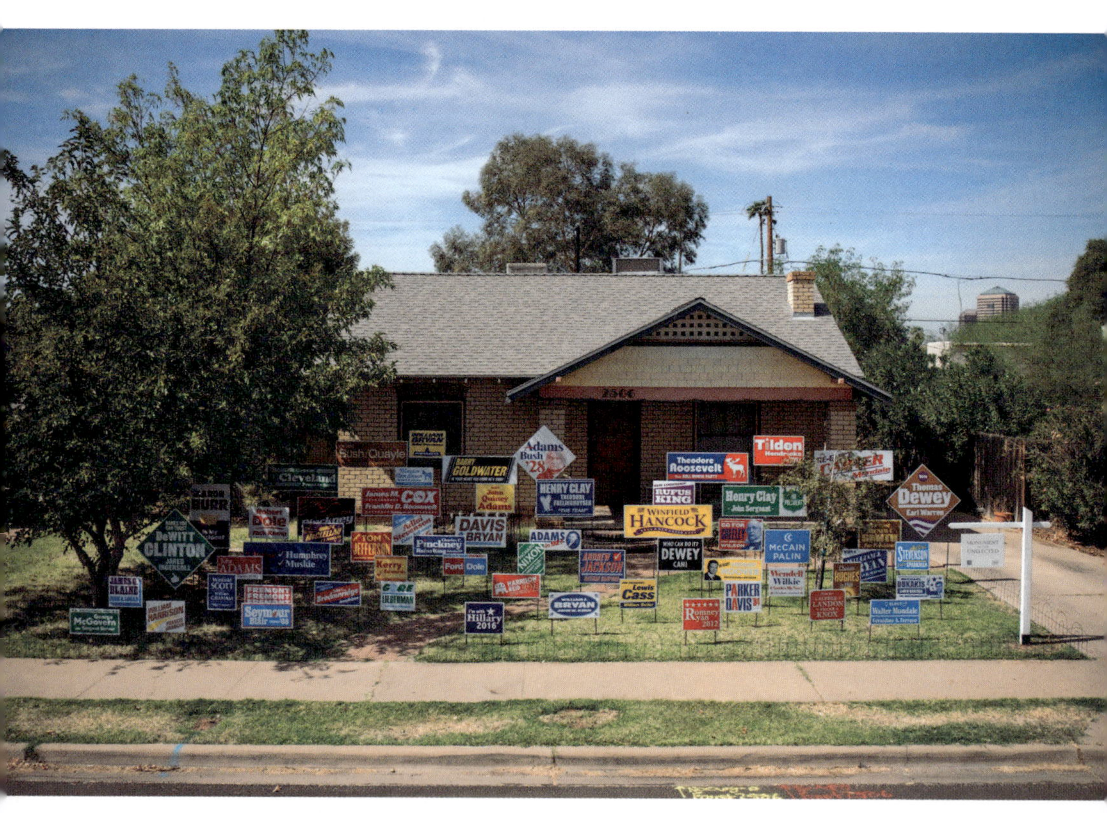

Nina Katchadourian, Monument to the Unelected, 2008 and ongoing. Mixed media installation, dimensions variable.

NOTICE WHAT YOU'RE NOTICING

What do you *really* want to make? Be a meta-observer of yourself to find out.

In 2008, multidisciplinary artist **Nina Katchadourian** was commissioned to produce work for an exhibition at the Scottsdale Museum of Contemporary Art in Arizona. It was a heated election year in the United States, and Katchadourian had noticed the political campaign signs cropping up in front lawns and vacant lots in the politically divided swing state. The artist found herself wondering about the afterlives of the signs for unsuccessful candidates – as well as the lost futures, or the 'paths not taken', that these signs represented.

Engaging her curiosity around the cultural phenomenon of the signage and the material archive that it formed, Katchadourian embarked upon a deep dive into the political history of the United States. With the help of graphic designer Evan Gaffney, she created lawn signs with a modern aesthetic for each losing presidential candidate since the country's founding. The artist has exhibited this evolving installation in various locales during each presidential election cycle since she initiated the project; each time the latest winner and loser are announced, she adds a sign to represent the newest runner-up.

'Sometimes the clue for what you really want to make is in thinking about what you're thinking about or noticing what you're already noticing,' Katchadourian told *The Creative Independent* in 2017. It's advice that she gives her students: projects begin to take shape when you are a 'meta-observer of yourself, of your own curiosities and obsessions', and explore why it is that you find a particular subject or phenomenon so compelling.

FIND YOUR MONT SAINTE-VICTOIRE

Revisit the same subject to explore how your perceptions change.

Over the course of his career, **Paul Cézanne** painted Mont Sainte-Victoire more than 70 times, but never made the same painting twice. By repeatedly returning to the same subject, Cézanne worked out some of his most influential ideas about the complex and shifting nature of perception.

The craggy limestone mountain, located in the painter's beloved Aix-en-Provence in southern France, first appeared in the backdrop of his 1870 painting 'The Railway Cutting'. By the mid-1880s it was a cardinal subject in his work, and one that would continue to occupy him until October 1906, when he died after catching pneumonia following an outing to paint the mountain in a thunderstorm.

Cézanne's attachment to Sainte-Victoire was profoundly personal. He had traversed its terrain as a youth, and in his mature years chose to build a studio in Les Lauves with the mountain in clear view. An *en plein air* painter whose philosophy revolved around nature, Cézanne associated the mountain with the essence of the Provençal countryside. Sainte-Victoire also appealed to him for its blocky inner geometry, which the artist emphasized with planes or patches of juxtaposed colour.

'The same subject seen from a different angle offers subject for study of the most powerful interest and so varied that I think I could occupy myself for months without changing place,' Cézanne wrote to his son in 1906. A famously slow painter, Cézanne worked in oil paint or watercolour to render Sainte-Victoire from multiple – often simultaneous – perspectives and in different lights. As he explored the effects of these shifting conditions in varied portrayals of his 'beau motif', the artist developed his theories of perception, which would play a crucial role in bridging Impressionism and Cubism.

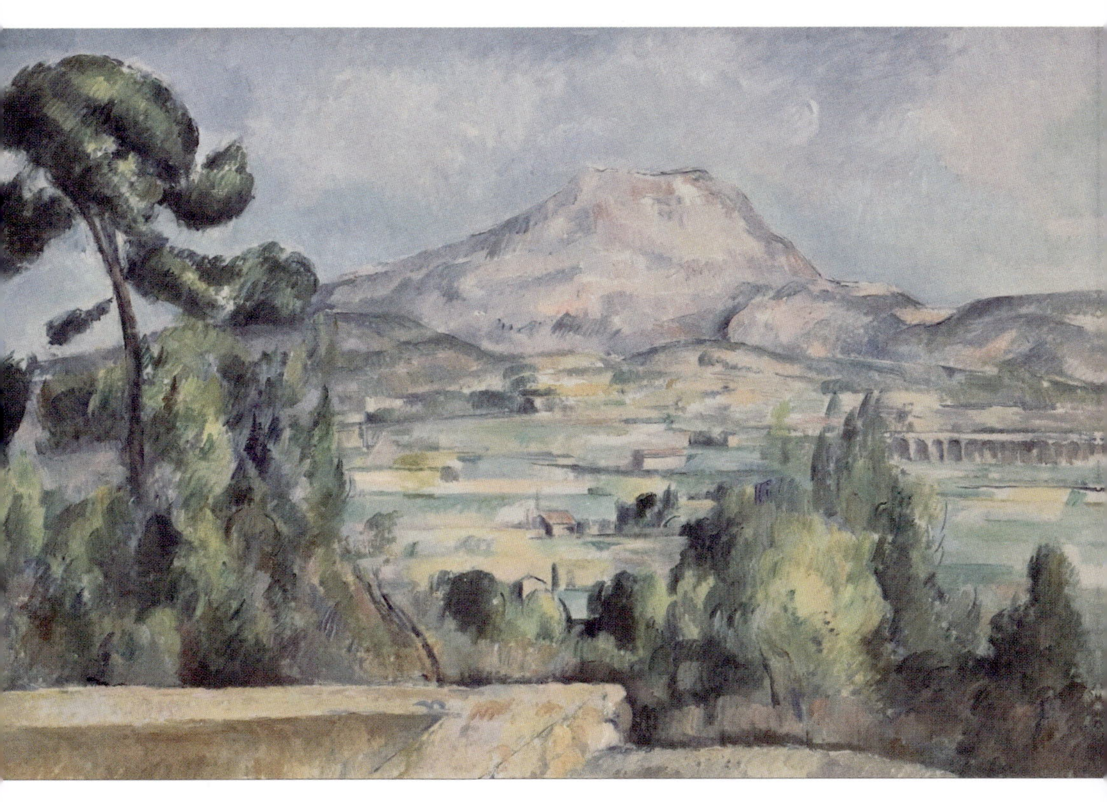

Paul Cézanne, Mont Sainte-Victoire, 1904–6. Oil on canvas, 57.2 x 97.2 cm (22½ x 38¼ in).

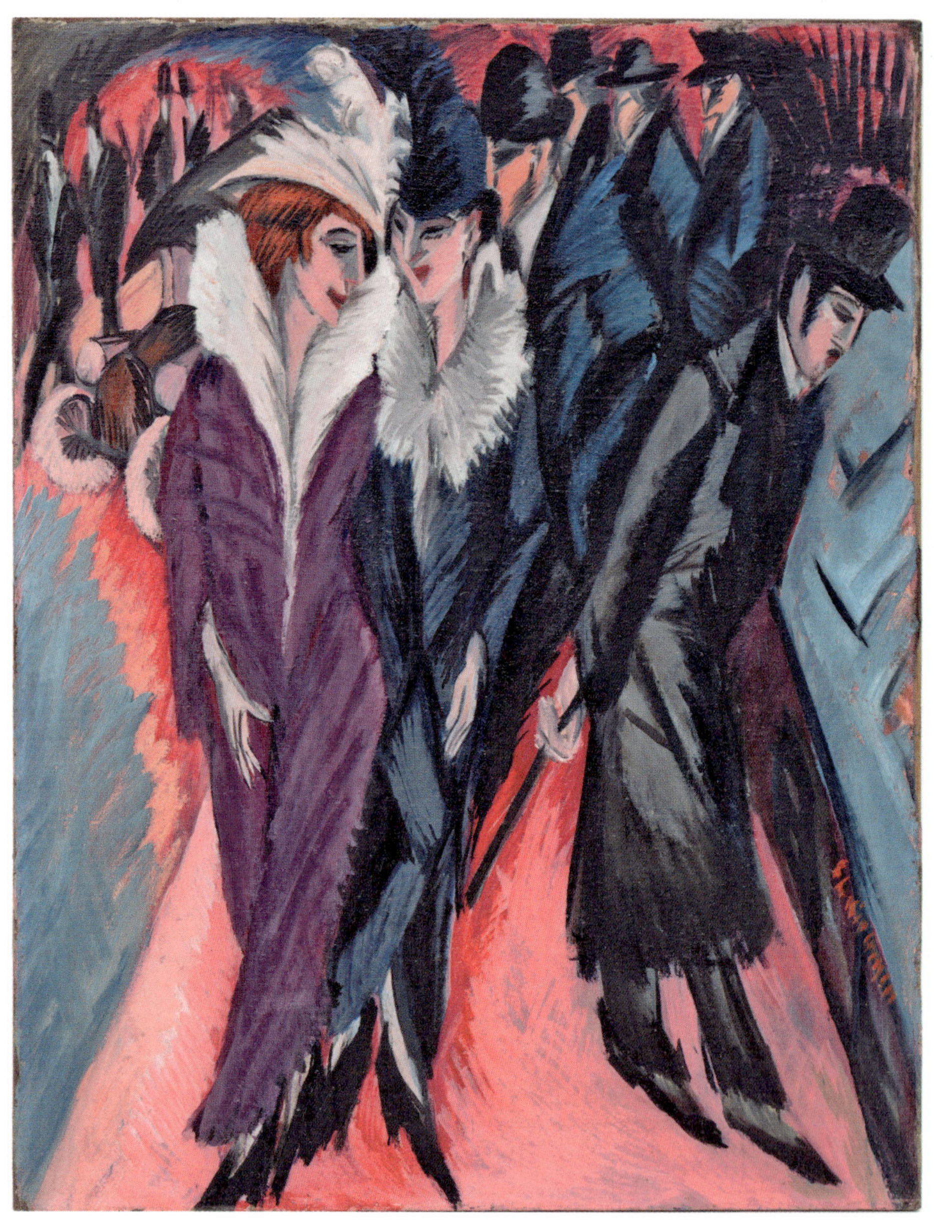

Ernst Ludwig Kirchner, Street, Berlin, 1913. Oil on canvas, 120.6 cm x 91.1 cm (47½ x 35⅞ in).

LOSE YOURSELF IN YOUR SURROUNDINGS

Let yourself dissolve so an image can cohere.

In 1911, German Expressionist painter and printmaker **Ernst Ludwig Kirchner** relocated from Dresden to bustling Berlin. He was in good company: other members of Die Brücke (The Bridge), an anti-bourgeois, anti-academic artistic cohort that he had cofounded in Dresden in 1905, also made the move. As the group rapidly began to splinter, Kirchner – who described the period as 'one of the loneliest times of my life', rife with 'agonizing restlessness' – took to Berlin's people- and car-filled streets with his sketchbook to capture the sights and sensations of the major metropolis.

These sketches, rendered with urgency and immediacy, formed the basis for the 'Street Scenes' series, a group of 11 paintings created by Kirchner between 1913 and 1915. Characterized by teetering perspectives and jagged forms, harsh angles and even harsher colours (including chartreuse, which echoed the garish new hues produced by streetlamps), this landmark body of work captured the frenetic, anxious, excited and erotic energy of Berlin in the years before World War I (the artist suggested that the works were conceptualized from 1911 to 1914).

Kirchner, who like his Die Brücke counterparts was interested in new ideas around free sexuality, viewed sex workers as emblematic of urban life. They became the subject of the 'Street Scenes' series, depicted with impenetrable mask-like faces in bold hues. In 1917, Kirchner wrote in a letter: 'It seems as though the goal of my work has always been to dissolve myself completely into the sensations of the surroundings in order to then integrate this into a coherent painterly form.' With the 'Street Scenes', he may have succeeded.

LEARN HOW YOU LEARN

Embrace the unique ways in which you process information.

Adeptly fusing quilting, weaving and embroidery with gestural painting and drawing, American artist **Amanda Valdez** makes bold, richly textured abstractions that upend staid distinctions between 'art' and 'craft'. While not overt in their meaning, her works are nonetheless shaped by the references and experiences that Valdez absorbs or accrues.

When she made *full Tanit* (2018), Valdez was studying pagan iconography in Renaissance painting. Her research led her to ancient goddess worship, and subsequently to Tanit, a Phoenician goddess associated with fertility and the moon; the three hand-dyed fabric blocks at the work's base loosely reference ruins at sites of worship. Around the same time, the artist was studying drawings by Abstract Expressionist Joan Mitchell. Inspired by the immediacy of Mitchell's mark-making, Valdez juxtaposed the embroidery in 'full Tanit' with a vigorous field of oil stick. All of these disparate influences converged to form the work.

Over time, Valdez has come to understand the non-linear and frequently somatic ways in which she processes information, and integrates that knowledge into her work. 'More than anything, my drawing practice has taught me about how I learn,' the artist explains. 'I study points of interest in art history and cultural theory regularly, however I actively avoid using that information didactically in my work, and also struggle with my cognitive processing. Through drawing, I observed that what I ingest is inherently changing me and that as I research my body is having a somatic experience apart from my brain. By thinking through my hands while drawing, I can subtly reveal the impact of the research and experiences I store in my body through the process of making art.'

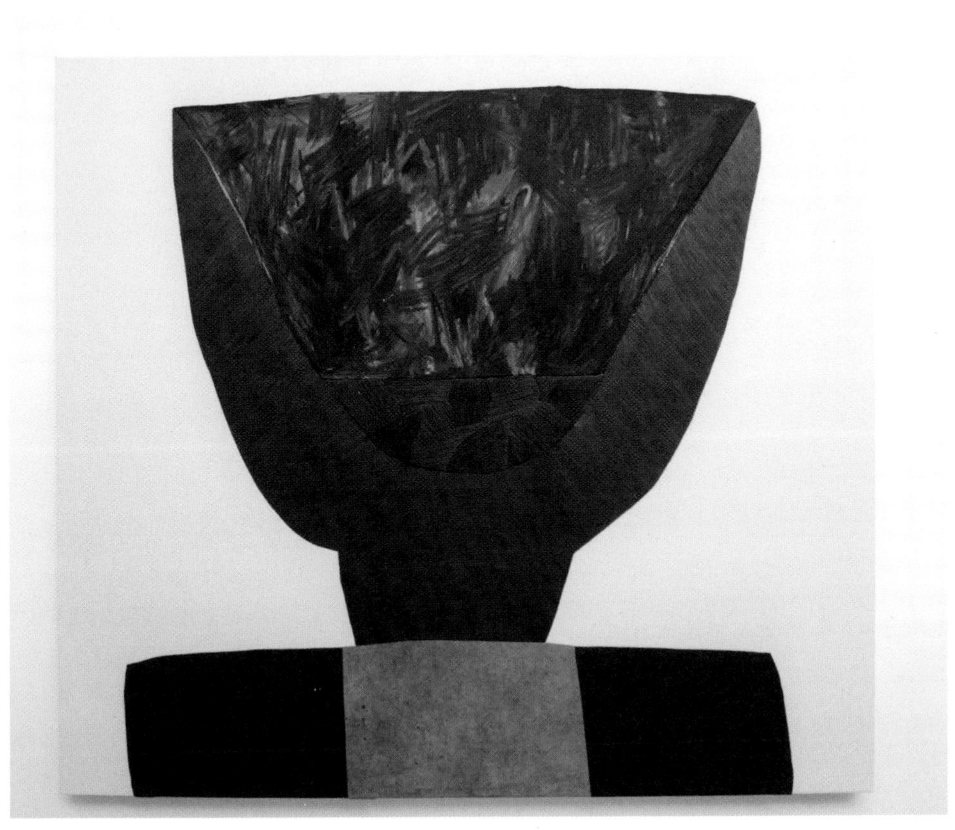

Amanda Valdez, full Tanit, 2017. Embroidery, hand-dyed fabric, oil stick on paper and canvas, 106.7 x 116.8 cm (42 x 46 in).

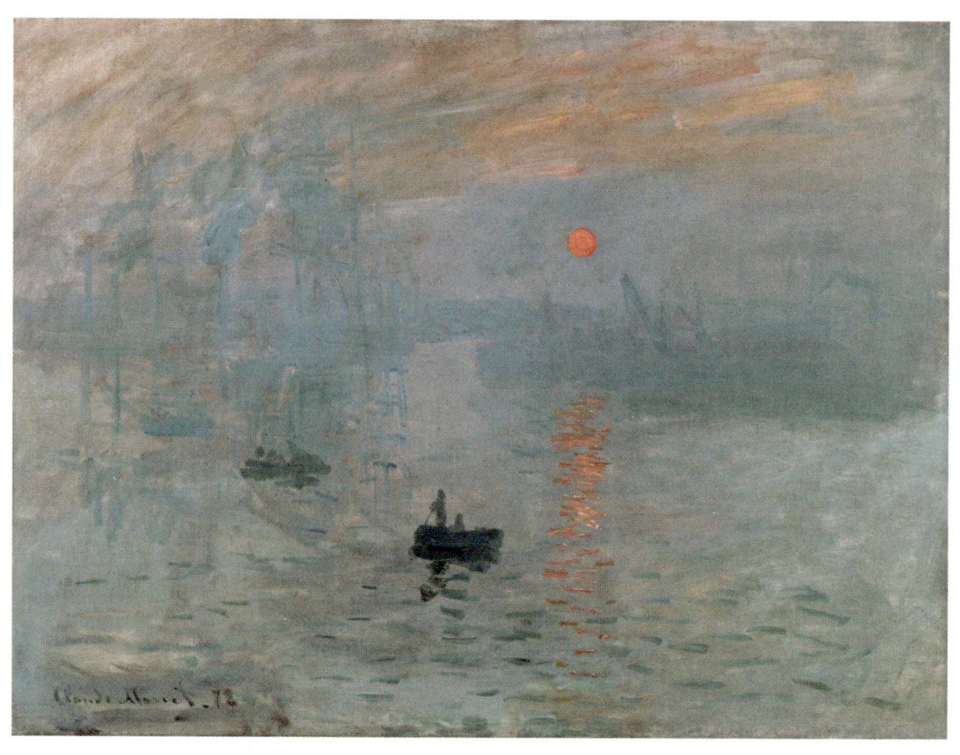

Claude Monet, Impression, soleil levant (Impression, Sunrise), 1872.
Oil on canvas, 48 x 63 cm (18.9 x 24.8 in).

CAPTURE WHAT IS ALIVE BETWEEN YOU AND THE SUBJECT

Convey the experience of an encounter in lieu of something static.

French painter **Claude Monet** was Impressionism's progenitor - so much so that his 1872 painting of an orange sun burning through a morning haze over the water at Le Havre, *Impression, soleil levant* ('Impression, sunrise'), gave the movement its name. Though the moniker, which was intended as an insult, was popularized in 1874 when the group held their first exhibition in Paris, Monet and other core artists in the movement were working in an Impressionist mode as early as 1863.

To make their landscape paintings, Monet and his cohort would take paint - synthetic paint had become available in portable tubes - outside to work directly from nature, operating *en plein air* at a time when it was unusual to execute more than a sketch outdoors. Applying small strokes of pure colour with a sketchy facture to a canvas that he had primed in a light colour, Monet, who was attentive to new developments in scientific theories of perception, captured his experience of seeing and encountering his subject in the world. 'For me, the subject is of secondary importance: I want to convey what is alive between me and the subject,' he said.

Because Monet was reproducing his fluctuating experience of a subject, rather than executing a static rendering of the subject itself, he made very different paintings of the same motifs - haystacks, cathedrals, his beloved Giverny - according to shifts in light and atmosphere. 'A landscape does not exist in its own right, since its appearance changes at every moment; but the surrounding atmosphere brings it to life - the air and the light which vary continually,' the artist explained in 1891.

2

MAKE

LIKE AN ARTIST

ON INSPIRATION & STARTING OUT

A JOKE, A SNEEZE, A DREAM, SCIENCE, POP CULTURE: THESE DIVERSE PHENOMENA HAVE ALL SERVED AS INSPIRATION FOR ARTWORKS DESCRIBED HERE. STRUCTURES AND PROMPTS CAN ALSO BE HELPFUL IN STARTING OUT, FROM CHALLENGING YOURSELF TO MAKE AS MUCH AS POSSIBLE, TO CHARTING A ROAD MAP TO MAKE SOMETHING IMPOSSIBLE.

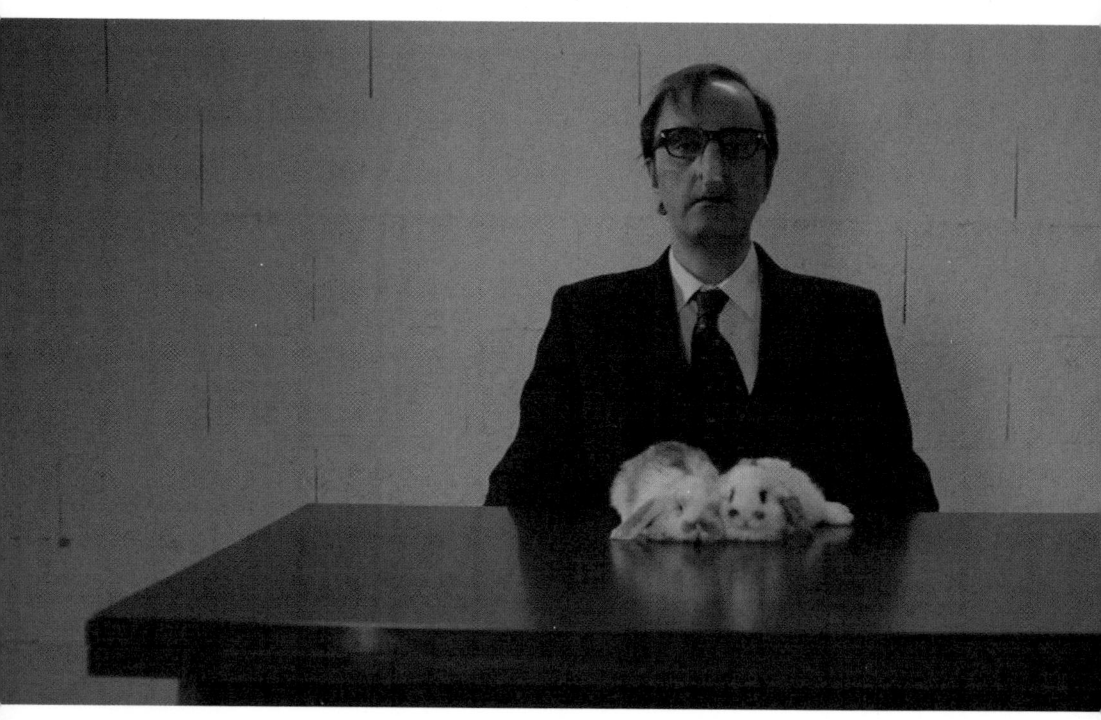

Mika Rottenberg, Sneeze (video still), 2012. Single-channel video installation, sound, colour; 3:02 min.

START WITH A SOUND, SMELL OR TEXTURE

**Begin with something simple or small.
Then, work outwards, building a structure around it.**

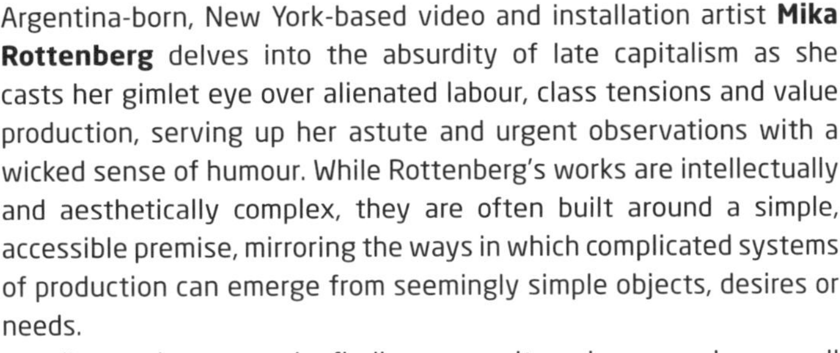

Argentina-born, New York-based video and installation artist **Mika Rottenberg** delves into the absurdity of late capitalism as she casts her gimlet eye over alienated labour, class tensions and value production, serving up her astute and urgent observations with a wicked sense of humour. While Rottenberg's works are intellectually and aesthetically complex, they are often built around a simple, accessible premise, mirroring the ways in which complicated systems of production can emerge from seemingly simple objects, desires or needs.

'I start the process by finding a core – it can be a sound or a smell or a texture,' the artist said of her working method in a 2010 *BOMB* interview. 'If I put a core detail in, say, the itch you feel in your nose when you are allergic to something, I then create a structure where you can throw in more details… There's a moment when I think, I have to be brave and just start building something.'

The single-channel three-minute video work 'Sneeze' (2012) – along with the later longer video 'NoNoseKnows' (2015) – centres around the simple act of sneezing, which was also the subject of 'Fred Ott's Sneeze' (1894), a 45-frame film by William K.L. Dickson from which Rottenberg drew inspiration. In 'Sneeze', men with comically large noses seated at bureaucratic desks sneeze loudly, producing an outpouring of live rabbits, raw steaks and, seemingly in a factory error, a single lightbulb. Around this familiar bodily function, Rottenberg constructs a narrative of the human body and the assembly line put at odds while posing questions about excess and waste.

"""

YOU ARE THE SUBJECT YOU KNOW BEST

Start with yourself.

Throughout her career, Mexican Magical Realist **Frida Kahlo** painted numerous self-portraits - so many that more than a quarter of the paintings she left behind fall into the category. 'I paint myself because I am so often alone and because I am the subject I know best,' said the artist. When Kahlo was 18 years old, she experienced a traumatic bus accident that broke her spinal column, ribs, pelvis and collarbone, and riddled her leg with fractures. She would undergo some 32 surgeries in her lifetime and lived with chronic pain and frequent bedrest. Kahlo often painted herself as she convalesced, studying her reflection in a mirror that was installed above the bed.

The artist portrayed herself with her hallmark facial hair, wearing colourful Indigenous dress that declared allegiance to her Mexican heritage; her likeness appeared amid flora and fauna native to Mexico, or alternatively, in empty rooms or strange, barren landscapes with a desolate cast. *The Two Fridas* (1939) is a double self-portrait that Kahlo made the year that she and painter Diego Rivera divorced. Against a stormy backdrop, the artist appears twice - once in lacy European dress and bearing surgical scissors, and once in Tehuana dress with a small oval portrait of Rivera in her hand. A long vein connects Fridas' two hearts, which have been laid bare. Kahlo, as the 'subject she knew best', used a combination of painterly skill and radical vulnerability to powerfully represent her inner emotional and psychic states, relaying the pain that she experienced in her body, in the society she inhabited, and in her tumultuous romantic relationship.

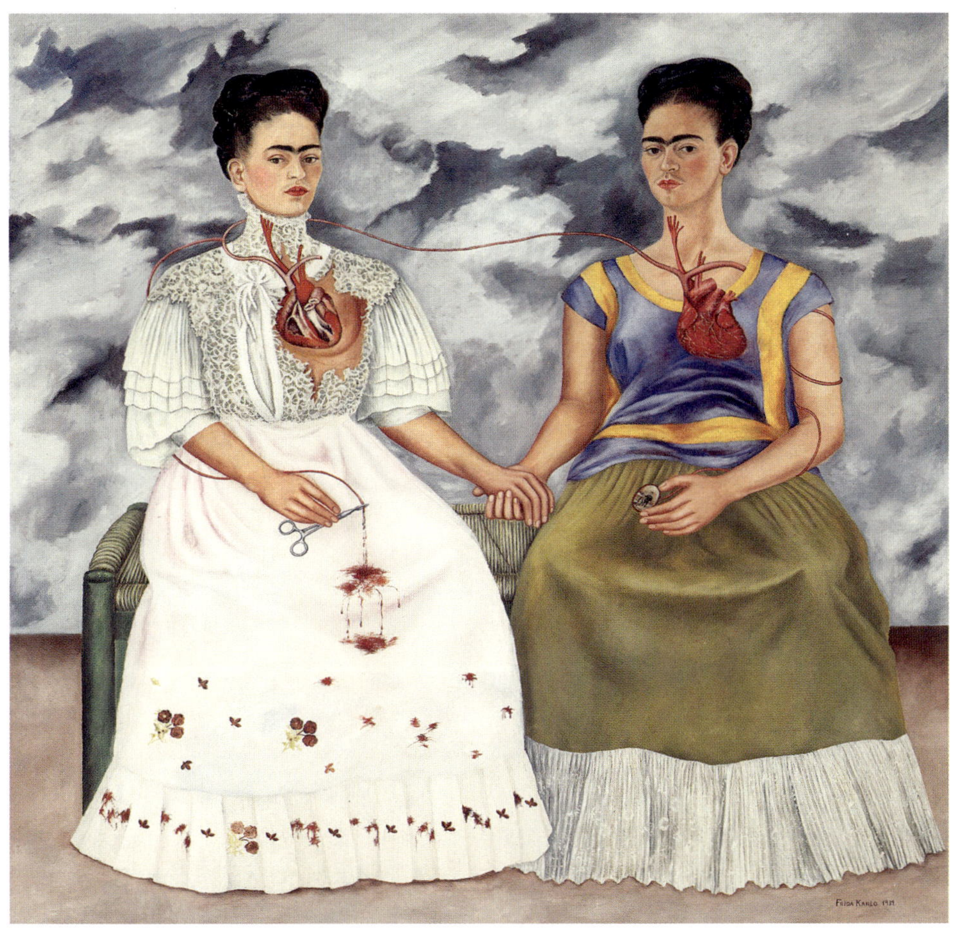

Frida Kahlo, The Two Fridas, 1939. Oil on canvas, 173.5 x 173 cm (68¼ x 68⅛ in).

BEGIN WITH A SINGLE MARK

Strip artmaking down to its elemental forms.

Marks are protagonists in the work of Ethiopian-born, New York-based artist **Julie Mehretu**. Her frequently sweeping paintings and drawings are built up from layer upon layer of precise marks, masses of geometric and calligraphic forms that reference a range of source material - including but not limited to architectural plans, flight patterns, urban maps and media photographs - and engage with urgent contemporary themes such as migration, climate change and global uprisings. Mehretu's work, even when it enters non-representational terrain, is mired in social and political realities of public space, as well as efforts to picture or conceptualize those phenomena diagrammatically, cartographically or photographically.

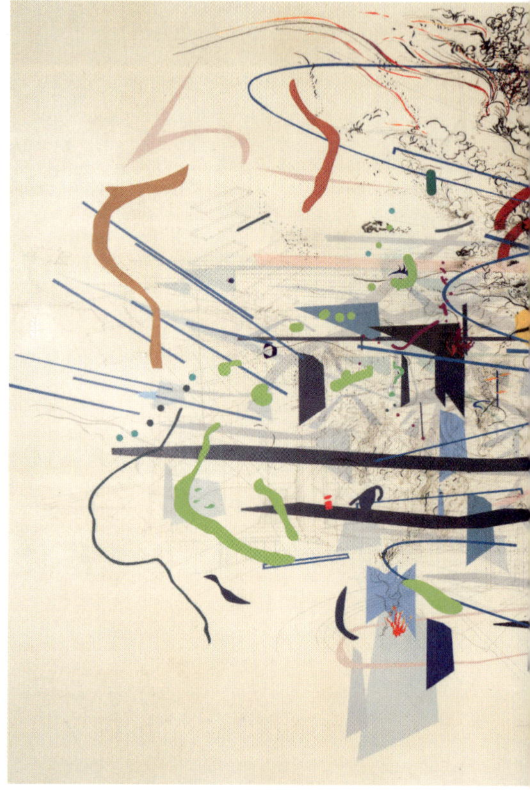

In conversation with *The Brooklyn Rail*, Mehretu identified an important turning point in her work that occurred during her graduate studies at the Rhode Island School of Design. Mehretu, who was making gestural paintings at the time, received an assignment from her professor Michael Young: make just one mark on a piece of paper. Mehretu made hundreds. 'They evolved on my wall like an enormous lexicon of my thinking,' she reminisced.

The prompt stripped artmaking, and in a sense worldmaking, down to its essentials. 'I learned something very profound and fundamental from this way of working - how to access the creative and inventive place within myself through drawing,' Mehretu explained. The exercise also prompted her to think of the marks as 'social agents in space, charting terrain, creating cities and cosmologies', a significant breakthrough in her practice and in social abstraction at large.

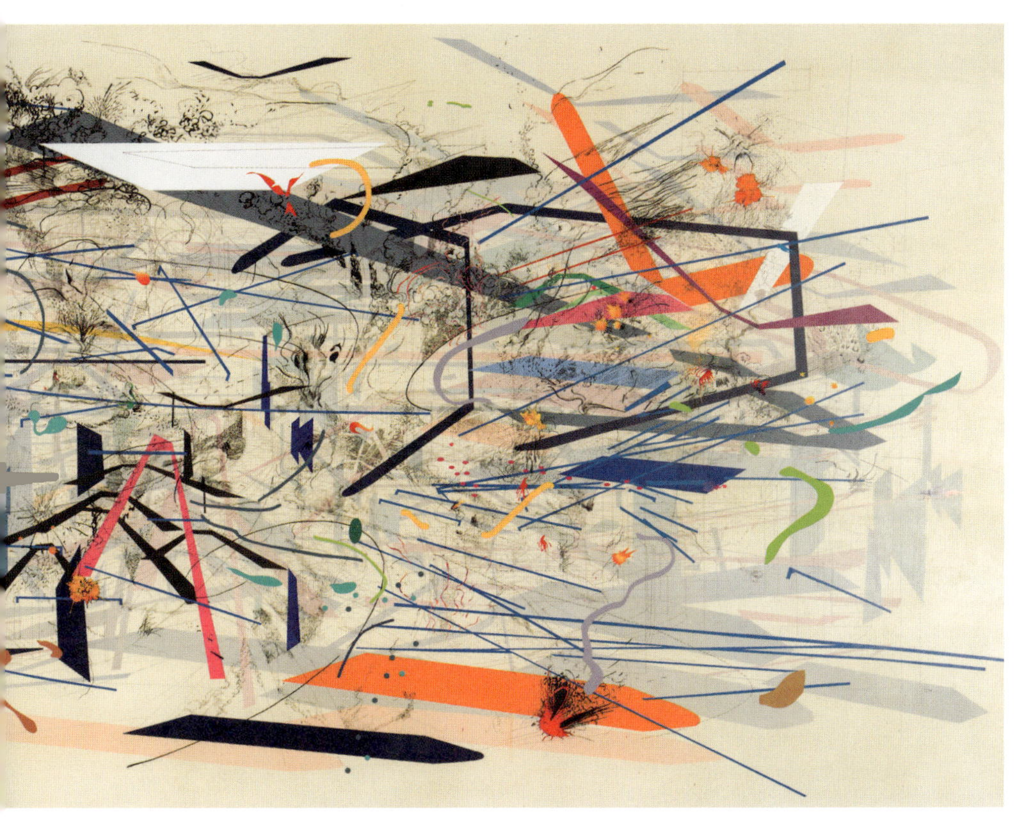

Julie Mehretu, *Retopistics: A Renegade Excavation*, 2001.
Ink and acrylic on canvas. 257.8 x 529.6 cm (101½ x 208½ in).

TAKE HUMOUR SERIOUSLY

Creatively tap into the tension, absurdity and – yes – comedy of jokes.

Meret Oppenheim's fur-covered tea cup, which takes its place alongside Salvador Dalí's lobster telephone as one of Surrealism's most iconic disagreeable objects, originated in a joke among friends. Oppenheim, a German-born Swiss artist whose eccentricity extended to her accessories, donned a bracelet made of fur-covered metal tubing (which she designed for the fashion house Schiaparelli) to a lunch with Pablo Picasso and Dora Maar at Paris's Café de Flore. Picasso jested that anything could be wrapped in fur, leading Oppenheim to quip: 'Even this cup and saucer. Waiter, a little more fur!'

Two weeks later, Oppenheim headed to the department store to purchase a cup, saucer and spoon, all of which she then covered with the flecked fur of a Chinese gazelle. Through this furry tea set, the artist - who was not only a Jungian, but also a patient of Carl Jung himself - mined the psychosexual tension that often nests at the heart of jokes, an energy that Surrealists tapped into via automatism. *Object* (1936), as it came to be called, subjected the refinement and polish associated with drinking tea to animalistic, erotic or even unknowable drives. What could the function of such a ridiculous object possibly be?

Alfred Barr, the director of the Museum of Modern Art in New York, purchased the work for $50 and convinced the museum to acquire it in 1946, despite the professed disgust of members of the board, who would only deign to add it to the institution's study collection. In the 1960s, it was added to the permanent collection: today, it is a jewel of the museum's holdings.

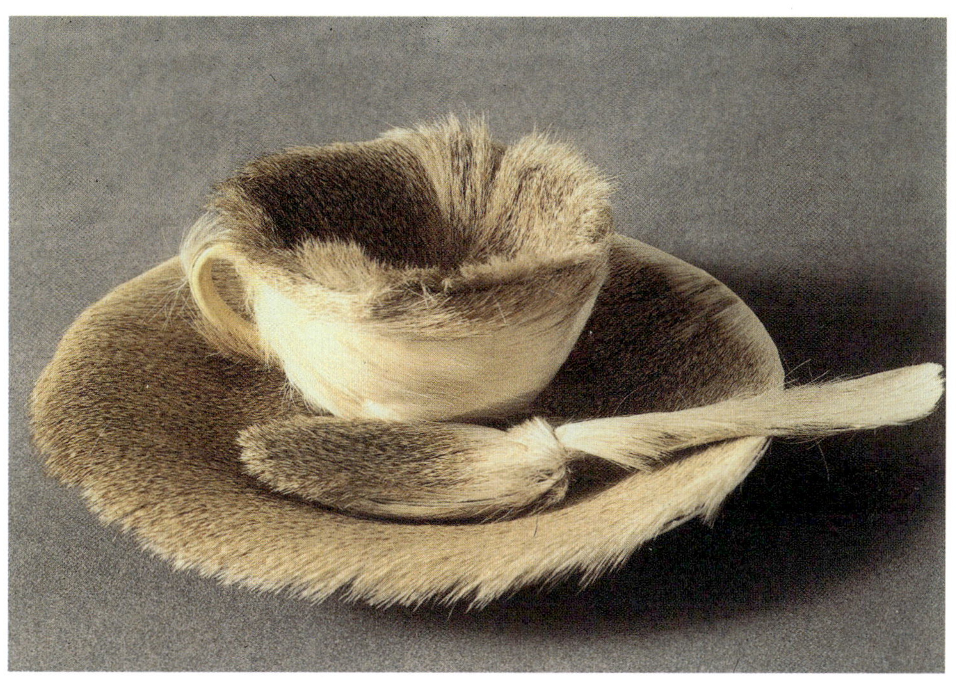

Meret Oppenheim, Object, 1936. Fur-covered cup, saucer, and spoon.
Cup 10.9 cm (4⅜ in) in diameter; saucer 23.7 cm (9⅜ in) in diameter; spoon 20.2 cm (8 in) long; overall height 7.3 cm (2⅞ in).

CAPTURE MOTION

Try to catch a world moving at warp speed.

In the *Technical Manifesto of Futurist Painting* (1910), Italian Futurist painter, sculptor and theorist **Umberto Boccioni** declared that he and his cohort were no longer interested in depicting fixed or static moments on canvas. Instead, they wanted to capture 'dynamic *sensation*', he said, adding that 'all things move, all things run, all things are rapidly changing'. Four years later, after having produced a series of paintings devoted to analyzing the movement of athletes, cyclists and horses, Boccioni argued that the world's only form was dynamism itself.

The Futurists, self-professed lovers of speed, technology and modernity (and, unfortunately, fascism), strove to render the movement that they saw roiling under the surface of all things. Adapting and heightening the Cubists' fragmentation of the picture plane, the Futurists creatively segmented and twisted forms to accommodate modern motion, adding force lines and blurs to their depictions of humans merging with bikes and cars as they moved into a new age.

Umberto Boccioni, Dynamism of a Cyclist, 1913. Oil on canvas, 95 x 70 cm (37⅜ x 27½ in).

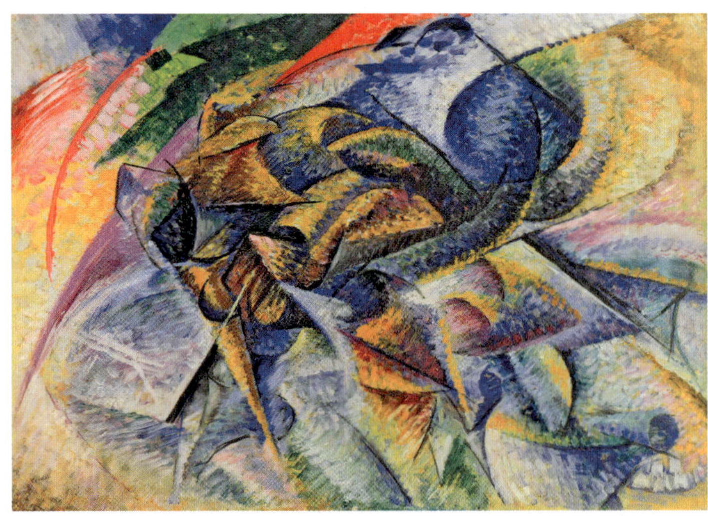

DEFINE SOMETHING IMPOSSIBLE, THEN DO IT

Map out impossibility to make it possible.

For over 50 years, **Lynn Hershman Leeson** has blazed a trail as a pioneering new media artist and filmmaker, achieving things that many would perceive to be impossible. An early cyber-feminist, she has consistently worked at the bleeding edge of technology and biology, making prescient art that examines how identity is constructed and mediated, surveilled and controlled, altered and augmented. In addition to creating what is credited as the first interactive video art disc, 'Lorna' (1979–84), Leeson has collaborated with leading programmers and scientists to explore artificial intelligence and genetic engineering, even developing two antibodies in 2018.

Often, Leeson made these groundbreaking works with little funding or – until recently, when the artist was already in her 70s – substantial public recognition. Teaching at the University of California, Berkeley in 1984, she gave her students a set of three simple instructions, which were later reprinted in curator Hans Ulrich Obrist's *do it (home)* compendium. First, define something that is impossible to accomplish. Next, map out a plan – a road map for achieving that elusive, impossible thing. Finally, and perhaps most importantly: do it.

'PEOPLE KEEP SAYING, "IT'S IMPOSSIBLE" . . . BUT I THINK THAT YOU CAN SOLVE PROBLEMS IF YOU ARE CREATIVE AND APPLY YOURSELF TO DOING IT.'

LYNN HERSHMAN LEESON

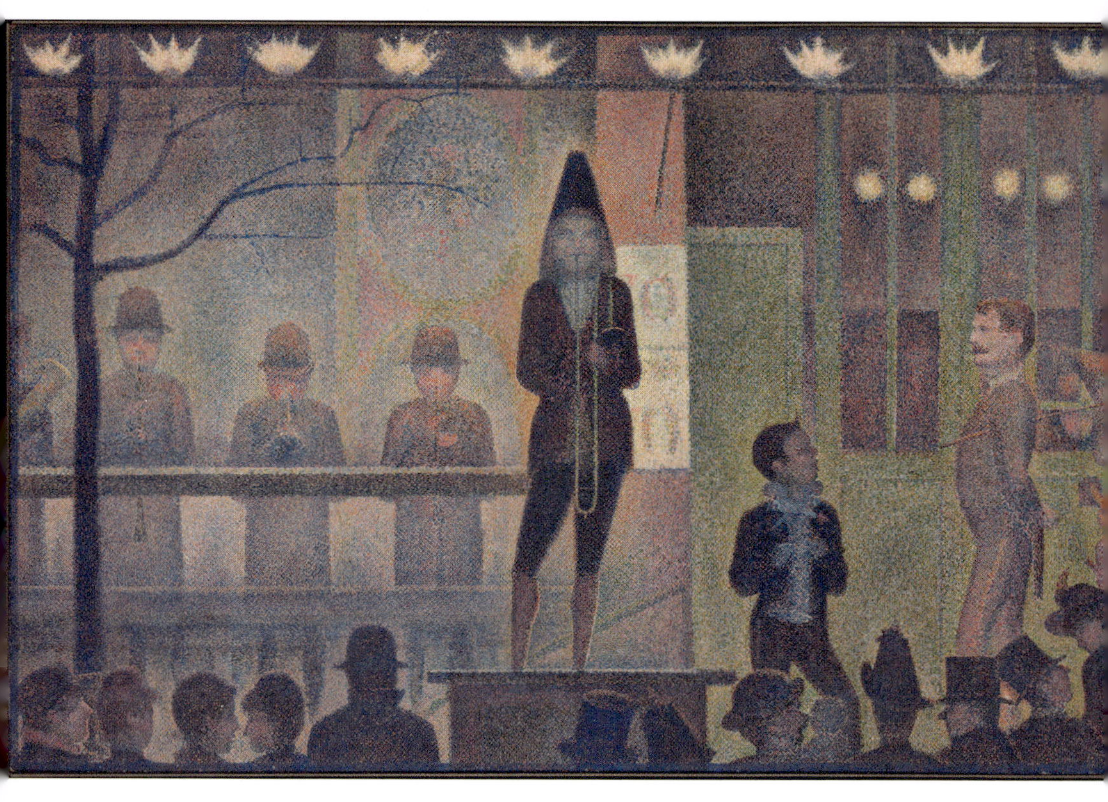

Georges Seurat, Parade de cirque (Circus Sideshow), 1887–8.
Oil on canvas, 99.7 x 140.9 cm (39¼ x 59 in).

FOLLOW THE SCIENCE

Excited by discoveries in other fields? Let that filter into your work.

French Neo-Impressionist painter **Georges Seurat** was fascinated by science. As he embarked upon his career, Seurat was among the artists taking note of new theories of colour, perception and optics published by scientists including American physicist Ogden Rood, German physicist Hermann Ludwig Ferdinand von Helmholtz, French mathematician Charles Henry and, perhaps most significantly, French chemist Michel Eugène Chevreul, who was responsible for some of the earliest scientific studies of colour perception and introduced a version of the colour wheel.

Beyond paying attention to the discourse around these developments, Seurat integrated them into his work in exciting ways (though academics differ in their opinions as to how well he understood the science). Along with the painters Paul Signac and Camille Pissarro, Seurat pioneered Pointillism, also known as Divisionism, in which tiny dots of pure, unmixed colour were meticulously placed side by side in a precise, predetermined schema so that they fused in the eye of the beholder – a phenomenon known as 'chromoluminarism' – rather than on the canvas itself.

Though many of Seurat's contemporaries questioned this scientific, systematic approach – Vincent van Gogh, who in fact had a brief flirtation with Pointillism himself, described it as the work of 'little green chemists who pile up tiny dots' – the style was enormously influential on the Fauves, who were inspired to use pure colour and hyper-saturated hues. 'They see poetry in what I have done,' mused Seurat. 'No, I apply my method and that is all there is to it.'

THE IMPORTANT THING IS TO CREATE

To know what you're going to draw, you have to begin drawing.

Pablo Picasso, a Spanish-born modernist who spent the bulk of his life in France, has an outsize presence in the history of art. Celebrated for his role in fragmenting the picture plane to cofound Cubism as well as his important subsequent contributions to Neoclassicism and Surrealism, Picasso experimented and evolved unrelentingly – often revisiting and reworking previous motifs or scenes in a new style – over the course of a career spanning nearly eight decades. He was prolific, too, producing upwards of 20,000 paintings, drawings, sculptures, prints and ceramics across his lifetime. A firm believer in the potency of studies and sketches, the artist boasted that he was able to produce hundreds over the course of several days. Some of his most famous paintings, such as *Le Rêve* (1932), were made in a single day.

When the photographer Brassaï, a close friend and peer who documented Picasso's work in the early 1940s, asked the artist about the inspiration for his many drawings, Picasso responded that 'ideas are simply starting points'. 'As soon as I start to work, others well up in my pen,' he explained. 'To know what you're going to draw, you have to begin drawing.' Approaching art as fundamentally mutable, Picasso was open to the many ways in which an image might evolve over the course of its execution and was sceptical of the notion that a picture could ever be finished. 'The important thing is to create,' he told artist and poet Jaume Sabartés. 'Nothing else matters; creation is all.'

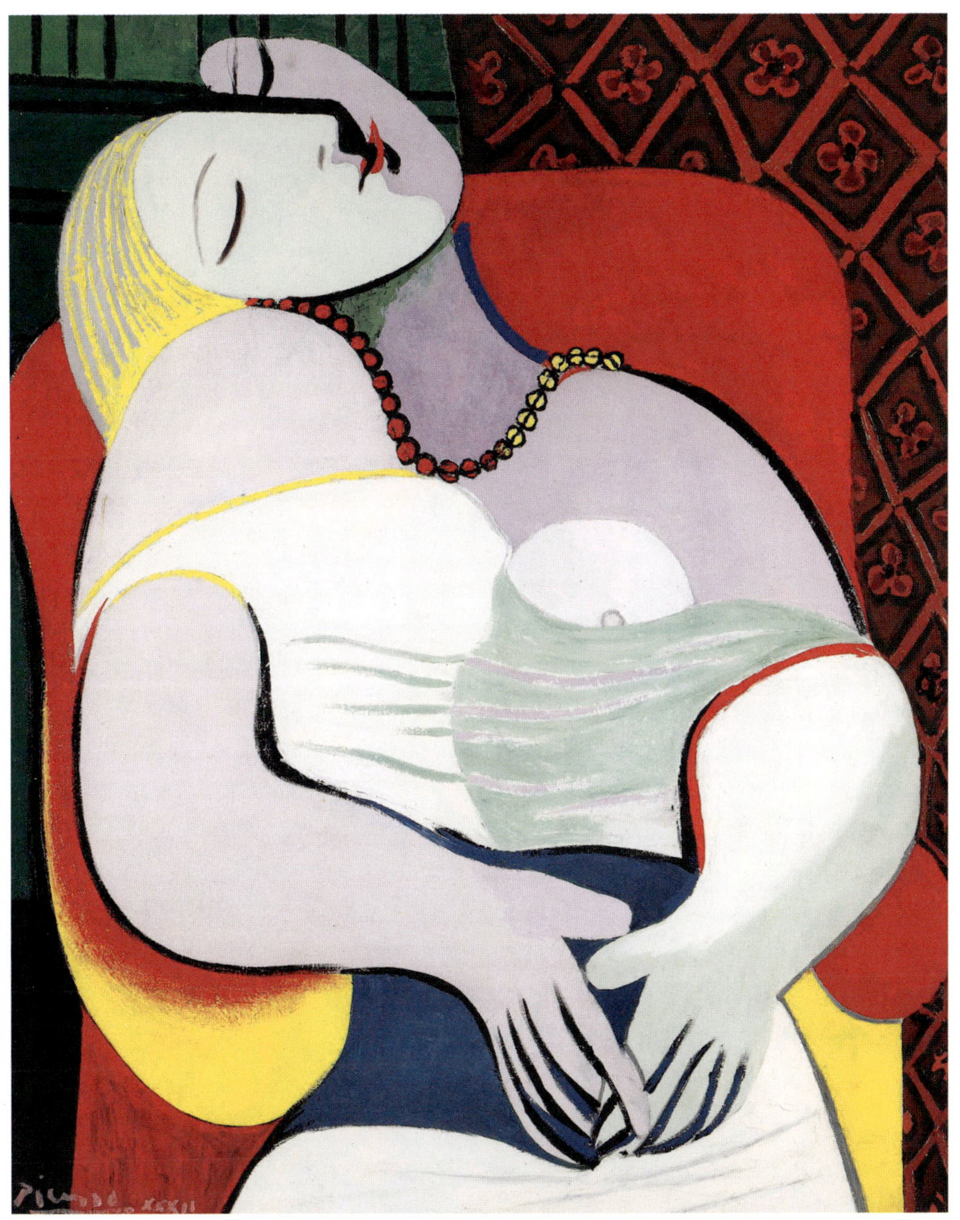

Pablo Picasso, Le Rêve (The Dream), 1932. Oil on canvas, 130 x 97 cm (51 x 38 in).

YOU MIGHT BE MORE INFLUENCED BY BEYONCÉ THAN PICASSO

Your influences and inspirations don't have to be historical.

As part of the MTV generation that came of age in the 1980s and 1990s, American multidisciplinary artist **Hank Willis Thomas** grew up on a regular diet of pop culture. Today, his work probes themes and imagery found in mass media, sports and advertising, focusing on the ways in which these intersecting phenomena represent, frame and commodify Blackness in the United States. In his explorations of the relationship between popular culture and identity, Willis also questions notions of freedom that are central to the country's branding.

Thomas began his artmaking career as a photographer, composing images that deploy the language of advertising and using erasure to intervene in existing adverts and thus deconstruct their treatments of race and gender. He came to work with sculpture as well, often employing industrial or mass-produced materials such as stainless steel, fibreglass, retroreflective vinyl and factory-made textiles, including the American flag. Driven by an orientation towards social justice, Thomas cofounded For Freedoms, an artist-run platform promoting civic engagement, in 2016.

'I'm much more influenced by Beyoncé than I am by Picasso,' Thomas said in the catalogue accompanying his 2020 survey show at the Crystal Bridges Museum of American Art in Arkansas, underscoring the artist's commitment to parsing the operations of pop culture. In a later interview, he added, 'I would not say that I consider myself a super-fan of Beyoncé in any real way. But I will say that seeing her perform live from a few steps away changed my life.'

Hank Willis Thomas, It Shows, 2010. Digital C-print, 109.9 x 76.2 cm (43¼ x 30 in).

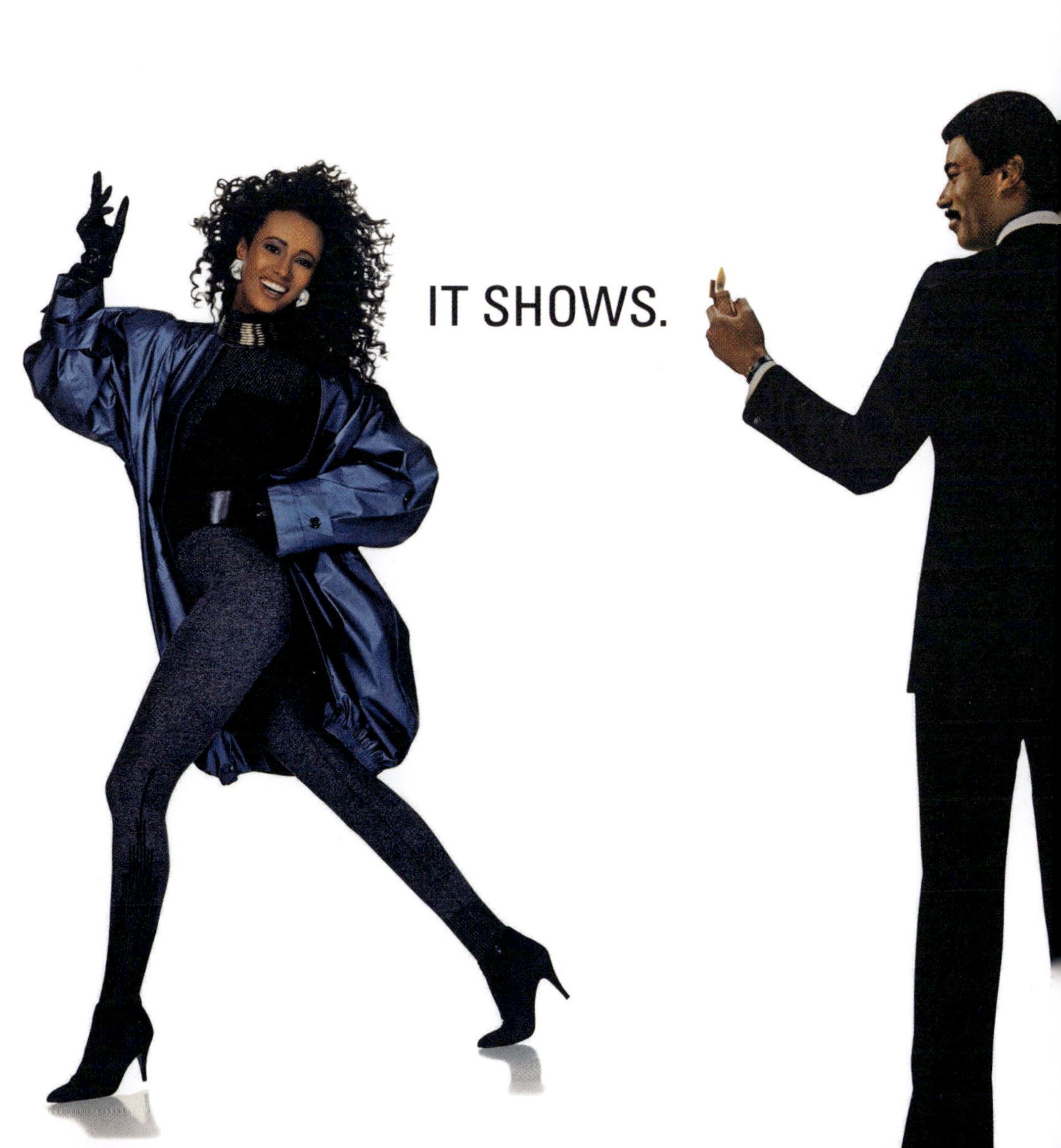
IT SHOWS.

'NO' DOESN'T MEAN THE PROJECT IS OVER

If you encounter a deadlock, don't quit; ask more questions.

'In all of my projects, there's a series of noes and impasses,' American artist and filmmaker **Jill Magid** said in a 2016 *Artforum* interview. 'I've learned that no doesn't mean the project is over, but rather that it is beginning. No needs to be unpacked. Why *no*? No what, exactly? No this? No that? What law or deeper issue does *no* reveal? What do I have to do so that *no* becomes a *yes*?'

In her conceptually driven projects, Magid inserts herself into bureaucratic, corporate, legal, military and other drily authoritative systems. As the artist interrogates these established structures, she strives to understand how power, permission and agency operate and relate to one another within their bounds – and where exactly those boundaries lie. Her multiyear project 'The Barragán Archives' (2013-16) addressed the complex legal legacy behind Mexican architect Luis Barragán's split archives and image rights. Instead of being brought to a standstill by the archive's partial inaccessibility, Magid explored its sequestered status and even made an unusual 'proposal' – using a diamond made from Barragán's ashes – in an effort to make the repository publicly accessible.

'WHAT IS CONSIDERED BANAL OR CLICHÉ MIGHT BE HIDING SOMETHING.'

JILL MAGID

FOLLOW YOUR DREAMS

Try out techniques to mine your unconscious.

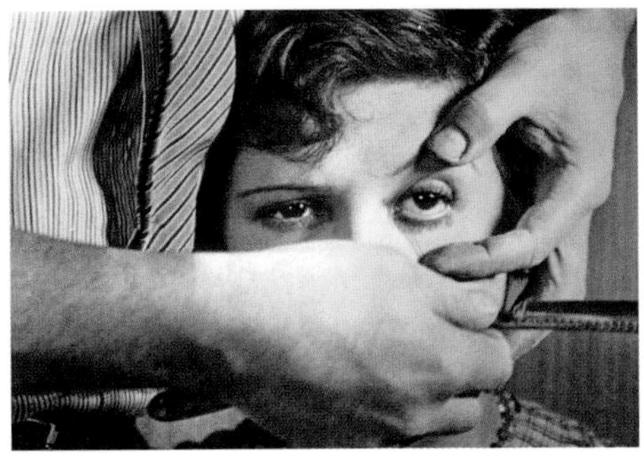

In André Breton's 1924 *Surrealist Manifesto*, the French writer argued for the importance of dreams, which he believed offered powerful insights but had been unfairly 'reduced to a mere parenthesis'. To access the unconscious in their artmaking, Surrealists turned to their dreams, as well as techniques that helped them relinquish control over the creative process, including automatic drawing, automatic writing, and collaborative games like Exquisite Corpse.

Spanish Surrealist **Salvador Dalí**, who referred to his paintings as 'hand-painted dream photographs' and innovated a 'paranoiac-critical method' that helped him to enter a delirious state, took dreaming very seriously. Sometimes, a work would stem directly from a dream; *Un Chien Andalou* (1929), a silent film that Dalí made with Spanish director Luis Buñuel, was inspired by dreams that each of the men had (about ants and the moon, respectively) and unfolded associatively rather than narratively. Dalí also explored hypnagogic states, holding a small object as he dozed off in his armchair; as soon as he fell asleep, the object would fall to the floor, waking him, and he would rush to his canvas to paint.

Luis Buñuel and Salvador Dalí, Un Chien Andalou (An Andalusian Dog), 1929. Film still, 17min.

TRANSLATE TO A NEW MEDIUM

Start with familiar imagery and transpose it to an unexpected material.

From 1904 to the onset of World War I, Geneva-born painter and wood engraver **Alice Bailly** lived in Paris, where she positioned herself at the bleeding edge of the city's avant-garde. Her style evolved continuously in response to her milieu. Bailly employed Fauvism's colourful palette and graphic outlines, and one of her paintings was featured in the Fauve section of the 1906 Salon d'Automne in Paris. She also applied Futurism's force lines to music and rhythmic motion, increasingly important motifs for her as her career progressed, and wielded Cubism's fragmented planes so deftly that, in 1913, the Orphist quality of her painting garnered her the admiration of poet Guillaume Apollinaire. Naturally, this chameleon declined to identify with a singular movement.

While stuck in Geneva during World War I, Bailly began to experiment with different media, incorporating collage and beading into her compositions. This period of material exploration gave rise to the artist's most distinctive body of work: from 1917 to 1923, Bailly produced some 50 '*tableaux-laine*', or wool pictures, in which she used short pieces of multicoloured yarn to transpose her fragmented, avant-garde forms into textile patches that simultaneously evoked brushstrokes and were emphatically woollen. 'Wool becomes before our eyes a precious, expressive and living material like oil, pastel, marble or gold,' writer Albert Rheinwald opined of Bailly's work in his 1918 monograph on the artist. Bailly elected to exhibit the wool pictures alongside her paintings, refusing a hierarchy of media implicitly rooted in a devaluation of women's work.

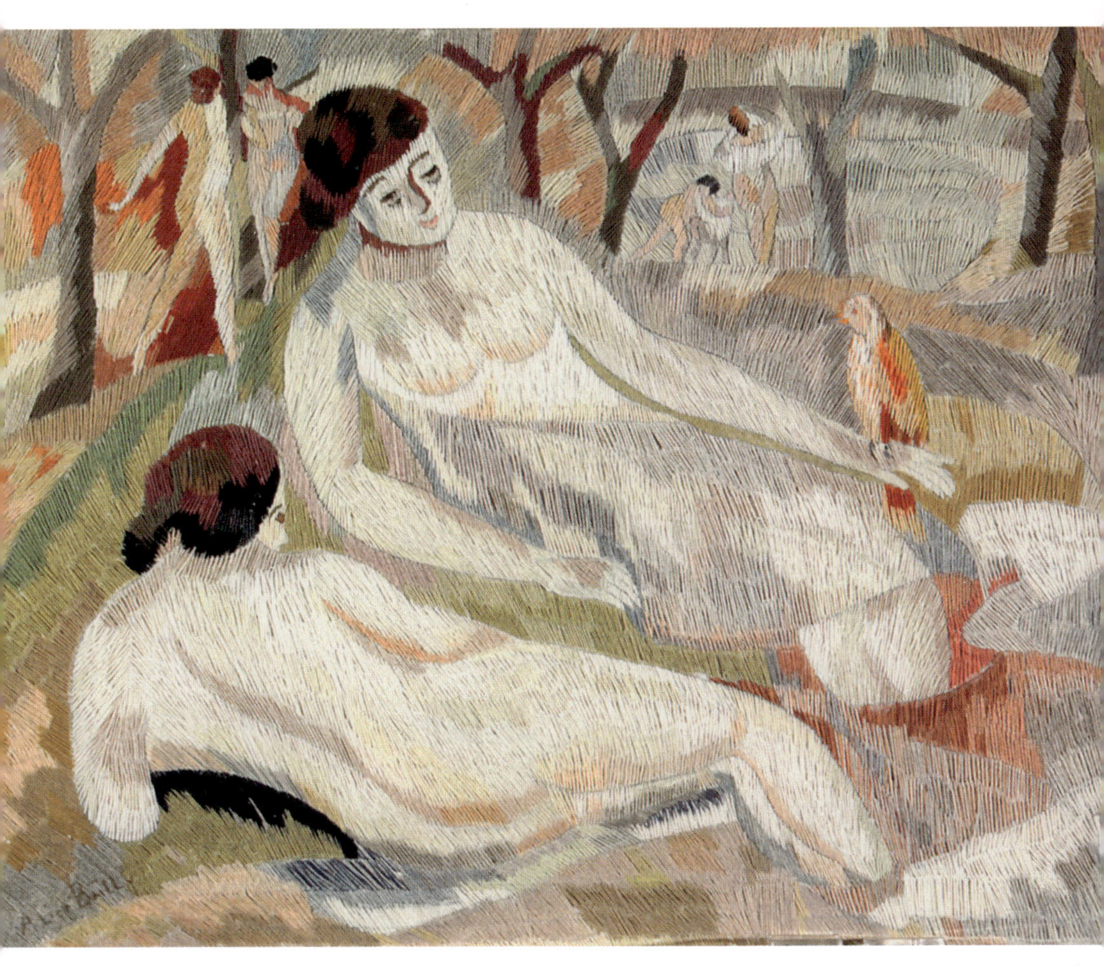

Alice Bailly, Après-midi d'automne (Autumn Afternoon), 1924–5. Wool and collage on canvas on cardboard, 73.5 x 94 cm (29 x 37 in).

ON PROCESS

HOW DOES THE MAKING OF A WORK UNFOLD? FOR SOME ARTISTS, ARTMAKING FUNCTIONS LIKE A MACHINE, WITH AN IDEA AS A MOTOR; FOR OTHERS, THE PROCESS LOOKS MORE LIKE A SERIES OF INVOLVED DECISIONS TOWARDS AN END; AND FOR STILL OTHERS, INTUITION, EXPERIMENTATION AND PLAY ARE IN THE DRIVER'S SEAT.

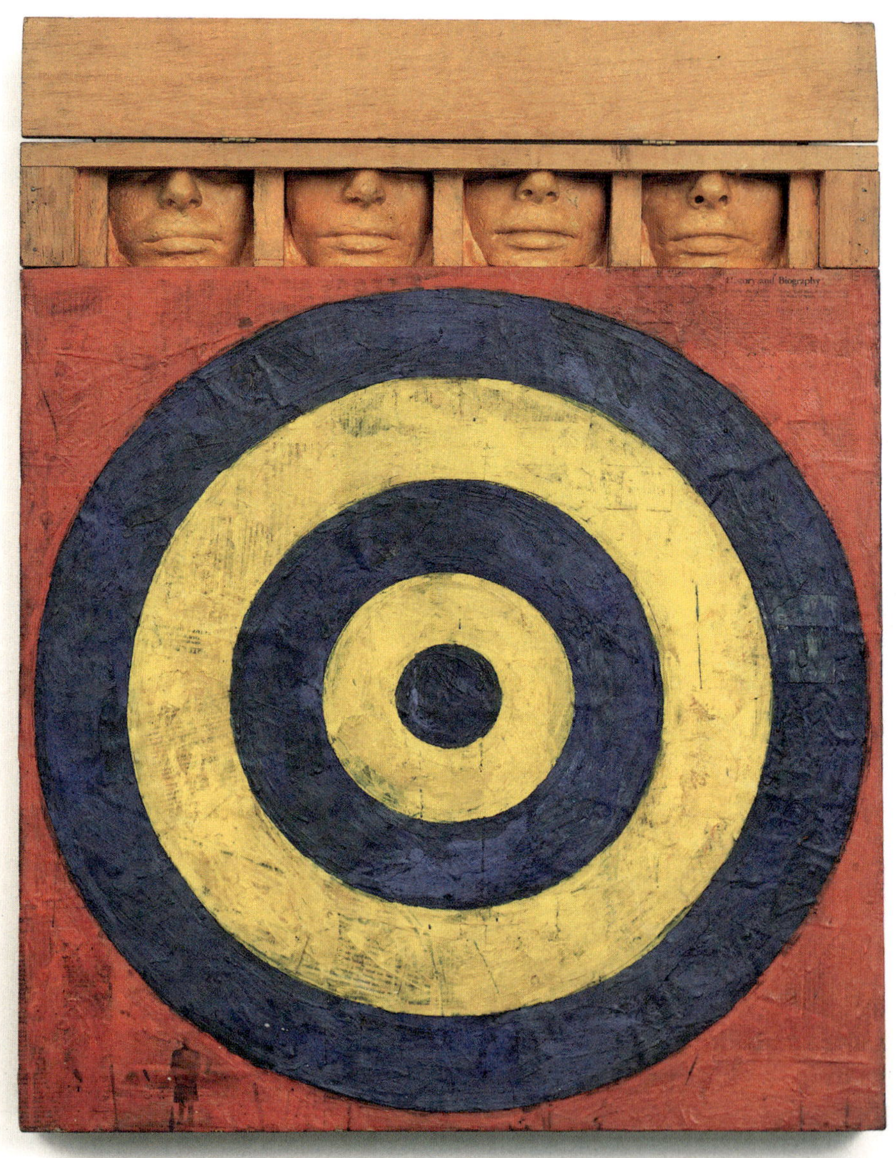

Jasper Johns, Target with Four Faces, 1955. Encaustic on newspaper and cloth over canvas surmounted by four tinted-plaster faces in wood box with hinged front, overall, with box open, 85.3 x 66 x 7.6 cm (33⅝ x 26 x 3 in); canvas 66 x 66 cm (26 x 26 in); box (closed) 9.5 x 66 x 8.8 cm (3¾ x 26 x 3½ in).

TAKE AN OBJECT.
DO SOMETHING TO IT.
DO SOMETHING ELSE TO IT.

Work through an existing image or form serially.

Having destroyed the bulk of his existing artwork in the autumn of 1954, a 24-year-old **Jasper Johns** set off in a bold new direction. In stark contrast with the Abstract Expressionist painting that was prevalent in New York City at the time, Johns' new, coolly enigmatic work took as its subject 'things that the mind already knows' – commonplace forms that weren't typically afforded much visual consideration. Setting the stage for Pop Art, Johns demonstrated the ways in which these everyday forms could be abstract, strange, variable and, in a sense, endless.

Flag (1954–5), his first major work in this mode, depicted an American flag made with built-up encaustic (pigmented hot wax) and bits of newspaper; close on its heels was *Target with Four Faces* (1955), a painting of a shooting target (a fundamentally geometric form, similar to the flag) made with encaustic topped with four niches containing plaster faces lopped at the eyes. Over the subsequent six years, the artist would explore and modulate the form of the target across dozens of paintings, drawings, prints and sculptures.

Writing in his sketchbook in 1964, Johns encapsulated the process by which he made variations on a concrete image: 'Take an object / Do something to it / Do something else to it. [Repeat].' In addition to flags and targets, maps, numbers and letters of the alphabet were important motifs for Johns in the 1950s and 1960s; later on, a pattern he saw from a car, Pablo Picasso's paintings and the cognitive optical illusion Rubin's vase would get the same serial and cyclical treatment.

THROW A PARTY

Make your artistic community integral to your work – and have fun while you're at it.

Parties were critical to Jazz Age painter **Florine 'Florrie' Stettheimer**'s practice, both as a context for displaying and discussing work and as subject matter. Stettheimer, who was also a poet and theatrical designer, was born into a prominent Jewish banking family in Rochester, New York. In the years during which she lived and studied in Europe, she familiarized herself with the avant-garde salon – evenings of intellectual exchange among artists, writers and cultural figures which took place in domestic quarters under the guidance of a host(ess).

After fleeing Europe for New York City with her family at the onset of World War I, the artist teamed up with her sisters Ettie (a writer) and Carrie (a set designer) to hold regular salons at their Manhattan apartment and Florrie's art studio. These fabulous events, which were attended by the likes of Marcel Duchamp, Georgia O'Keeffe and Francis Picabia, facilitated fertile conversations among figures in art, literature, theatre and dance. Often, Florine Stettheimer would debut new artworks at these events as an alternative to exhibiting work in more conventional gallery contexts.

Stettheimer's social milieu was also a frequent subject of her work, which drew inspiration from Art Deco fashion illustration. Said to have thrown parties as an excuse to paint them, Stettheimer depicted the New Yorkers in her circle as they picnicked, shopped, visited museums, lounged at the beach and attended the Stettheimer salons. In *Studio Party* (*Soirée*) (1917-19) she portrayed a cast of colourful characters at a salon night at her studio, her own nude self-portrait regally presiding over the action.

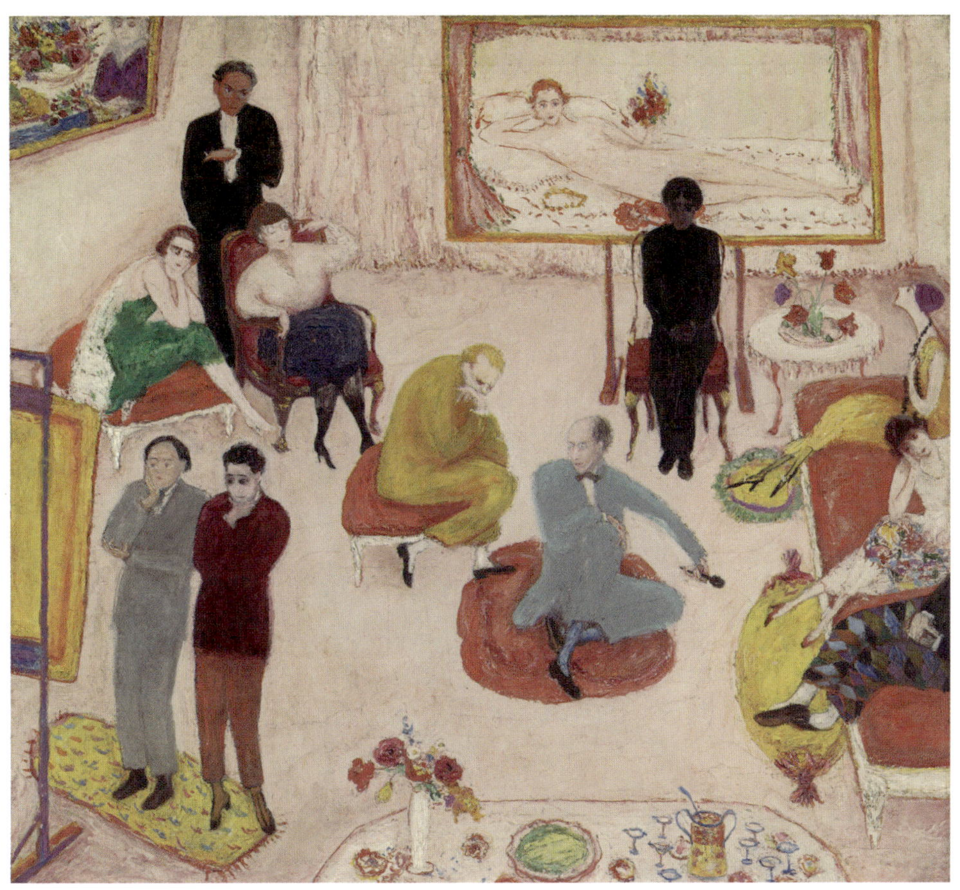

Florine Stettheimer, Studio Party (Soirée), 1917–19. Oil on canvas, 71.8 x 76.2 cm (28¼ x 30 in).

'OUR PARTIES / OUR PICNICS / OUR BANQUETS / OUR FRIENDS / HAVE AT LAST A RAISON D'ÊTRE / SEEN IN COLOR AND DESIGN / IT AMUSES ME / TO RECREATE THEM / TO PAINT THEM.'

FLORINE STETTHEIMER

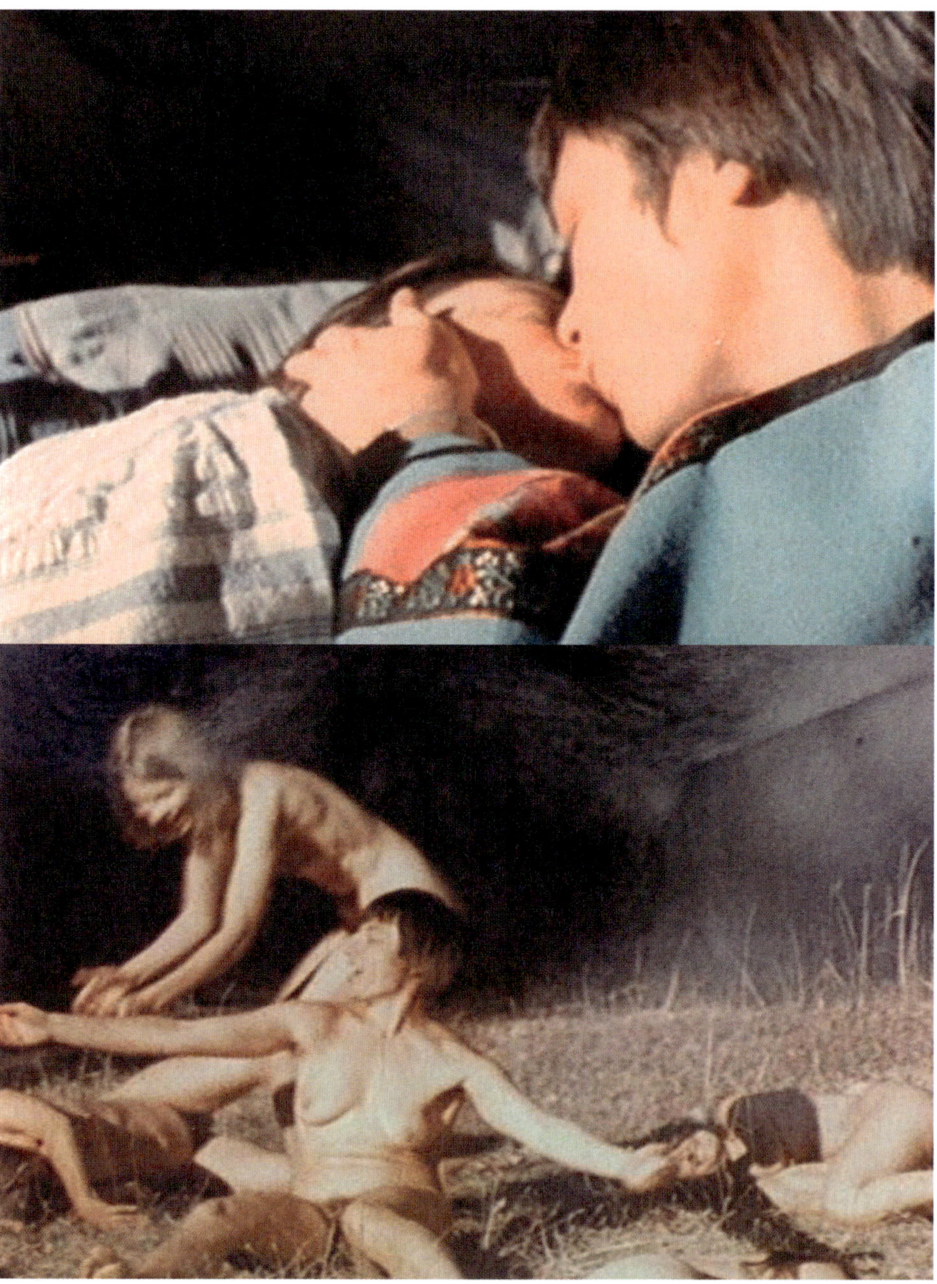

PLEASURE YOURSELF IN THE JOY OF MAKING

When you have an idea, follow it with gusto and pleasure.

In 2018, experimental filmmaker **Barbara Hammer** delivered a performance lecture at the Whitney Museum of American Art in New York titled 'The Art of Dying or (Palliative Art Making in the Age of Anxiety)'. As a 79-year-old artist with a terminal diagnosis, Hammer had been reflecting on her life and practice, which were thoroughly enmeshed. Across more than five decades, she explored themes such as lesbianism, feminism, sex and illness in her work, producing over 90 moving image pieces along with performances, works on paper, installations and photographs.

Hammer's 'Dyketactics' (1974), an early work in her repertoire that she cheekily described as a 'lesbian commercial', was among the first films of its kind: a celebration of women's bodies and pleasure from a lesbian point of view. The 4-minute 16mm film was composed of 110 layered shots of women cavorting in the countryside. The women danced and touched, sometimes with the camera nestled between their bodies. The prominence given to touch in 'Dyketactics' cemented into a philosophy in the film *Sync Touch* (1981), which Hammer described as 'a lesbian/feminist aesthetic proposing the connection between touch and sight to be the basis for a "new cinema"'.

As Hammer's work shifted and evolved, she consistently kept lesbian jouissance and representation at the fore. 'When you have an idea, follow it with gusto and pleasure,' Hammer advised in her talk at the Whitney. 'Be open. Open to your intuition. And pleasure yourself in the joy of making.'

Barbara Hammer, Dyketactics, 1974. Transferred 16mm, 4:3, colour, sound, 4 min.

YOU ARE CONSTANTLY MAKING DECISIONS

Let a larger intention direct the many choices you make as you execute a work.

'I am not a proponent of the idea of an artist as someone who kind of magically makes things and has no real control or isn't willfully producing a certain kind of thing,' American figurative painter **Kerry James Marshall** told Tracy Zwick in a 2013 interview. 'It is labor-intensive, and it is research-intensive. You are making one decision after another, trying to get at something you think is important.'

The Chicago-based artist, who was born in the civil rights organizing hub of Birmingham, Alabama and moved to Los Angeles shortly before the Watts Uprising, has made the representation of Black subjects and a Black aesthetic central to his magnificent paintings, subverting a Western pictorial tradition that has historically written self-possessed subjects of colour out of the picture.

Marshall's *School of Beauty, School of Culture* (2012), a portrayal of a Black beauty salon, is tightly packed with art historical and cultural references. An anamorphic head of a blonde Disney princess - a reference to the famous skull in Hans Holbein the Younger's Renaissance double portrait *The Ambassadors* (1533) - signals the dearth of non-white representation in Western painting; the reflection of the photographer's own image in the mirror, a nod to Diego Velázquez's *Las Meninas* (1656), addresses the intractable physical presence of the artist and specific constellation of identities; and a large poster of a painting by Chris Ofili, the first Black artist to win the Turner Prize, gestures at the expansion of the canon. Each intentioned reference is part of Marshall's larger project of depicting and celebrating Black life.

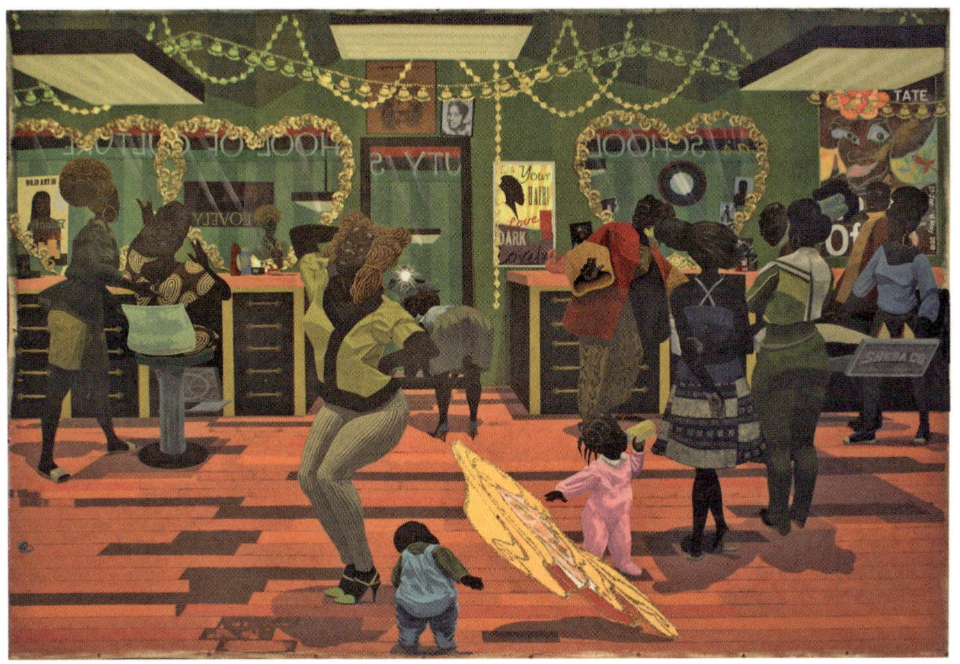

Kerry James Marshall, School of Beauty, School of Culture, 2012. Acrylic and glitter on canvas, 274 x 401 cm (8 ft 11⅞ in x 13 ft 1⅞ in).

'I CAME IN MAKING CHOICES ABOUT HOW I DEPLOY AESTHETICS AND IMAGERY STRATEGICALLY.'

KERRY JAMES MARSHALL

TRUST THE PROCESS

As you develop working methods that are uniquely your own, believe in the imminence of breakthroughs.

'What I tell younger artists is to have faith in their process,' says Canadian photographer **Michael Flomen**. 'To continue to push through the difficult moments in their artmaking and trust that something new and meaningful to them will reveal itself and stimulate them on their breakthrough.' A longtime master printer with a penchant for experimentation, the self-taught artist has spent the past two decades producing camera-less photographs under the cover of darkness in the countryside, using large-format film and analogue photographic papers.

In *Taps* (2019), which he made in fields in the summertime, Flomen works with the bioluminescent light of fireflies, placing the insects directly onto light-sensitive film and allowing them to expose the film over time. The artist begins his intuitive process by meditating in the landscape where he plans to make images, bringing his senses to the present moment as he orients himself to the surrounding nature and his subconscious.

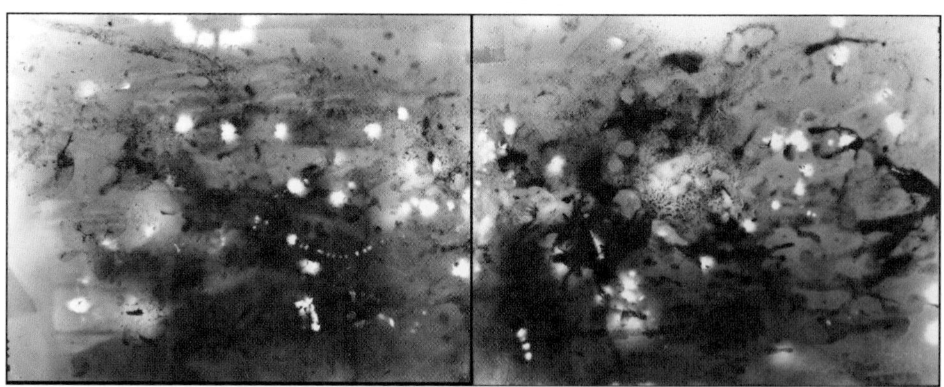

Michael Flomen, Taps, 2019. Edition of 3. Gelatin silver print, 110 x 277 cm (43½ x 109 in).

THE IDEA BECOMES A MACHINE THAT MAKES ART

Let a concept motor a project.

A progenitor of conceptual art as well as Minimalism, American artist **Sol LeWitt** was an early exponent of the notion that the concepts that drive a work are more important than the way the work is executed. LeWitt, who worked across painting, drawing, sculpture and text, outlined some of his ideas on the matter in his 1967 essay 'Paragraphs on Conceptual Art': 'When an artist uses a conceptual form of art, it means that all of the planning and decisions are made beforehand and the execution is a perfunctory affair. The idea becomes a machine that makes the art.'

LeWitt's 'Wall Drawings', made from 1968 to 2007, exemplify the artist's concept-driven approach. Each wall drawing is executed according to a set of written or diagrammatic instructions, such as a 'wall divided vertically into fifteen equal parts, each with a different line direction and colour, and all combinations' with the specified colours 'Red, yellow, blue, black pencil'. Though the artist carried out the earliest wall drawings himself, they could soon be drawn by any trained assistant; the art was in the instructions.

> **'THE FEWER DECISIONS MADE IN THE COURSE OF COMPLETING THE WORK, THE BETTER. THIS ELIMINATES THE ARBITRARY, THE CAPRICIOUS, AND THE SUBJECTIVE AS MUCH AS POSSIBLE.'**
> SOL LEWITT

EXPLORE SCALE SHIFTS

Interrogate perception by experimenting with scalar extremes.

Six matchboxes could easily hold all of the sculptures produced by Swiss artist **Alberto Giacometti** between 1942 and 1945, wrote art historian Karin von Maur. From 1935, when Giacometti parted ways with the Surrealists, until the end of World War II, the artist created his attenuated, waiflike figures on an increasingly - hyperbolically - diminutive scale. While many critics at the time erroneously characterized these sculptures as preparatory studies, the artist approached his scaled-down personages as meaningful interrogations into the experience of sight itself. Giacometti cited his own sense of seeing people at a distance as he traversed the streets of cosmopolitan cities such as Paris or Geneva; his new scale engaged with the reflexive scrambling that occurred as he adjusted his perspective to find his bearings in urban space. (The material shortages experienced by artists during World War II may also have contributed to the decision to produce smaller works.)

'I found a large figure untruthful, even though I found a small one intolerable; apart from that, they often became so small that they crumbled to dust at a single touch of my knife,' lamented Giacometti. After 1945, the artist slowly began scaling up his figures again as he zeroed in on his major themes of walking men and standing women. Though he was able to reach new elevations - the loftiest of his 'Tall Figures' from 1960 approached 3 metres (10 feet) in height - Giacometti's sculptures always retained their slenderness, remaining diametrically opposed to the volumetric.

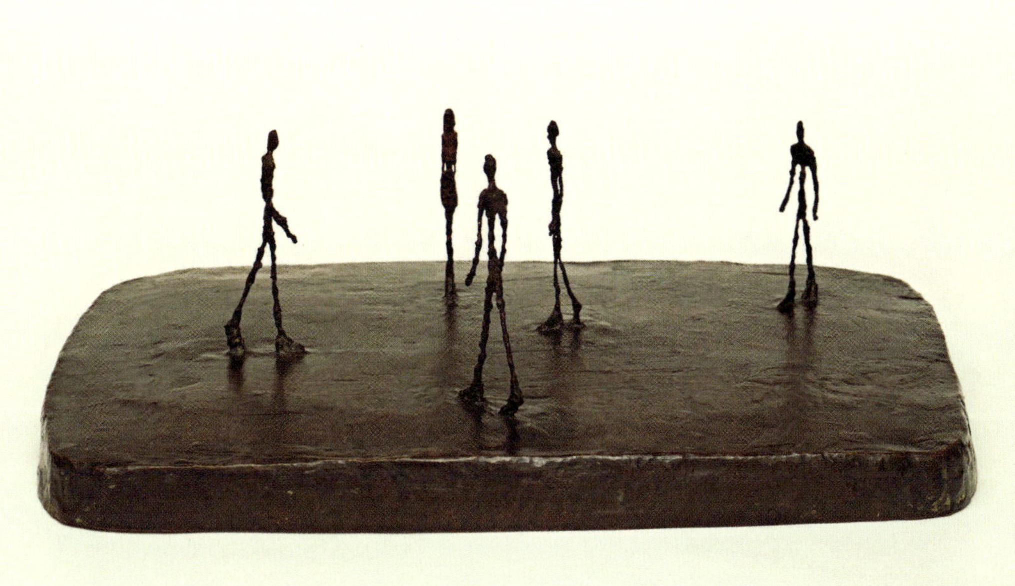

Alberto Giacometti, The City Square, 1948-9. Bronze, 24 x 64.7 x 43.4 cm ($9\frac{7}{16}$ x $25\frac{1}{2}$ x $17\frac{1}{16}$ in).

MESS AROUND WITH A SYMBOL

Take a symbol that is meaningful to you and explore it from every angle.

Paradoxes, wordplay, visual puns and a trickster spirit are among the hallmarks of American artist **David Hammons**. With remarkable visual economy, Hammons works with the detritus of the urban landscape to comment on the experience of marginalized Black communities in America, while handily skewering art world pretences.

'Outrageously magical things happen when you mess around with a symbol,' Hammons told Kellie Jones in a rare interview in 1988. One particularly potent symbol for Hammons is basketball, which first featured in his work that decade. Declaring himself 'enraged' at the sport, which often reneges on its empty promises of professional success, Hammons explored the iconography of basketball from every angle, whether he was fusing a basketball hoop with an ornate chandelier, bouncing a basketball covered with Harlem-sourced dirt onto paper to form abstractions, or, in the case of the public sculpture *Higher Goals* (1986), crowning bottle-top-decorated telephone poles with basketball hoops to depict a desire out of reach.

'YOU DO ALL THE CORNY THINGS, CONSTANTLY EMPTY THE BRAIN OF THE IGNORANT AND THE DUMB AND THE SILLY THINGS AND THERE'S NOTHING LEFT BUT THE BRILLIANT IDEAS. PRETTY SOON YOU GET IDEAS THAT NO ONE ELSE COULD HAVE THOUGHT OF BECAUSE YOU DIDN'T THINK OF THEM, YOU WENT THROUGH THIS PROCESS TO GET THEM.'

DAVID HAMMONS

HARD WORK MATTERS

'Genius' requires sustained effort.

The atmospheric, dynamic compositions of nineteenth-century Romantic painter and printmaker **J.M.W. Turner** infused landscape painting – especially the maritime variety – with a churning energy befitting the industrial age. In his writings, Victorian art critic John Ruskin recounted a conversation between Turner and close mutual friend William Kingsley, who declared that 'want of power in a certain painter to depict what was not before him showed a want of genius'. Turner retorted, 'I know of no genius but the genius of hard work.'

Turner's contemporaries frequently described him as a diligent worker whose advancements in his career – such as his notable election to the Royal Academy at the tender age of 26 – were entirely attributable to his work ethic, as he lacked social graces and his humble upbringing deprived him of a ready-made network. While such characterizations may have been linked to the predilections of Victorian biographers, there was more than a grain of truth to them: in addition to teaching and running his own art gallery, Turner produced some 32,000 works in his lifetime.

J.M.W. Turner, Snow Storm, 1842. Oil on canvas, 91 cm x 122 cm (36 in x 48 in).

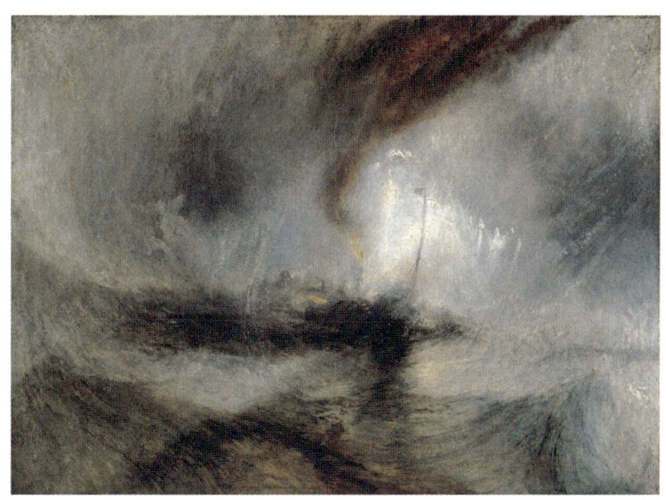

ON FORMS & MATERIALS

FROM PARING DOWN FORM TO ITS ESSENCE TO PURSUING EXCESS OR REPETITION, FROM REPURPOSING REFUSE AS MATERIAL TO WORKING WITH IMMATERIALITY, ARTISTS DEVELOP THEIR OWN APPROACHES TO FORMAL AND MATERIAL MATTERS.

LISTEN TO YOUR MATERIALS

Let the medium lead the way.

Anni Albers, whose abstract wall hangings and weavings earned her the first solo show ever devoted to a designer at the Museum of Modern Art in New York in 1949, played a critical role in establishing the place of textiles in the realm of modernist art. In 1922, the German-born artist enrolled in the Bauhaus, where she studied weaving, the only medium open to her as a woman, under Gunta Stölzl. Albers went on to immigrate to the United States with her husband, painter Josef Albers, to teach at Black Mountain College, North Carolina in 1933. During a 1936 trip to Mexico, the textile artist encountered pre-Colombian inscriptions in Oaxaca. This affecting experience and subsequent trips - as well as copious research - through the 1940s led her to develop her pictorial weavings. In 1963, she also added printmaking to her repertoire.

Albers' textile work and writing evince a unique sensitivity to her medium of choice. In a 1968 oral history interview conducted for the Archives of American Art at the Smithsonian Institution, she lamented that contemporary artists could easily acquire synthetic paints and ready-made panels, in contrast to the Renaissance, when paints had to be ground and canvas had to be prepared. 'There is nothing that teaches you the care that materials demand,' Albers said. 'When the painter or the weaver or someone has to prepare the material, you learn what the material tells you and what the technique tells you... that frees you from this too-conscious searching of your soul which very often turns just into this kind of intestinal painting.' In an essay written 14 years later, 'Material as Metaphor', Albers would add that she 'learned to listen to [threads] and to speak their language'.

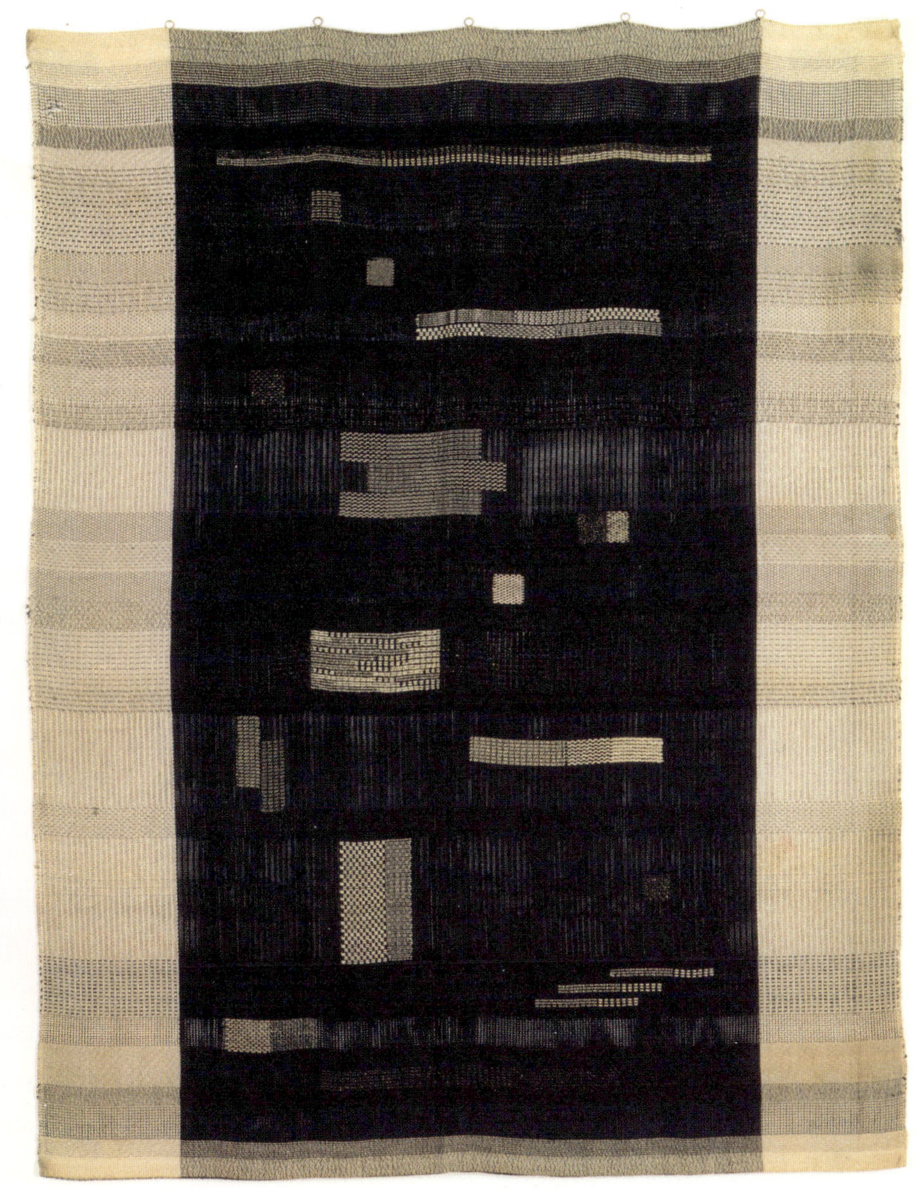

Anni Albers, Ancient Writing, 1936. Woven fabric, 150.5 x 111.8 cm (59¼ x 44 in).

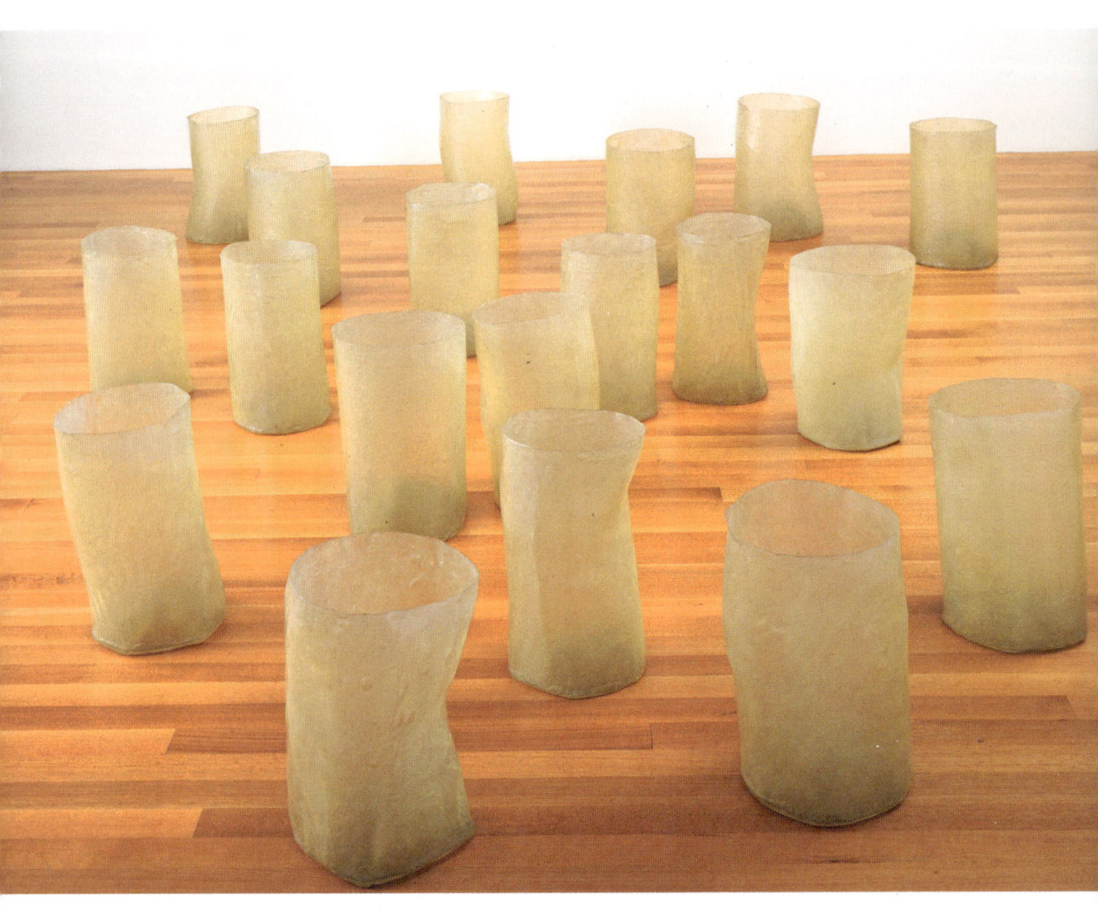

Eva Hesse, Repetition Nineteen III, 1968. Nineteen tubular fiberglass units, 48 to 51 cm (19 to 20¼ in) high x 27.8 to 32.3 cm (11 to 12¾ in) diameter.

REPEAT YOURSELF

Consider the aesthetic and conceptual potential of repetition.

Across the hallmark sculptures that she produced in then-new materials such as fibreglass and latex from the mid-1960s until her premature death in 1970, American Post-Minimalist **Eva Hesse** returned to the same abstract forms, motifs, materials and gestures. Conjuring up a softened, biomorphic version of Minimalism's rigid seriality, a work by Hesse would often feature a repeated shape: circles, tubes, strings. Early drawings also regularly featured stacks of cubes.

Hesse's *Repetition Nineteen III* (1968), in the collection of the Museum of Modern Art in New York, consists of a group of 19 fragile, bucket-like forms, each about 50 centimetres (20 inches) tall, made from fibreglass and polyester resin. As the buckets visually echo one another, their repetition likewise highlights the subtle differences between them, the places where one sags or another juts. The viewer is generously invited to become receptive to such nuance. In Hesse's oeuvre, forms also recur across different media: circles, for example, appear in sculptures of coiled rope, low tables covered with washers, and drawings on graph paper.

'Why do you repeat a form over and over again?' Cindy Nemser asked Hesse in a 1970 interview. 'Because it exaggerates,' the artist responded. 'If something is meaningful, maybe it's more meaningful said ten times.' For Hesse, repetition wasn't just an aesthetic strategy; it was a conceptual one, too. 'Repetition does enlarge or increase or exaggerate an idea or purpose in a statement,' the artist said, explicating the potency of her work.

BEAUTY ARISES FROM THE RELATIONS BETWEEN FORMS

Turn your attention to composition.

Dutch painter and theorist **Piet Mondrian**, who cofounded De Stijl (The Style) in 1917, was adamant about making art that would reflect the beauty and harmony of the natural world without evoking any specific concrete objects in that world. In the 1920s, the artist – who was already primarily working with vertical and horizontal lines – developed the style for which he is known, producing non-objective abstractions that adhered to a rigorous lexicon of straight lines and rectilinear forms in primary colours, all held in an asymmetrical balance.

For Mondrian, who was interested in Hegelian dialectics, the push–pull between forms, rather than the forms themselves, made the picture. In his essay 'Plastic Art and Pure Plastic Art', published in *Circle* in 1937, Mondrian wrote: 'Throughout the history of culture, art has demonstrated that universal beauty does not arise from the particular character of the form, but from the dynamic rhythm of its inherent relationships, or – in a composition – from the mutual relations of forms. Art has shown that it is a question of determining the relations. It has revealed that the forms exist only for the creation of relationships.'

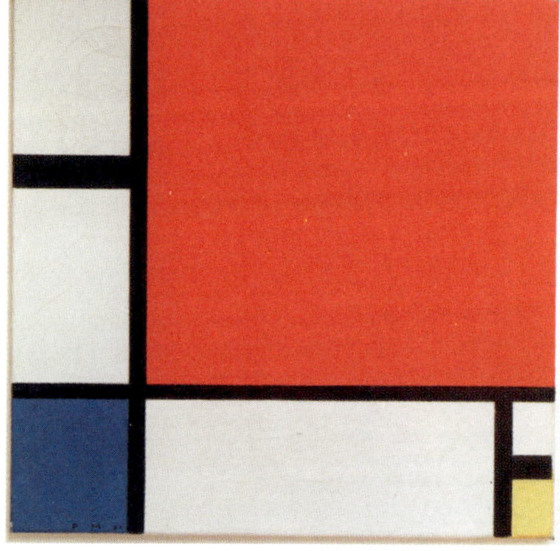

Piet Mondrian, Composition with Red, Blue and Yellow, 1930. Oil on canvas, 45 x 45 cm (17¾ x 17¾ in).

APPROACH CHOREOGRAPHY AS READY-MADE

The everyday systems and energies around you are ripe for appropriation.

'It's a fact of the expanding universe that today you will travel faster and farther than yesterday – no matter what,' says American artist **Madeline Hollander**. 'My choreographies, culled from everyday scenes, attempt to work with this preexisting momentum on every scale.'

A former ballet dancer, Hollander approaches seemingly banal or manufactured systems and sequences, from the raking of beaches to the winking of brake lights, with keen curiosity and a choreographer's eye. In her 2018 performance 'New Max', four dancers in a room outfitted with four air conditioning units moved their bodies in a strategic choreography that drew upon athletic warm-ups and frostbite prevention techniques to generate enough heat to raise the surrounding temperature from 65 degrees Fahrenheit (about 18 degrees Celsius), the temperature at which art is typically stored, to a toasty 85 degrees Fahrenheit (about 29 degrees Celsius). Adapting Marcel Duchamp's more sculpturally oriented theory of the ready-made to movement-based practices, Hollander has produced astoundingly innovative work.

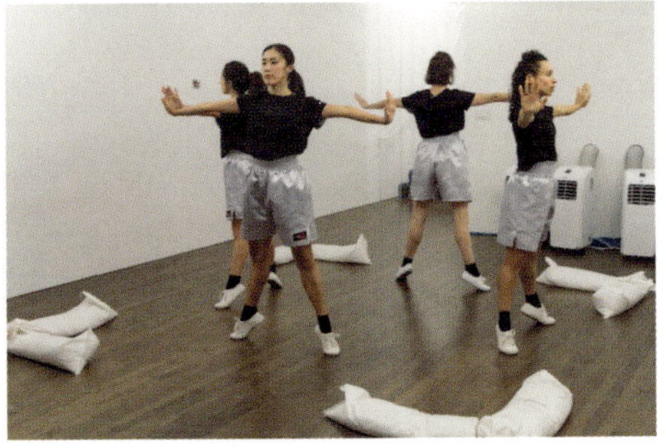

Madeline Hollander, performance documentation of New Max, 2018. The Artist's Institute, New York.

WORK DIRECTLY WITH NATURE

Approach the natural world as a medium.

Cuban-American artist **Ana Mendieta** was studying painting at the University of Iowa when she realized that a different, expanded medium might afford her art more vigour, and proceeded to enrol in the school's new interdisciplinary MFA Intermedia Program led by Hans Breder. 'I wanted my images to have power, to be magic,' Mendieta declared. 'I decided that for the images to have magic qualities I had to work directly with nature. I had to go to the source of life, to mother earth.'

In addition to creating feminist performance art pieces that employed organic materials such as feathers and blood, Mendieta held intimate performances in nature in an attempt to reassert her bond with the earth: a womb from which she had been cast, she believed, when she was exiled from her home in Cuba at the age of 13. While travelling with her MFA cohort between Iowa and Mexico, Mendieta embarked upon her 'Silueta' series (1973-80), private performances – documented in photographs – in which she left the trace of her presence on the land through methods as varied as carving her silhouette into the ground, igniting a self-effigy composed of branches, and covering her naked body with flowers. Mendieta's 'Siluetas' coincided with the advent of Land Art, which transcended the literal and capitalistic constraints of the gallery system by sculpting the environment itself. Yet, in contrast to many of her conceptual artist peers, Mendieta was not interested in 'mastering' the landscape through a large-scale, long-lasting installation; instead, her earth-body performances explored the tenor and texture of her own relationship with the natural world.

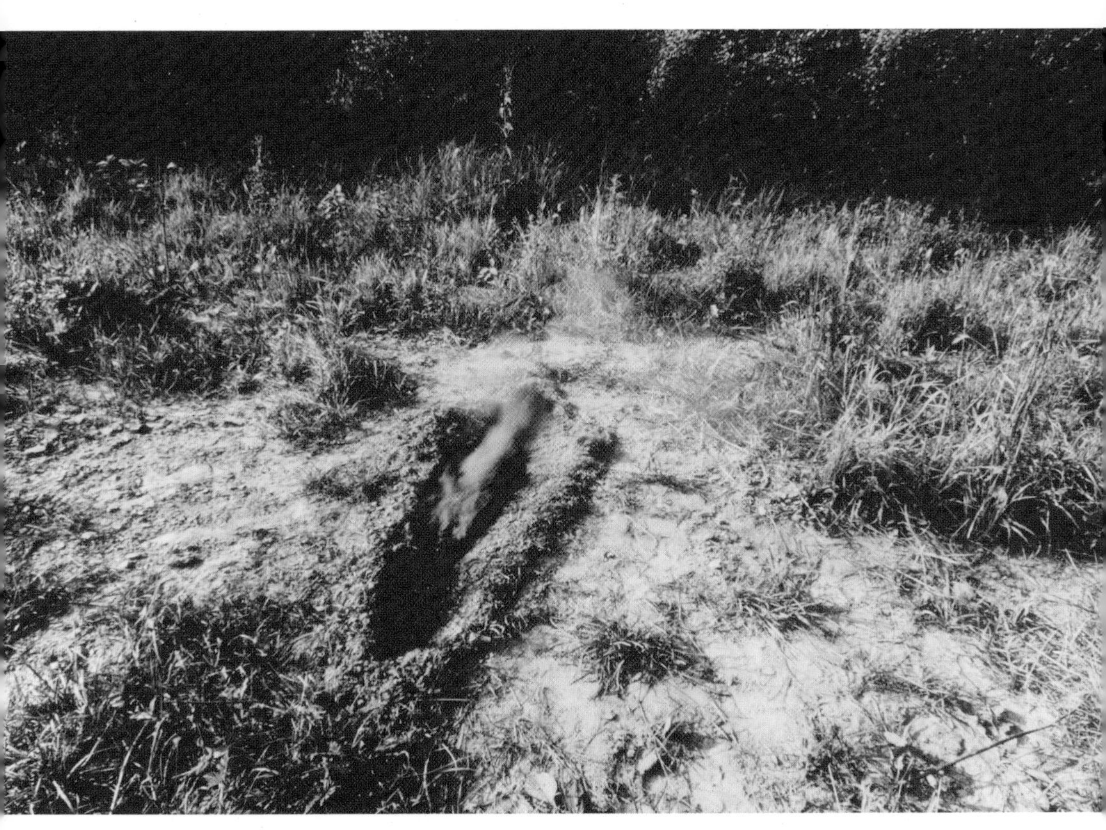

Ana Mendieta, Untitled from the series Silueta, 1978. Gelatin silver print, 33.6 x 49.5 cm (13¼ x 19½ in).

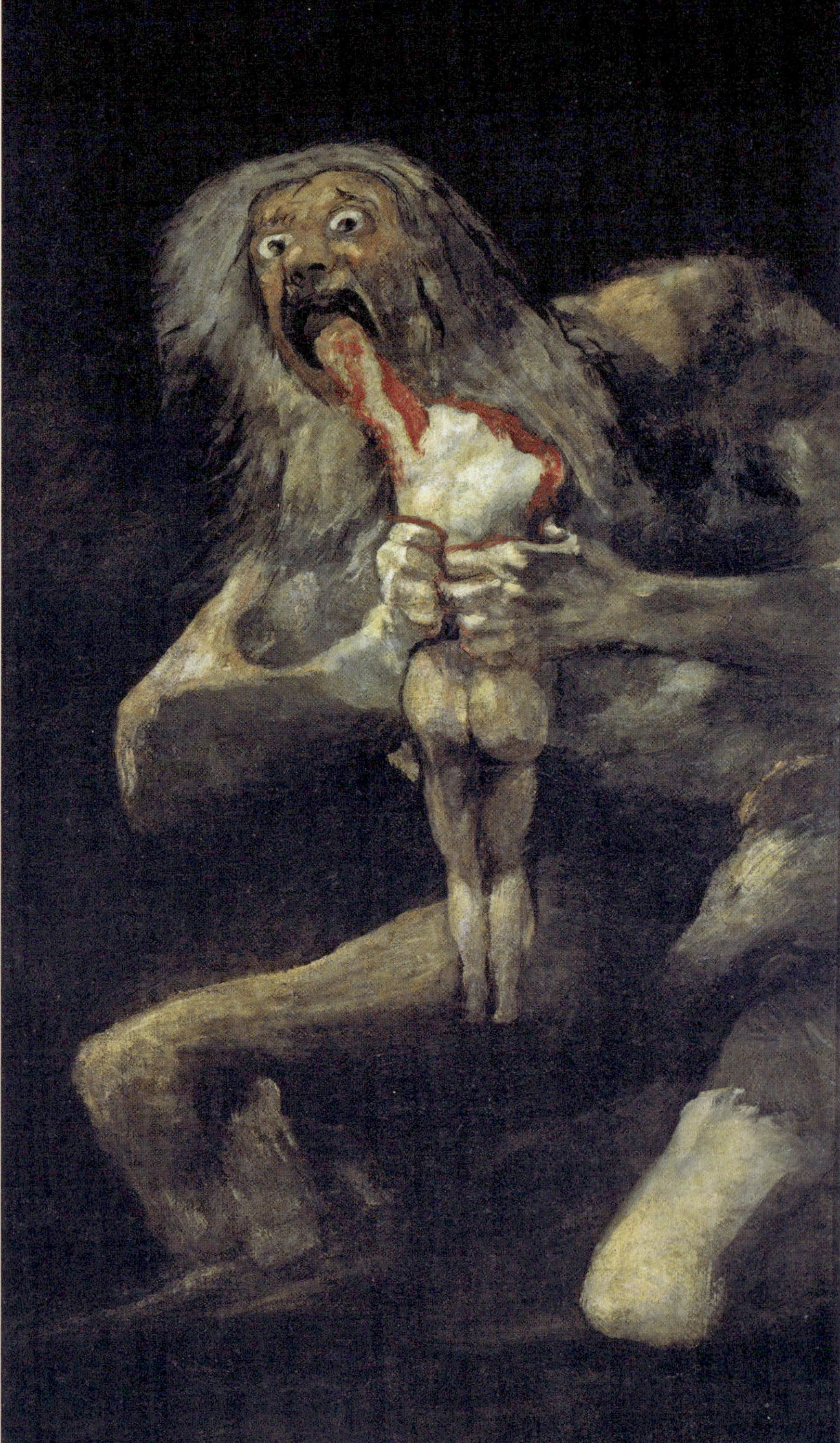

COLOUR IS NOT ESSENTIAL

A restrained palette can pack a punch.

Spanish artist **Francisco Goya**, whose charged compositions are viewed as a crucial link between the Old Masters and modernists, considered colour to be superfluous to the creation of a compelling image. 'In art there is no need for colour; I see only light and shade,' declared the artist. While an achromatic approach naturally characterized Goya's etchings, it increasingly distinguished his painting, as well.

In Goya's early work as a court painter to the Spanish crown, it was not unusual for pastel hues to feature in his compositions. However, around the time of the Napoleonic Wars - a period during which Goya made some of his most iconic works about war's real cost, such as *The Third of May 1808* (1814), a gory painting representing atrocities committed by the French - the artist's palette adopted sootier hues, capturing the grim mood.

From 1819 to 1823, Goya laboured over the 'Black Paintings', 14 epic depictions of mythological violence and pagan turmoil: a wild-eyed Saturn devouring his son, witches flocking to a silhouetted chimera, Judith on the verge of decapitating Holofernes. The artist, at that point a solitary septuagenarian who had distanced himself from the royal court, painted the works directly onto the walls of his farmhouse outside Madrid. (After his death, they were removed from the house and transferred to canvas, before being ultimately deposited at the Prado Museum in Madrid.) Identified by French writer André Malraux as the beginning of modern art, these particularly harrowing paintings set a dark tone with a nocturnal palette dominated by brown and black with occasional contrasting shocks of white.

Francisco Goya, Saturn Devouring His Son, 1819–23. Mixed media mural transferred to canvas, 143.5 x 81.4 cm (56½ x 32 in).

PLAY COLOURS LIKE NOTES

Use colour thoughtfully to tap into sensory, emotional and psychological states.

In 1896, **Wassily Kandinsky**, a rising law professor who made art and music on the side, left his native Russia to study painting in Munich under Anton Ažbe and Franz von Stuck. Fifteen years later, Kandinsky cofounded the avant-garde group Der Blaue Reiter (The Blue Rider), and his vividly hued, lyrical non-representational paintings and associated critical writings distinguished him as one of the progenitors of Western Abstraction. Kandinsky taught theories of colour and form, design theory and painting at the Bauhaus from 1922 to 1933, at which point the school closed under Nazi pressure and the artist immigrated to Paris, where he explored forms that skewed towards the more biomorphic.

A painter who drew inspiration from music, Kandinsky associated sounds with colours, perhaps due to the neurological condition synaesthesia. 'The sound of colours is so definite that it would be hard to find anyone who would express bright yellow with base notes, or dark lake with the treble,' he wrote in his 1912 book *Concerning the Spiritual in Art*, noting that certain hues could also be associated with smells, textures, tastes, emotions, physical sensations and psychological effects – connections to which sensitive individuals were uniquely attentive. 'Generally speaking, colour directly influences the soul,' wrote Kandinsky. 'Colour is the keyboard, the eyes are the hammers, the soul is the piano with many strings. The artist is the hand that plays, touching one key or another purposively, to cause vibrations in the soul.' For the artist, a careful consideration of hues and their inter-relationships was necessary to, and even a driver of, creation.

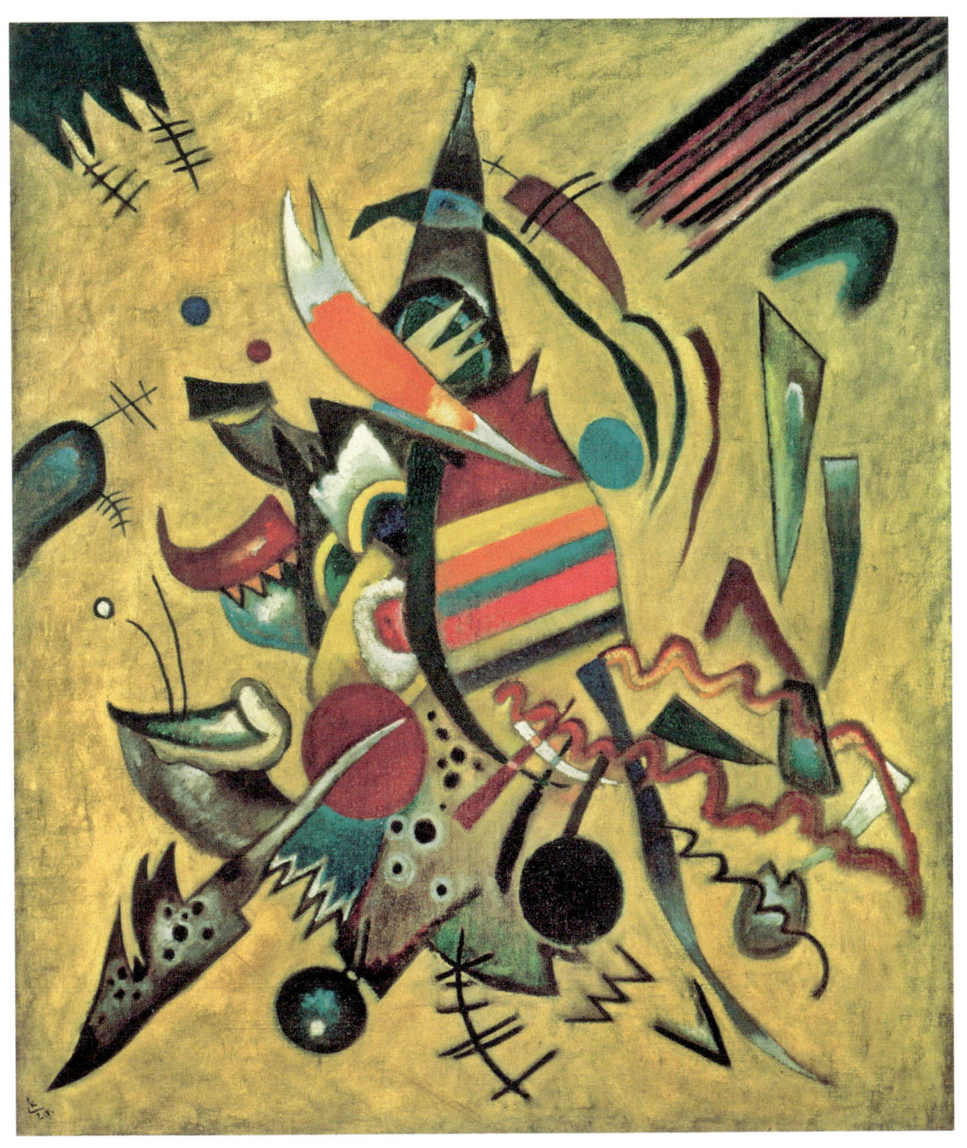

Wassily Kandinsky, Points, 1920. Oil on canvas, 110.3 x 91.8 cm (43⅜ x 36⅛ in).

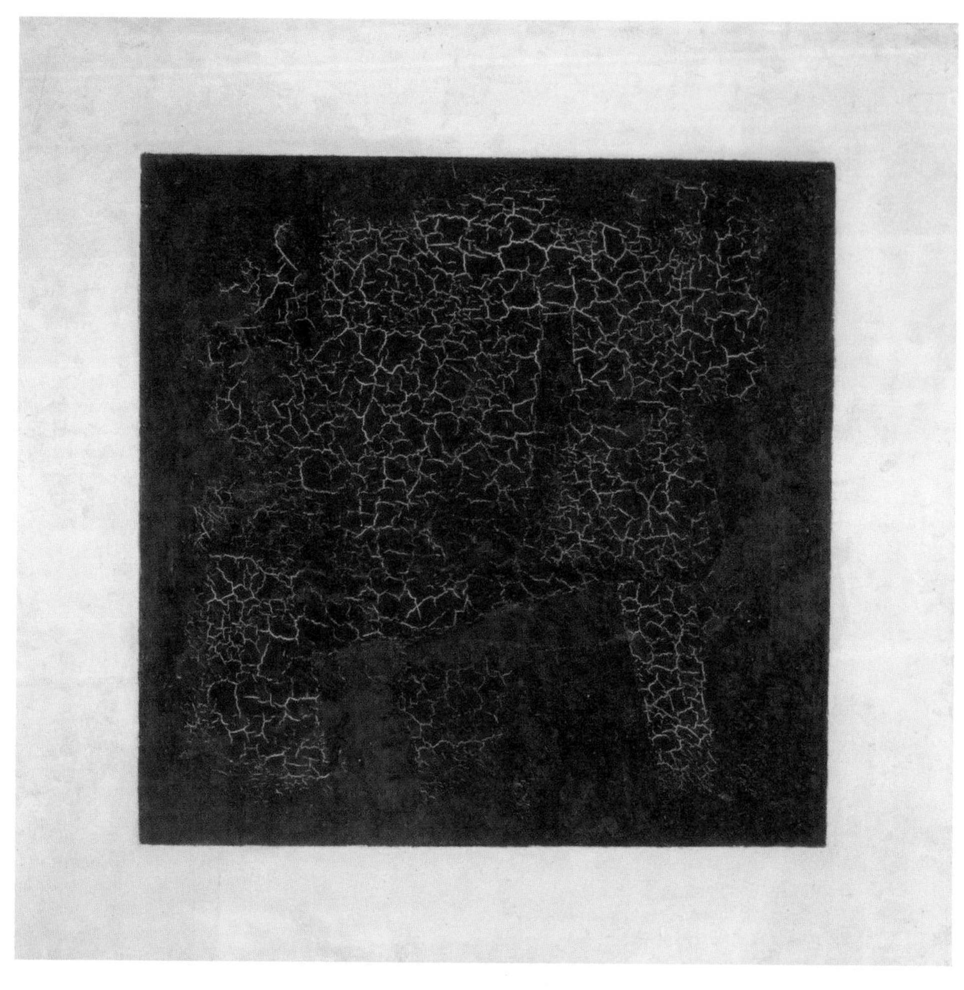

Kazimir Malevich, Black Square, 1915. Oil on linen, 79.5 x 79.5 cm (31¼ x 31¼ in).

BE RADICALLY SIMPLE

Explore the zero of form.

Ukrainian-Russian artist **Kazimir Malevich** was an established Cubo-Futurist painter when he made his first depiction of a black square on a white ground as a set element for *Victory Over the Sun* (1913), an absurdist Russian Futurist opera in which a cast of characters triumphs over the sun, time and rationality. Two years later, at 'The Last Futurist Exhibition 0,10' in Saint Petersburg – a show whose title hinted that it would herald the 'zero of form' – Malevich unveiled a painting of a plain black square on a white ground, unlike any of his previous works fragmenting figurative subjects into planes. Suprematism, a movement devoted to pure geometric abstraction, was born, along with a manifesto that declared: 'Everything has vanished, there remains a mass of material, from which the new forms will be built.'

Black Square – which is believed to have been made in 1915, though Malevich, for whom the future could not come fast enough, dated it to 1913 – jolted and agitated viewers. The groundbreaking abstract painting's refusal of anything other than what Malevich would later call 'the supremacy of pure artistic feeling' diverged radically from the canon of representational art. Highlighting the significance of what he had done as he shocked viewers' sensibilities, Malevich hung the painting high in a corner, the spot where a religious icon might be displayed in a Russian Orthodox home. As he reflected on this significant moment in his 1927 treatise *The Non-Objective World*, Malevich wrote, 'There was no "empty square" which I had exhibited but rather the feeling of non-objectivity.'

USE WHAT'S AVAILABLE

Reflect your environment, circumstances and history with found or readily available materials.

'Throughout my career, I've been using materials that are close to hand,' Ghanaian-born, Nigeria-based artist **El Anatsui** told the *Guardian* in 2020. 'That's one of the issues I sorted out after art school: you should always work with what's available.' After graduating, Anatsui began branding pictograms into wooden discs, typically used for produce displays, that he found in the market. Work made from other readily available materials followed, including local clay, other used wooden objects and milk tin lids.

For the past two decades, Anatsui has made gleaming abstract tapestries from another form of quotidian refuse: liquor bottle-tops. After sourcing the tops from recycling centres, the artist and his studio assistants cut, hammer and fold the small pieces of metal, evoking the pounding of gold into foil by Ghanaian artisans. Anatsui then weaves the bottle-tops together using copper wire, creating masterfully patterned, malleable metal sheets that can be displayed in a variety of ways. For Anatsui, the bottle-tops nod to legacies of colonialism, acknowledging the relationship between gold, alcohol and enslavement in the history of transatlantic trade. Anatsui's choice to use recycled materials also underlines problems surrounding consumption and sustainability.

If you choose to work with the materials around you, Anatsui explained, 'it will reflect your environment, circumstances and history'. He continued: 'If an artist uses only very rare materials, it can stifle creativity, because you won't want to make any mistakes with a precious material. With something that's so common, however, you can experiment without any hindrance.'

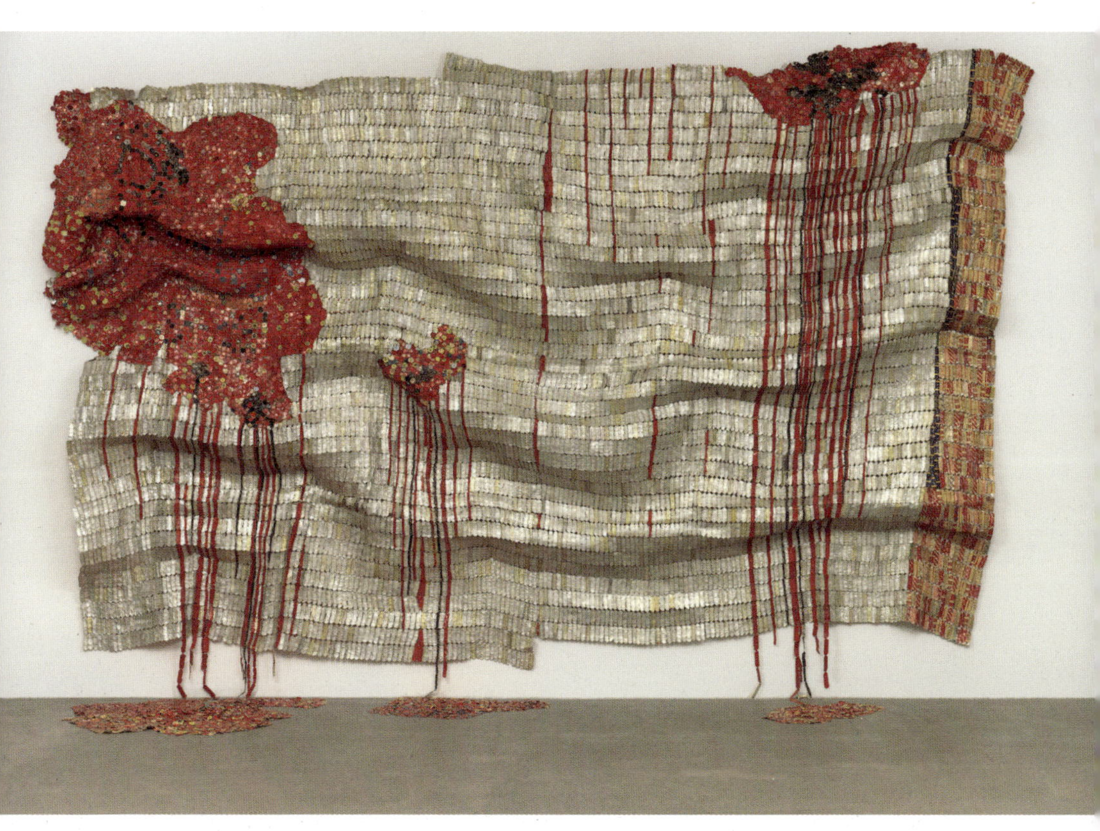

El Anatsui, Bleeding Takari II, 2007. Aluminium and copper wire, 393.7 x 576.6 cm (12 ft 11 in x 18 ft 11 in).

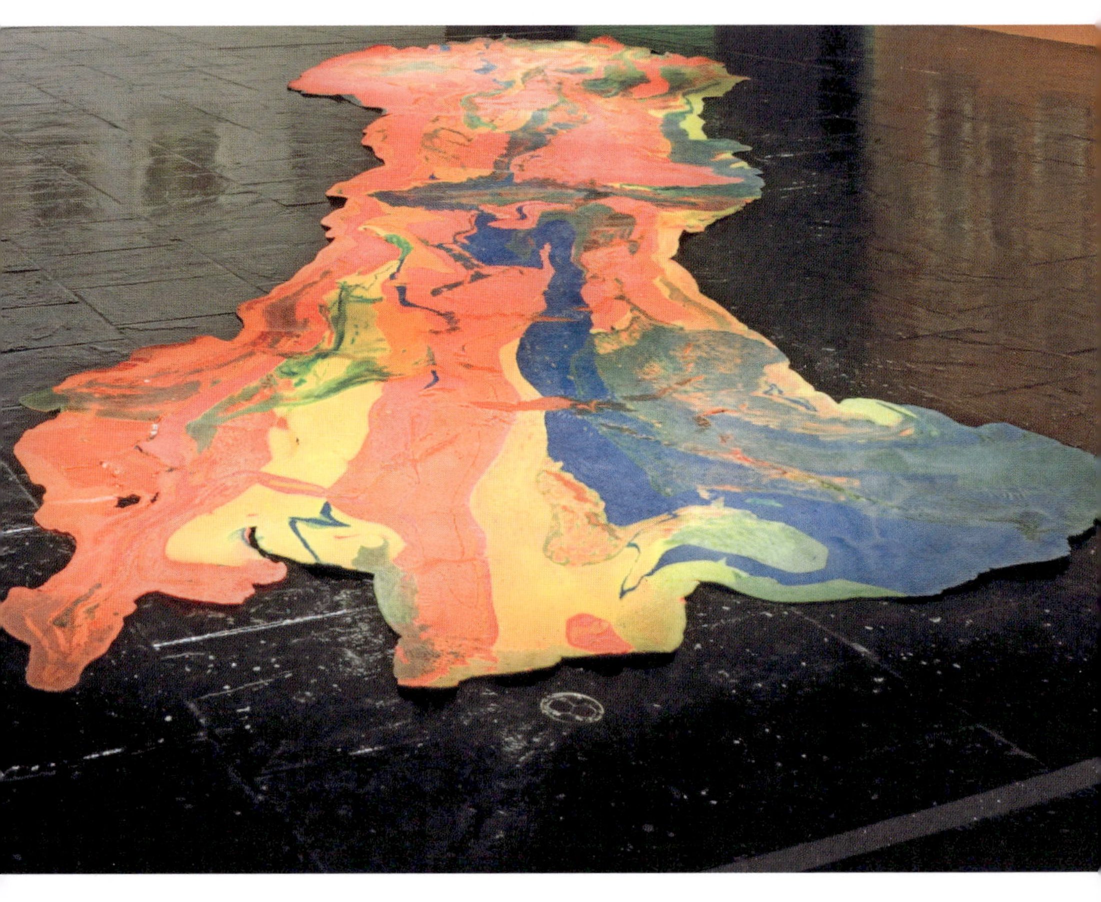

Lynda Benglis, Contraband, 1969. Pigmented latex, overall (irregular): 7.6 x 295.3 x 1011.6 cm (3 x 116¼ x 398¼ in).

BE EXCESSIVE

Allow your art to be unrestrained, exuberant and messy.

'What's wrong with excess?' **Lynda Benglis** once asked art historian Robert Pincus-Witten. When the American artist burst onto the scene in the late 1960s, the clean lines and neat, intentional, factory-style forms of Minimalism were de rigueur. Benglis, in stark contrast, poured pigmented liquid latex onto the floors or corners of gallery spaces, allowing the rubbery material to direct its own unfolding as it oozed into place before finally solidifying at the nexus of painting and sculpture. (She also went on to apply this technique to liquid metal.) The pour's emphasis on materiality and process aligned it with Minimalism; its uncontrolled, magmic appearance differentiated it. 'I was not interested in taking art to a final conclusion,' Benglis reflected in a 2012 interview with the Tate. 'I felt I wanted art to be much more excessive and it was about more, not less.'

When Benglis was invited to participate in the group exhibition 'Anti-Illusion: Procedures/Materials' at the Whitney Museum of American Art in New York in 1969, she proffered *Contraband* (1969), a Day Glo-coloured latex pour stretching over 10 metres (33 feet) in length. After other artists in the show expressed concerns about having their work shown near hers, the curators decided to install the piece on a ramp by the entrance, rather than in the way in which the artist had envisioned, sprawling out on the gallery floor. Refusing to see her delightfully exuberant spill curtailed, Benglis withdrew from the show. The Whitney wisely bought the work in 2008.

LET MEMORIES FIND A FORM

Return to a resonant memory. It may take a shape you didn't expect.

Arshile Gorky, who was born Vostanik Manoog Adoyan in the village of Khorkom in present-day Turkey, fled the Armenian genocide for the United States, where he adopted a new name and made art for the remainder of his days. Though he disliked revisiting the more traumatic elements of his past, Gorky often turned to halcyon memories to inspire his biomorphic paintings and drawings. The 'Garden in Sochi' series and the 'Khorkom' series, two related bodies of work from the 1930s and 1940s, are held up as prime examples of Gorky's virtuosity with organic form and fluid rhythm, epitomizing his capacity to make work that simultaneously reflected the natural world and took on a life of its own.

Gorky, like the Surrealists with whom he is often associated, was interested in mining his subconscious, and the artist's memories and myths from childhood - particularly pertaining to his father's garden - are the source from which these two striking abstract series spring. In 1945, Gorky was asked by New York's Museum of Modern Art which elements of his background were important to understanding his work. 'I was taken away from my little village when I was five years old, yet all my vital memories are of these first years,' the artist responded. 'These were the days when I smelled the bread, I saw my first red poppy, the moon, the innocent seeing. Since then these memories have become iconography, the shapes, even the colours; millstone, red earth, yellow wheatfield, apricots etc.'

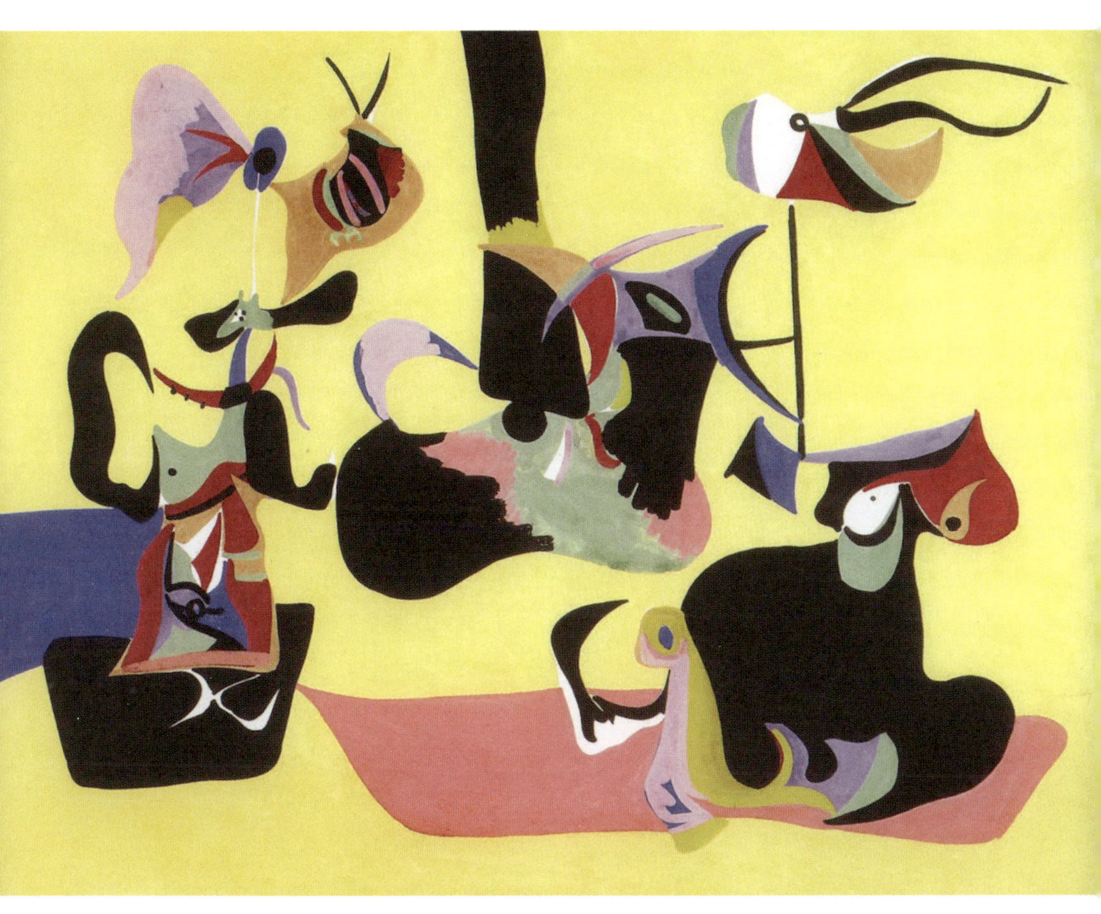

Arshile Gorky, Garden in Sochi, 1940–41. Gouache on board, 53.3 x 70.5 cm (21 x 27¾ in).

BREAK IT DOWN

Approach dots and lines like parts of a house.

Swiss-born German painter and draughtsman **Paul Klee**, who today is as celebrated for his art as he is for his pedagogy, began his career as an illustrator before becoming involved with more avant-garde movements such as Der Blaue Reiter (The Blue Rider), a German Expressionist group operating from 1911 to 1914. His linear-minded work would go on to blossom with luscious patches of colour following an influential trip to Tunisia in 1914. In 1920, the year that Klee was invited to teach at the Bauhaus in Weimar, the artist wrote in his 'Creative Credo': 'The formal elements of graphic art are dot, line, plane and space - the last three charged with energy of various kinds.'

From 1921 to 1931, Klee taught painting, bookbinding, glass painting and weaving at Bauhaus. In that productive period, he produced nearly 5,000 works, about half of his total oeuvre; he also generated over 3,000 pages of lecture notes, a portion of which constituted his *Pedagogical Sketchbook*, published in 1925, which crystallized many facets of Bauhaus theory. Breaking down the relationship between the dot, the line, the plane, colour and geometry, Klee demonstrated how a picture could be built step-by-step over time. 'When a dot begins to move and becomes a line, this requires time,' he explained in his 'Credo'. 'Likewise, when a moving line produces a plane, and when moving planes produce spaces... Does a pictorial work come into being at one stroke? No, it is constructed bit by bit, just like a house.'

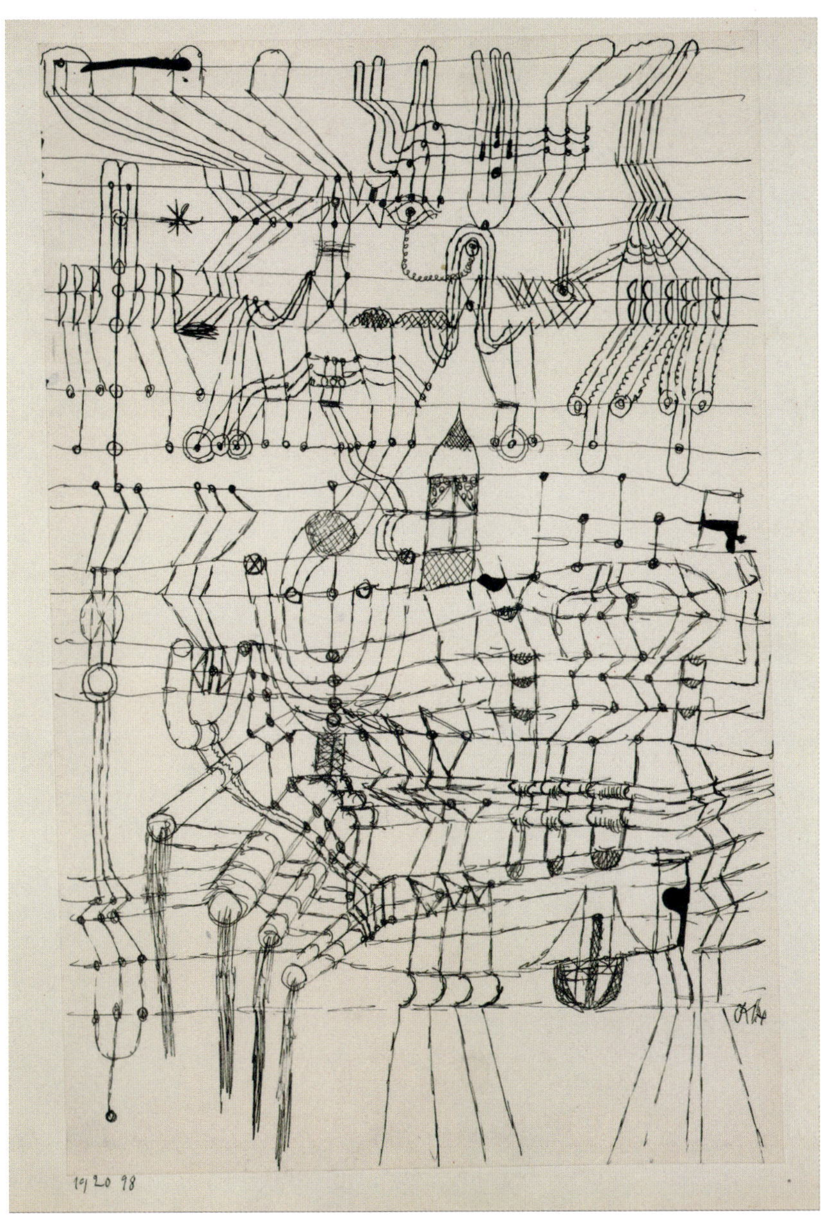

Paul Klee, Drawing Knotted in the Manner of a Net, 1920. Ink on paper mounted on cardboard, 31.1 x 19.1 cm (12¼ x 7½ in).

ON FINISHING & AUDIENCE

THE NOTION THAT AN ARTWORK CAN BE FINISHED OR COMPLETED RAISES QUESTIONS. HOW DO YOU KNOW WHEN IT'S DONE? WHAT IF YOU DON'T FINISH IT? AND WHAT PART DOES THE VIEWER PLAY IN THE WORK'S COMPLETION?

A PAINTING IS FINISHED LIKE A CONVERSATION IS FINISHED

If you've said what you want to say, stop.

The Lebanese American visual artist, poet and novelist **Etel Adnan**, who passed away in 2021, made intimately scaled paintings that drew inspiration from the timeless, elementary yet infinite lexicon of the landscape: sun, sea, sky. Her lucid geometric compositions are straightforward without being stark; bold stripes and slabs of pure colour, thickly applied with a palette knife, surround a central circle or square, or gracefully amalgamate to limn a mountain. Glowing with the natural warmth and easy generosity of a California sunset (uncoincidentally, Adnan painted the views from her home in Sausalito, often focusing on Mount Tamalpais), these images have a poetic simplicity that evokes the feeling, memory or afterimage of a landscape rather than a landscape itself. In addition to paintings, and tapestries inhabited by similarly geometric forms, Adnan produced leporellos, in which she would render with ink, gouache or watercolour various combinations of abstraction, landscape, observational imagery and poetry, all unfurling across the long horizontal of an accordion-fold book.

An artist who operated according to intuition, allowing one stroke of paint to lead her to the next, Adnan advised painters to stop working on a piece when encumbrance began to feel like a risk. 'A painting is finished like a conversation is finished. You have this feeling that you said it, and that if you add, you will clutter. You will spoil what you have done,' she told curator Hans Ulrich Obrist in 2020. 'How is anything finished? It's your instinct that tells you.'

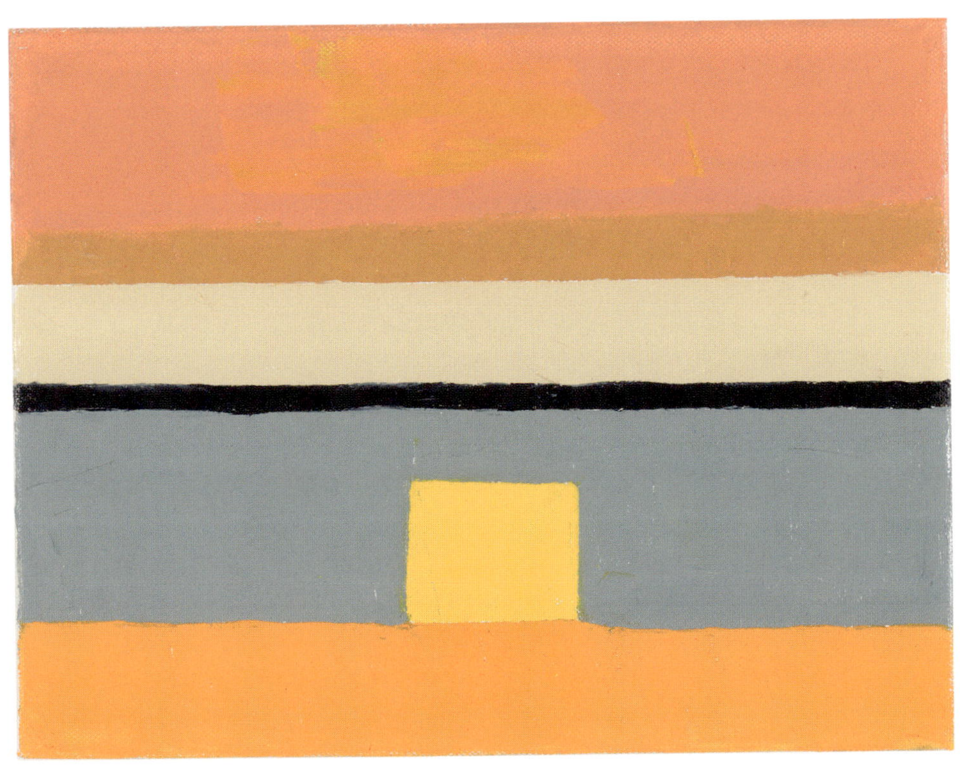

Etel Adnan, Untitled, 2010. Oil on canvas, 24 x 30 cm. (9½ x 11¾ in).

THE SPECTATOR MAKES THE PICTURE

Value the viewer's contribution to the creative act.

For the proto-conceptual artist **Marcel Duchamp**, the viewer was indispensable: a necessary component to the completion of an artwork. The French-born artist, primarily associated with Dada and Cubism, is celebrated for pioneering the ready-made, boldly appropriating a pre-existing object – typically a banal mass-produced one, such as a bottle rack, a bicycle wheel or a urinal – and presenting it as art by recontextualizing or repositioning it. As a novel aesthetic gesture that demonstrated the critical function of context in the production of meaning and the role of choice in artistic creation, the ready-made rerouted art history.

Whereas other artists, Duchamp said, might be satisfied with a 'retinal art', he wanted a 'cerebral' one: art that activated, and was in turn activated by, the observer's mind. What would an out-of-place bicycle wheel be without a viewer to gamely engage with it and see it anew? Duchamp believed that the spectator acted as a bridge between the artist's intention in making a work and the work's ultimate realization; the viewer's gaze, he suggested, was uniquely capable of the alchemy that transformed a raw idea into art.

'All in all, the creative act is not performed by the artist alone,' Duchamp said at a meeting of the American Federation of Arts in Houston in April 1957. 'The spectator brings the work in contact with the external world by deciphering and interpreting its inner qualifications and thus adds his contribution to the creative act.'

Marcel Duchamp, Bicycle Wheel, 1913. Metal wheel mounted on painted wood stool, 129.5 x 63.5 x 41.9 cm (51 x 25 x 16½ in).

'THE IDEAS [IN THE WORK] ARE MORE IMPORTANT THAN THE ACTUAL VISUAL REALIZATIONS.'

MARCEL DUCHAMP

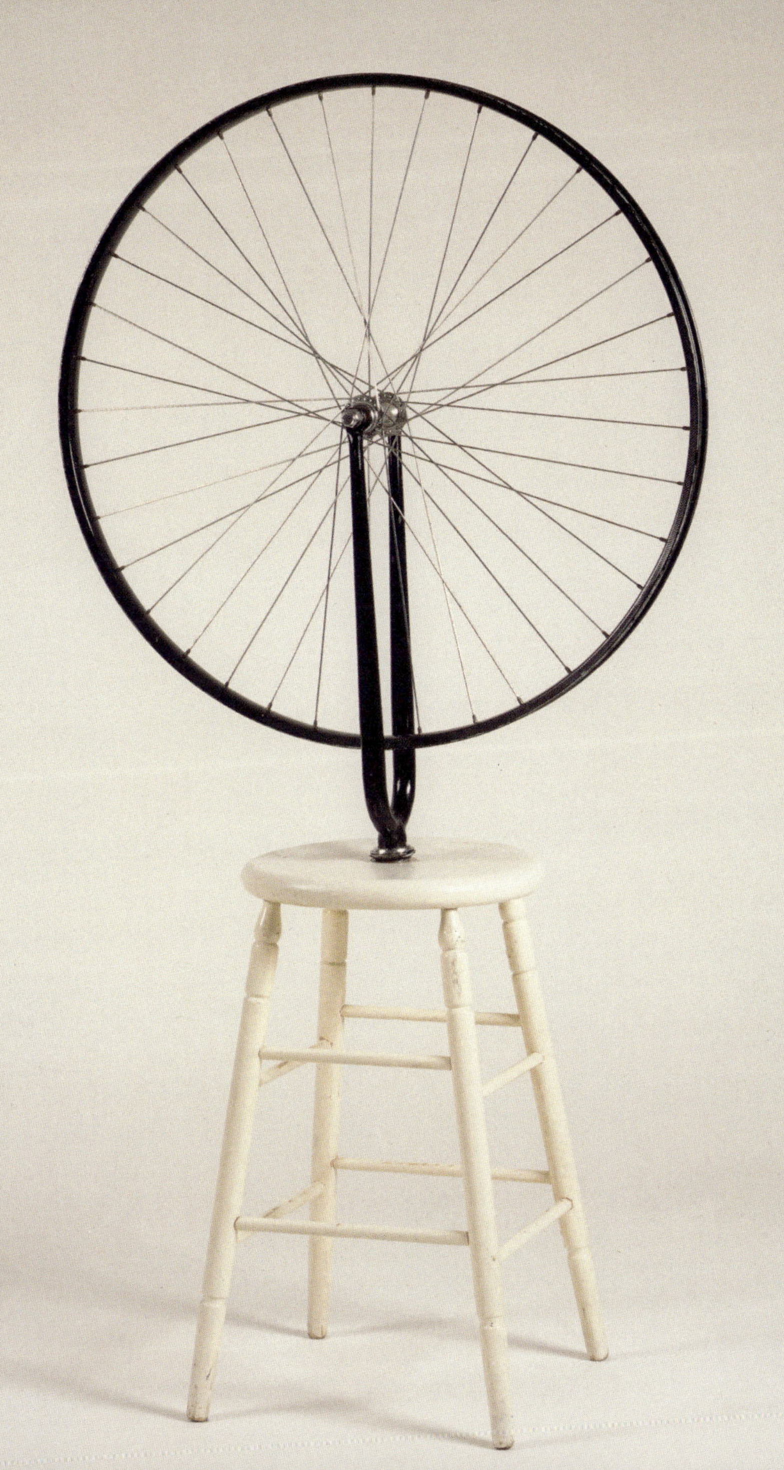

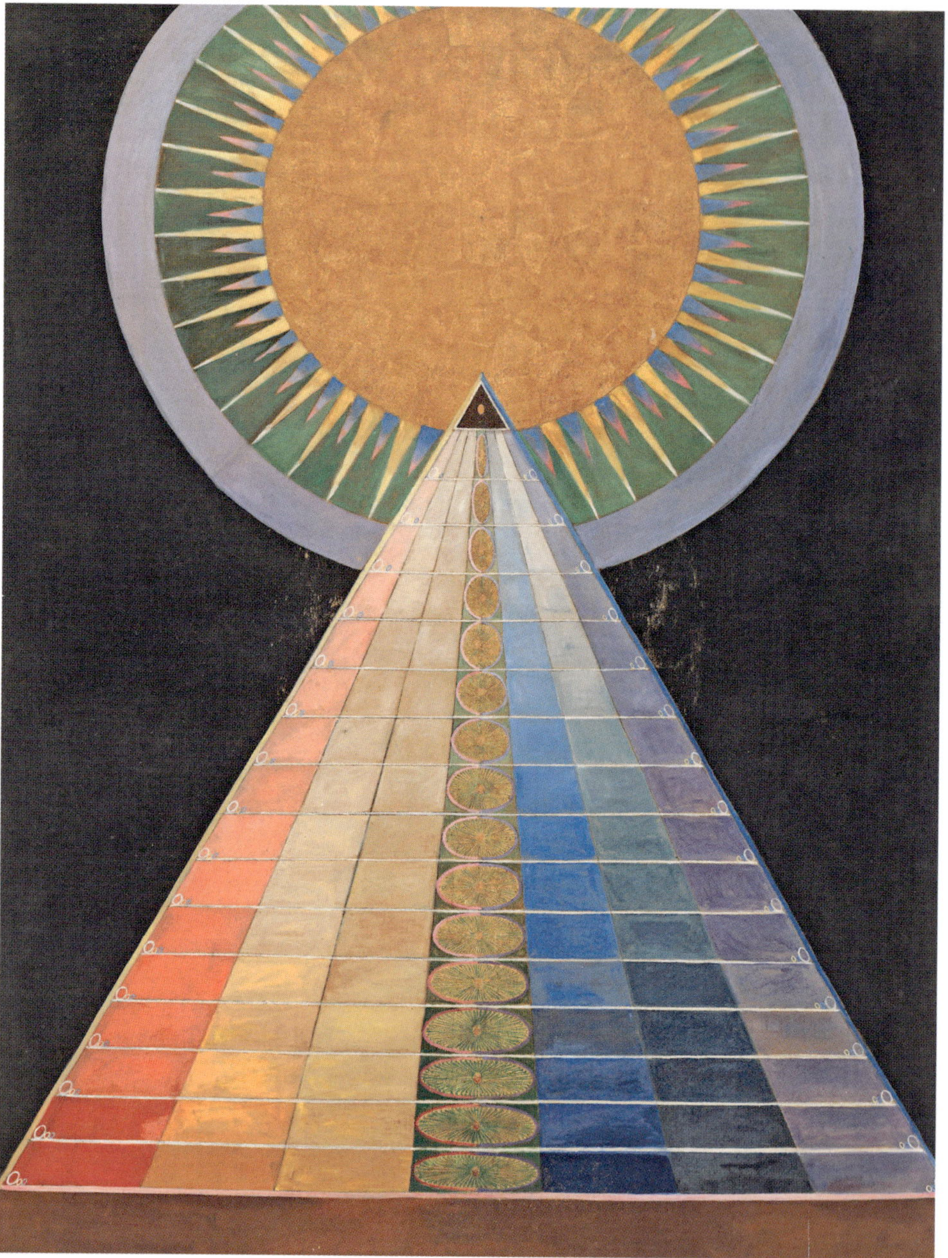

PAINT FOR THE FUTURE

Make work with future generations of viewers in mind.

Swedish spiritualist painter **Hilma af Klint**, who died in relative obscurity in 1944, seems to have had an inkling that she was light years ahead of her time - and drew solace from her belief that future generations would understand her work in ways that her contemporaries couldn't. After studying at the Royal Academy of Fine Arts in Stockholm, one of the first European art academies to admit women, af Klint established herself as a figurative painter and botanical illustrator. Her subsequent involvement with theosophy and spiritualism, and view of herself as a medium or channel, led her to create stunning symbolic abstractions as early as 1906, several years before non-representational modernist painting was supposedly pioneered by artists such as Kazimir Malevich, Piet Mondrian and Wassily Kandinsky.

Af Klint, who was fighting an uphill battle as a woman artist working in an overtly occultist mode in the late nineteenth and early twentieth centuries, largely kept her groundbreaking abstractions private but continued to make them devotedly. When she died, she left some 1,200 drawings and paintings behind - with the stipulation that they be kept out of sight until 20 years after her death, when society might be more ready for them. It took a bit longer: after the Moderna Museet in Stockholm rejected an offering of her work in 1970, af Klint flew under the radar until 1986, when her work was featured in a group show in Los Angeles. When New York's Guggenheim Museum held her first major US survey in 2018, the audience that af Klint had anticipated finally arrived. The acclaimed exhibition was the best-attended show in the museum's history, with over 600,000 visitors (and more than 30,000 exhibition catalogues sold - beating the museum's previous record, set by Kandinsky).

Hilma af Klint, Altarpiece, No. 1, Group X, Altarpieces, 1907. Oil and metal leaf on canvas, 237.5 x 179.5 cm (93½ x 70⁷⁄₁₀ in).

LEAVE THINGS UNFINISHED

Relay immediacy and flux with an unfinished appearance.

'The truth is that there's only one Impressionist in the rue Le Peletier group: that is **Berthe Morisot**,' wrote art critic Paul Mantz admiringly after seeing the third Impressionist group show in Paris in 1877. Morisot, the sole woman included in the first Impressionist exhibition in 1874, was an integral member of the movement. Drawing on her own experiences, and what was accessible to her considering constraints placed on upper-class women's movements in public space at the time, Morisot painted the everyday life of the French bourgeoisie. She typically depicted women: at their toilette, caring for children, lounging in gardens or performing household tasks (working-class maids and nurses were among her subjects). Morisot also regularly painted her daughter, Julie.

The artist rendered these figures using rapid brushstrokes, sensual daubs of paint that communicated the impression of the encounter, the sense of the moment slipping away. Often, she left the edges of her canvas bare, suggesting a sense of immediacy. 'My ambition is limited to the desire to capture something transient, and yet, this ambition is excessive,' she wrote in her sketchbook. The loose brushwork for which Morisot was known only became looser when she began to paint directly onto unprimed canvas in 1880. In her 1885 self-portrait, Morisot depicted herself as an artist, palette in hand, in a pose evocative of Rembrandt van Rijn's famed 1659 self-portrait. Between the sketchy brushstrokes and swathes of the canvas laid bare, the painting had an air of being unfinished, as if her very subjecthood were in flux.

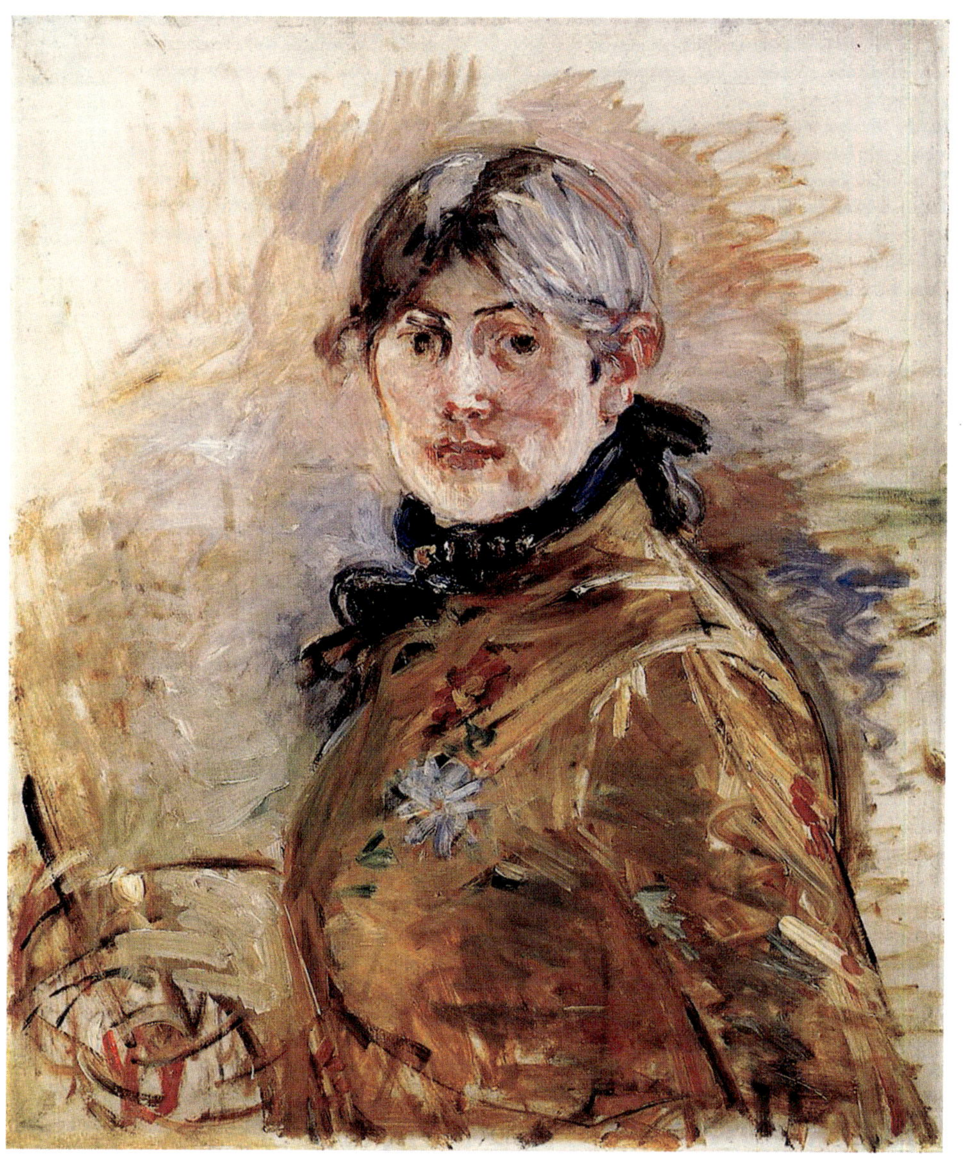

Berthe Morisot, Self-Portrait, 1885. Oil on canvas, 50 x 61 cm (19¾ x 24 in).

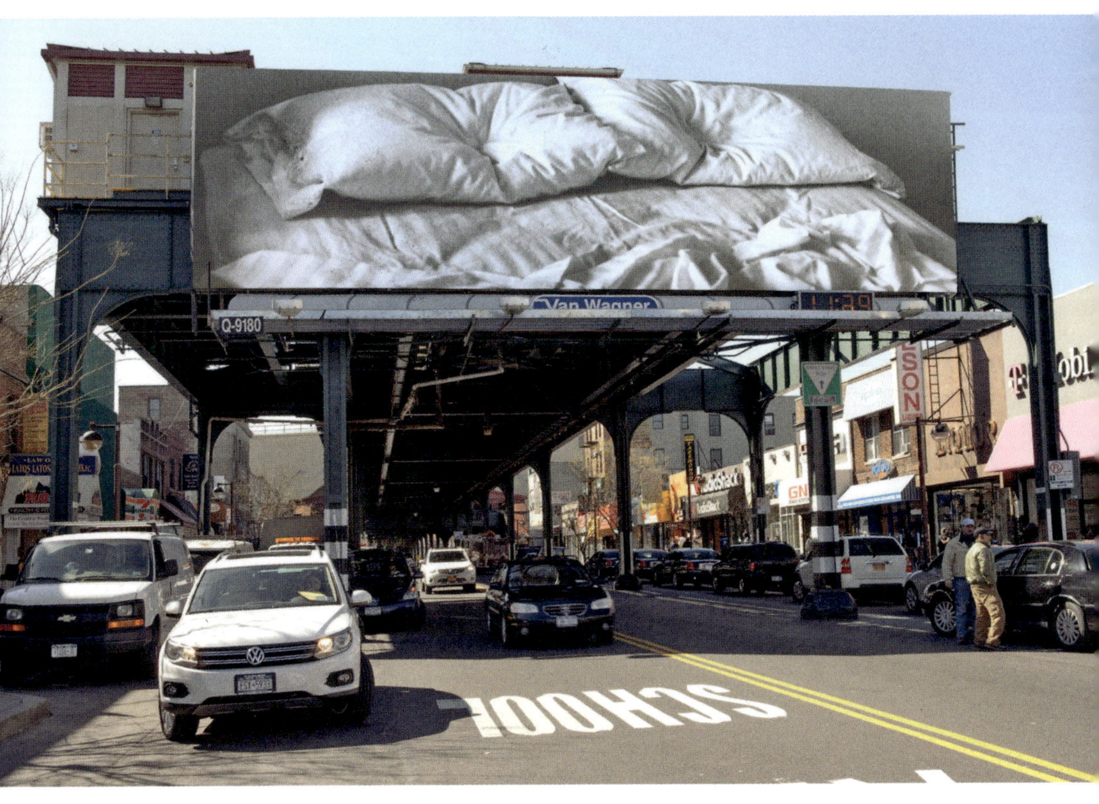

Felix Gonzalez-Torres, Untitled, 1991. Billboard. Dimensions vary with installation. 31st Street near Ditmars Boulevard, Queens, NY. 1 of 6 outdoor billboard locations throughout the New York City area, with 1 indoor location, as part of the exhibition Print/Out. The Museum of Modern Art (MoMA), New York, NY. 19 Feb. - 14 May 2012.

ASK WHO YOUR PUBLIC IS

Know who and what you're making your work for.

For Cuban-born American artist **Felix Gonzalez-Torres**, the public – his art's real and imagined audience – was constantly at the fore, shaping his work and driving his artistic decision-making. In conversation with critic and curator Robert Storr in 1994, Gonzalez-Torres said: 'One thing that I want to emphasize as much as I can with my students is, "Who is your public? What are you making this for?" That is better than trying to get some signature form or look or way of working.'

In his poignant sculptures and installations, Gonzalez-Torres brought Minimalist and conceptual strategies to bear on his personal politics and poetics. The artist and activist's staunch commitment to his public manifested in the frequently participatory quality of his work – for example, viewers were invited to take a wrapped sweet from a pile, or a poster from a stack – and was wrapped up with his status as an openly gay man living at the height of the AIDS epidemic, striving to make the individual and collective heartbreak of the crisis widely known and acknowledged.

In 1992, the year after Gonzalez-Torres's partner Ross Laycock died of AIDS-related complications, the artist mounted billboards in New York City featuring a black and white photo of a vacant bed with indentations for two absent heads. The image made a personal moment of loss, and the private gay intimacy that was tied up with that loss, radically, emphatically public. 'When people ask me, "Who is your public?", I say honestly, without skipping a beat, "Ross",' the artist told Storr.

VEX THE ENDING

Maybe the question isn't 'When and how is a painting finished?' but 'Can and should it be?'

New York painter, animator and zine-maker **Amy Sillman** – an equally formidable critic and essayist – makes sweeping, luscious oil paintings that are dialectical and digressive in nature. Often oscillating between abstraction and figuration, or inhabiting both poles at once, her deeply layered paintings bring together graphic and gestural marks in a glorious hodgepodge that foregrounds process itself, acting as a shifting picture of the exploratory nature of pushing coloured pigment around a canvas. Sillman deftly demonstrates how abstraction might be imbued with qualities like doubt, language and a sense of humor – her paintings are rich in puns – as well as a queer kind of corporeality.

In a 2018 conversation for *Interview*, Matt Mullen asked Sillman how she knew when one of her highly worked paintings was done. As the artist cited a 'gut reaction' and a 'weird feeling', she added: 'Every painting I've ever done has like 100 paintings under it.' Sillman proceeded to push back against the question itself, challenging the premise that her paintings could ever be truly finished, and thus finite or foreclosed. 'I want to expand the question of when something is done,' she said. 'I want to vex the ending… I like the idea that if you make a work that has no clear ending, then you must play with the ending. Because if you don't, you're not highlighting the weird, lovely openness of abstraction.'

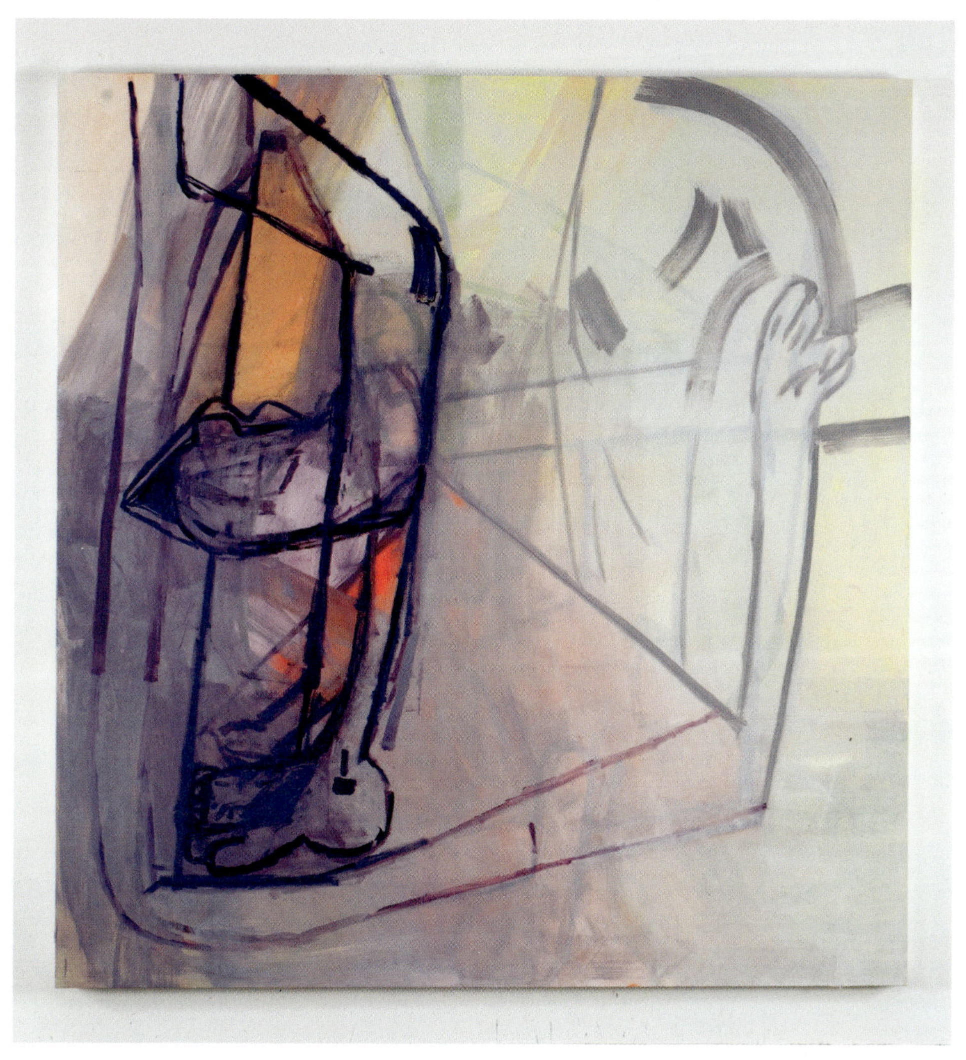

Amy Sillman, Clubfoot, 2011. Oil on canvas, 231.1 x 213 cm (91 x 83⅞ in).

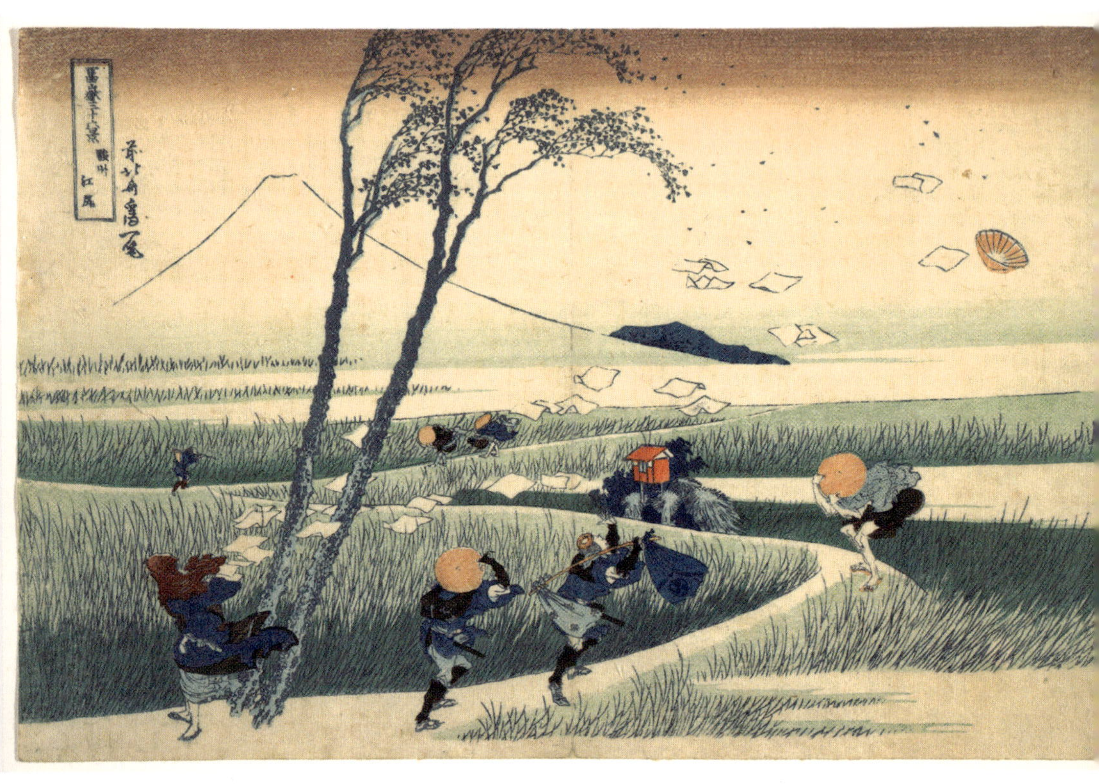

Katsushika Hokusai, Ejiri in Suruga Province (Sunshū Ejiri), from the series Thirty-six Views of Mount Fuji (Fugaku sanjūrokkei), c.1830–32. Woodblock print; ink and colour on paper, 25.1 x 37.5 cm (9⅞ x 14¾ in).

NEVER STOP MAKING

Mastery takes (lots of) time and (lots of) practice.

Ukiyo-e painter and printmaker **Katsushika Hokusai**, who is beloved for his depictions of the Japanese landscape and seascape, started making art when he was a child – and never stopped. 'From the time I was six, I was in the habit of sketching things I saw around me,' Hokusai wrote in the postscript to *One Hundred Views of Mount Fuji* (1834-9), his three-part illustrated book of woodblock prints portraying Japan's highest mountain, released not long after his colour print series on the same subject, 'Thirty-six Views of Mount Fuji' (*c*.1830-32).

For Hokusai – who depicted Mount Fuji from a variety of perspectives, in all kinds of weather, across various contexts, and populated by a range of people and animals – the mountain served as a symbol of artistic immortality and aesthetic striving; Mount Fuji was also believed to be a source of immortality in Taoist tradition. Reflecting the epic character of *One Hundred Views of Mount Fuji*, the artist, who was 75 years old when the first volume was released, changed his signature to 'Manji, Old Man Mad about Painting'.

In the book's postscript, Hokusai expounded upon his journey to mastery. 'Around the age of fifty, I began to work in earnest, producing numerous designs. It was not until after my seventieth year, however, that I produced anything of significance,' he wrote, adding that at this rate, if he lived to 110, every single dot and line that he painted would be alive. Hokusai, who died at the age of 88, was enormously prolific; he is believed to have created some 30,000 works in his lifetime, including paintings, sketches, woodblock prints and illustrated printed books.

YOU MIGHT NOT NEED A VIEWER

A work of art can be a self-sustaining system.

'A "sculpture" that physically reacts to its environment can no longer be regarded as an object,' wrote **Hans Haacke** in 1967. The German-born, New York-based conceptual artist – who in the intervening years has made work exposing unscrupulous real-estate activities, administering sociopolitical polls and surveys to gallerygoers, planting a populist garden in Germany's national parliament, and installing a stock ticker in a bronze horse skeleton – offered an alternative framework. He explained that his sculptures could be 'better understood as a "system" of interdependent processes [which] evolve without the viewer's empathy'.

Though Haacke would come to turn his focus to more overt institutional critique, his initial interest in systems skewed towards the biological and cybernetic. In the early 1960s, when Haacke was in his 20s, the artist created 'dripper boxes' – boxes containing water that the viewer could activate and move through manual manipulation or inversion. These works, which were concerned with basic physics, proposed that a sculpture could be a system or an event rather than an object.

Haacke made a momentous leap in 1963 when he conceived of a subsequent aqueous sculpture, *Condensation Cube*, which he would first execute in 1965. The work consisted of a clear cube containing distilled water that responded to its ambient surrounding conditions, such as light, heat or currents of air, by cycling through stages of evaporation, condensation and precipitation. Though the physical presence of a viewer would likely affect these external factors, Haacke's self-sustaining system didn't require an onlooker to operate; viewers were an unessential element of a larger system.

'A SYSTEM IS NOT IMAGINED, IT IS REAL.'
HANS HAACKE

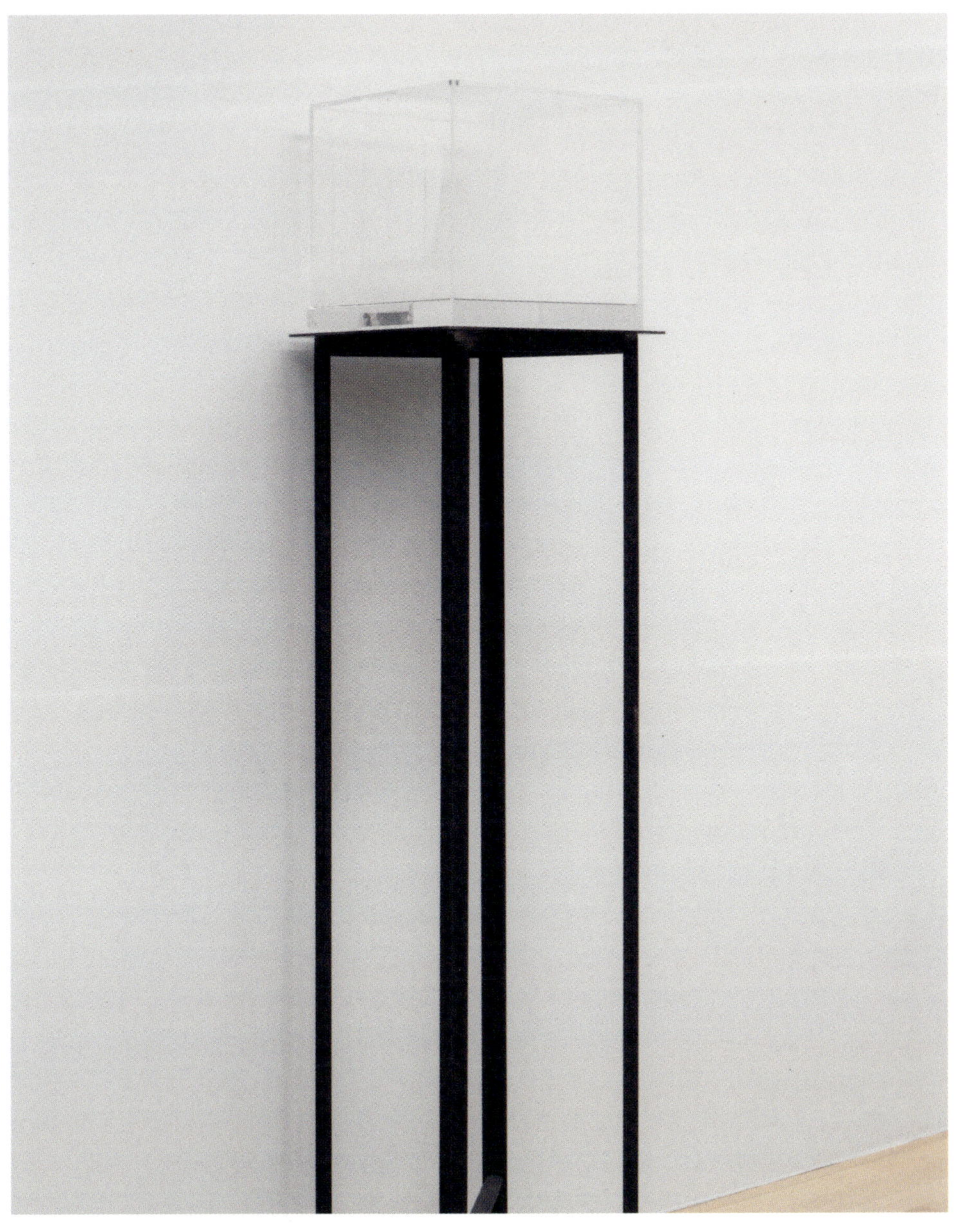

Hans Haacke, Condensation Cube, 1963–8. Perspex, steel and water, 30.5 x 30.5 x 30.5 cm (12 x 12 x 12 in).

3

WORK LIKE AN ARTIST

ON MAINTAINING A STUDIO PRACTICE

THE STUDIO IS THE PHYSICAL SITE OF ARTISTIC PRODUCTION AS WELL AS A MINDSET AROUND THAT PRODUCTION. HERE, ARTISTS TAKE AN EXPANSIVE VIEW OF THE STUDIO AND THINK THROUGH THEIR RELATIONSHIP WITH WORK AND DEADLINES.

WORK IN ACCORDANCE WITH YOUR NATURAL RHYTHMS

The best schedule for your personal creative process might not be 'nine-to-five'.

'My life has been regulated by insomnia,' **Louise Bourgeois** said in an interview with Douglas Maxwell in 1993. 'It's something that I have never been able to understand, but I accept it.'

The psychoanalytically oriented sculptor, painter, installation artist and printmaker, who came of age repairing fabrics at her parents' tapestry restoration business outside of Paris, had suffered from bouts of insomnia since 1939, shortly after she relocated to New York City. In her later years, she kept paper - graph paper, music paper, blue letter paper - by her bed, anticipating those midnight hours and positioning herself to use them creatively: to make writings and drawings driven by 'a deep need to achieve peace, rest and sleep'.

During strings of sleepless nights between November 1994 and June 1995, Bourgeois produced 'The Insomnia Drawings', a suite of 220 works on paper sketched with red or blue pen or pencil. The drawings are alternately whimsical and melancholic, characterized by resonant visual motifs such as clocks and houses, spirals and mazes, trees and waves. They also feature poetic annotations in French and English, tapping into the artist's lifelong habit of journalling.

By honouring her idiosyncratic rhythms and impulses, Bourgeois was able to produce a uniquely intimate and uninhibited body of work. Reading as collected fragments of her unconscious mind, 'The Insomnia Drawings' parse mature anxieties as well as the entrenched childhood traumas that the artist sought to exorcize in her sculpture.

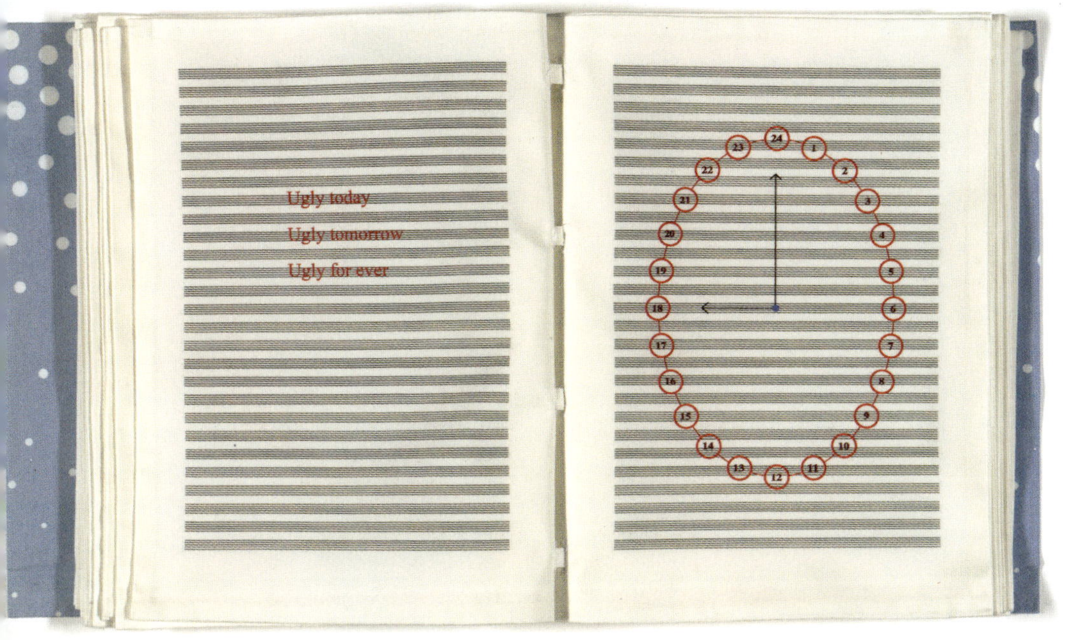

Louise Bourgeois, Untitled, no. 12 of 24, from the illustrated book *Hours of the Day*, 2006. Version 1 of 2. Digital print, composition (a and b): 26.3 x 17.8 cm (10⅜ x 7 in); page (a and b): 33 x 22.8 cm (13 x 9 in).

'NIGHT: WATCH FOR EMERGING EMOTIONS, HARD TO SPOT OUT, WAIT AND BREATHE RIGHT.'

LOUISE BOURGEOIS

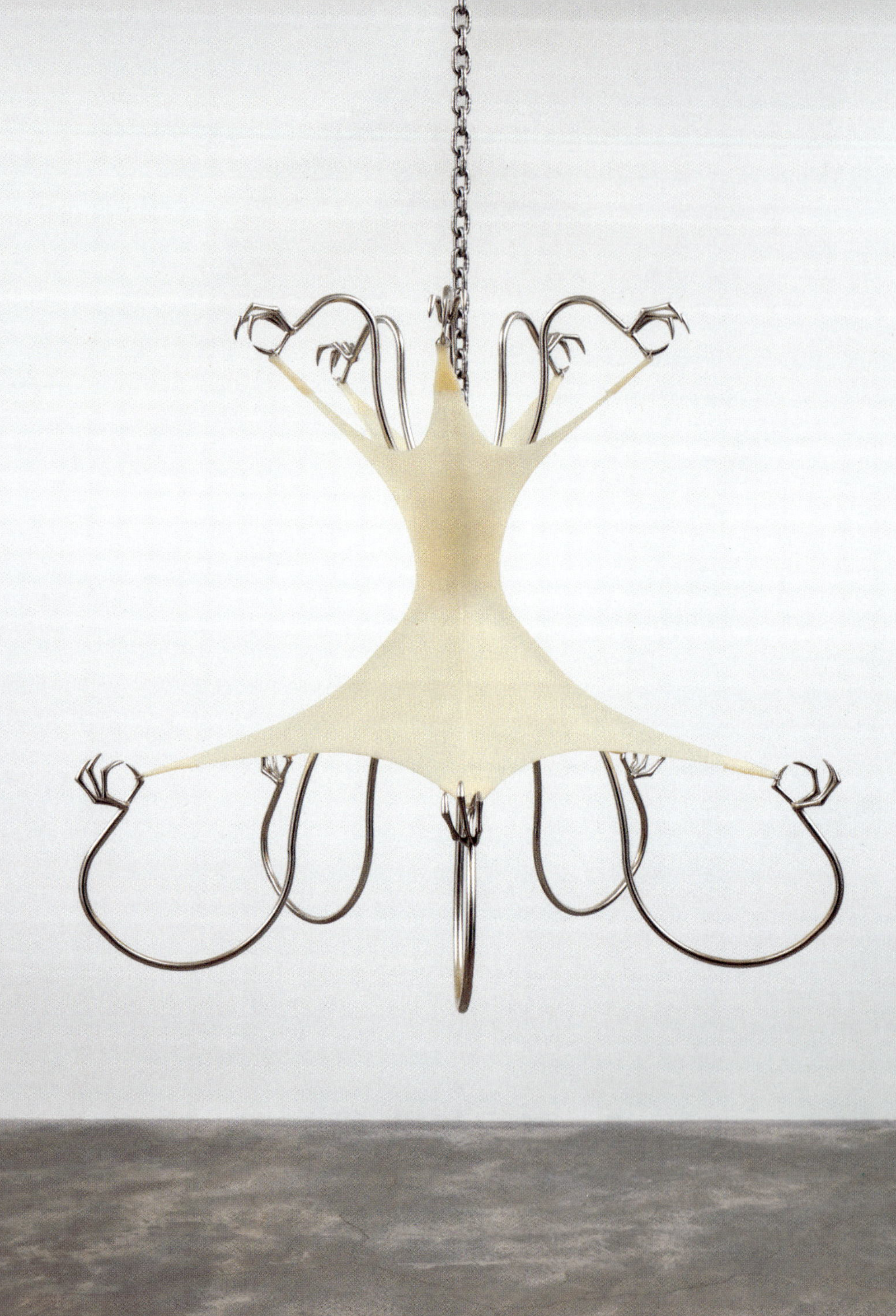

SET YOUR OWN DEADLINES

Making art on a deadline isn't romantic, but it's useful.

To produce her humorous, curiously menacing sculptures, American artist **Hannah Levy** works with materials such as nickel-plated steel, glass, fleshy silicone and even carved marble. While her vaguely anthropomorphic creations may appear as if they have materialized of their own accord, they are the result of meticulous craftsmanship - and serious deadline-setting.

'I'm not the most organized person, which I think is true of a lot of people who end up in creative fields, and deadlines are really what keep me going,' says Levy. 'It might be a show, a studio visit, or just wanting to have a photo of a finished work to send to a friend to prove to myself that I've been doing something. I'm constantly tricking myself into having a set schedule and making a finished object. It's very easy to fall in love with the process of making, and end up in a kind of endless loop of material experiments. Making art on a deadline isn't romantic, but it's useful.'

Levy took her own advice in the creation of *Untitled* (2020), an expanse of stretched silicone held gingerly in place by metal claws and suspended from a chain. For example, the artist made the claws finger by finger, cutting steel rods into pieces before welding them together, carving them and sanding them to a high polish - and that's for each individual finger, before the fingers are welded together and sanded yet again. Levy views the steps in this extremely regimented process as small deadlines that keep her on task.

Hannah Levy, Untitled, 2020. Nickel-plated steel, silicone, 182.9 x 152.4 x 152.4 cm (72 x 60 x 60 in).

FORGET ABOUT 'WORK'

Challenge normative dichotomies around labour and leisure.

Layering, contorting and juxtaposing found materials as sundry as peacock feathers, steel I-beams and petrified wood, Swiss-born American artist **Carol Bove** creates abstract sculptural assemblages with poetic elan. Crackling with unexpected resonances and dialogues, her visually balanced compositions imbue everyday objects and materials with talismanic power.

Ruminating on her two-decade artmaking practice in the 2015 book *Akademie X: Lessons in Art + Life*, Bove zeroed in on her personal relationship with work and productivity. 'I decided to stop using the word "work" as an experiment,' the artist explained. As the word 'work' vanished from her vocabulary, she began to rethink leisure, too. 'I let go of the notion that I deserved a certain amount of downtime from being productive or from being active,' said Bove. 'The labor/leisure dichotomy became uncoupled and then dissolved.' It's not unusual for artists to challenge consensus reality in the art that they produce. Bove's experience suggests that artists might do well to question normative thinking around the art's production, too.

'WORK DIDN'T EXIST, SO ALL THE PSYCHOLOGICAL PAYOFF OF WORK FOR WORK'S SAKE HAD NOWHERE TO GO.'

CAROL BOVE

THE STUDIO IS A CONSTANT SITE OF PERMISSION

Allow yourself uncertainty and the space to explore it.

After studying painting, **Carolee Schneemann** established herself in downtown New York in the 1960s and 1970s as a pioneer of body art, orchestrating cutting-edge performances, installations and films. Pieces like 'Meat Joy' (1964), an erotic eight-person performance that viscerally celebrated 'flesh as material', and 'Interior Scroll' (1975), in which the artist pulled from her vagina and then read aloud a written response to criticisms of her work, confronted societal taboos around female sexuality and female creative production. In the ensuing decades, Schneemann's boundary-pushing art continued to engage with subject matter viewed as uncomfortable or transgressive, from female aggression to the ravages of war to interspecies connection.

The artist was able to produce such radical work because she permitted herself to, giving herself free rein to experiment in the space of the studio. Speaking about her practice in 2009 in *The Studio Reader*, Schneemann said: '[The studio] is the constant site of permission – permission of uncertainty and the rarity of the circumstance in which I can address only my materials and the influences which may or may not bring them into a new form... but the permission is that I can be in a solitary concentration.'

'IT'S ALL ABOUT GIVING YOURSELF PERMISSION, WITHOUT HAVING TO RELY ON EXTERNAL FACTORS: WHICH ARE THE ONES THAT CONSTRICT US, CONSTRAIN US AND TRY TO REDEFINE OUR EXPERIENCE. YOU HAVE TO HACK, CHOP, CUT YOUR OWN PATH.'

CAROLEE SCHNEEMANN

THE STUDIO IS A FACTORY

Rethink the studio as a hub for collective mass production.

In an interview with **Andy Warhol** published in *Kulchur* in 1964, Warhol's studio assistant Gerard Malanga asked the Pop artist: 'What is your profession?' 'Factory owner,' Warhol responded. Warhol, who started out as a commercial illustrator, began transforming appropriated images into paintings in the early 1960s. Driven by an interest in mass production, mass media and consumer society, in 1962 he began to employ the commercial technique of photo-silkscreen printing to reproduce tabloid photographs of celebrities and media images of disasters. Working assembly line-style with studio assistants, Warhol de-emphasized the artist's hand as he challenged notions surrounding artistic singularity and authority. 'The reason I'm painting this way is that I want to be a machine,' he told G.R. Swenson in an *ARTnews* interview in November 1963.

Late that same year, Warhol opened a studio at a former factory on East 47th Street in Manhattan, where he would remain until he lost his lease in 1967 – he was really a factory *renter*, not an owner – at which point he moved to a new location on Union Square West, relocating again in 1974 and 1984. The first and most famous iteration of 'the Factory', dubbed 'the Silver Factory' for the futuristic silver spray-paint and aluminium foil that swathed its interior, was a vibrant site of cultural and creative production where artists, poets, musicians, actors, drag performers and celebrities convened. The variously anonymized, mechanized and collective artistic labour that occurred there resulted not only in silkscreens but also hundreds of films and photographs, numerous multimedia happenings, a tape-recorded novel and a record.

Andy Warhol, Four Marilyns, 1962. Acrylic, silkscreen ink and graphite on canvas, 73 x 55.2 cm (28¾ x 21¾ in).

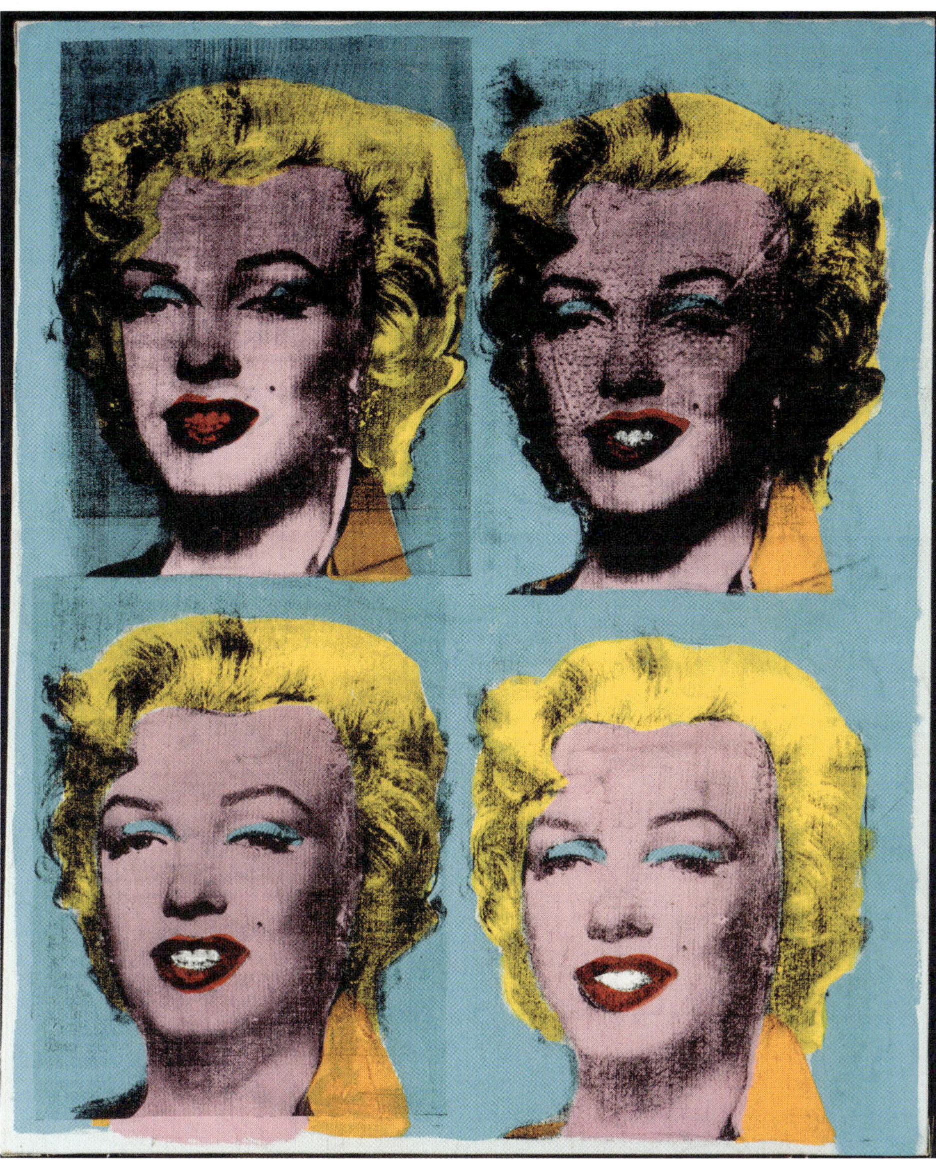

EVERYWHERE IS A STUDIO

Expanded notions of artmaking pair well with an expanded studio.

The conceptual artworks of Japanese-born avant-garde artist, musician and filmmaker **Yoko Ono** are divorced from many of the physical, technical and financial restraints that can accompany artmaking. Exhibiting a radical sense of unboundedness and itinerancy, her prominent works have included the dispersal of a container of perfume-scented flies across New York City and the planting of 'Wish Trees' in locales as far-flung as San Francisco, Tokyo and Buenos Aires; viewers are invited to follow the flies, or tie a written wish to the tree.

Ono, for whom the flow of new ideas is constant, has written a number of instructional artworks that lack a physical component beyond the page. Collated in her 1964 book *Grapefruit*, these poetically nonsensical instructions come to fruition in each reader's imagination, extending the studio immeasurably. Speaking with curator Hans Ulrich Obrist about her unconventional practice, Ono said: 'Look, for an artist everywhere is a studio.' The possible contexts for artistic production are vast if not endless.

'IN YOUR MIND YOU CAN DO THINGS THAT YOU CAN'T DO PHYSICALLY, WHICH IS VERY INTERESTING.'
YOKO ONO

WORK *EN PLEIN AIR*

Capture something essential about the natural world by painting outdoors.

En plein air painting – painting outside directly from nature rather than in the confines of a studio – may be most closely associated with Impressionism, but many attribute its conception to the early nineteenth-century English Romantic landscape painter **John Constable**. Best known for his depictions of rural Suffolk, Constable would work outside with his paintbox on his knees at a time when artmaking outdoors was typically reserved for preparatory sketches, not finished paintings. Through his direct immersion in nature, Constable produced paintings that reflected the atmospheric variances and climatic nuances of the English countryside.

Writing to artist John Dunthorne in 1802, Constable surmised that engagement with nature was critical to unmannered artistic excellence: 'However one's mind may be elevated, and kept up to what is excellent, by the works of the Great Masters – still Nature is the fountain's head, the source from whence all originally must spring – and should an artist continue his practice without referring to nature he should soon form a *manner*.'

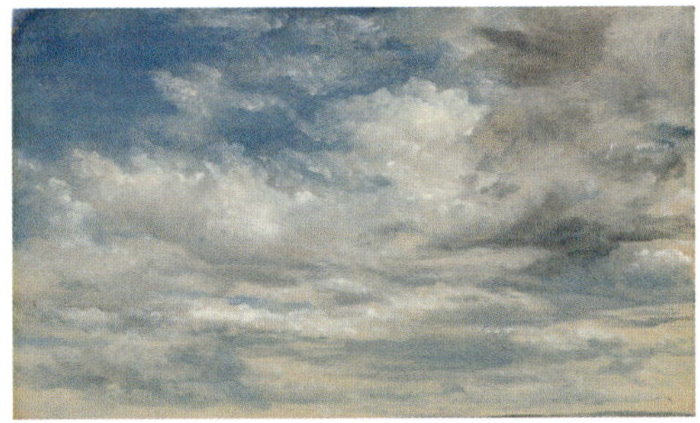

John Constable, Cloud Study, 1822. Oil on paper laid on panel, 28.6 x 48.3 cm (11¼ x 19 in).

TIME IS THE MOST EXPENSIVE MATERIAL YOU WILL EVER USE

Recognize time's value and weight.

Baltimore-based artist **Abigail Lucien**, who was raised in Cap-Haïtien, Haiti, and Florida, works across sculpture, language, drawing and time-based media to probe inherited colonial structures, challenge systems of cultural assimilation and engage systems of belief, care and possibility. Past works include a multi-use comb cast in bronze, a chapbook of experimental poetry and a post-tropical landscape constructed from painted steel architectural elements, citrus and fans.

For a 2021 group show at SculptureCenter in New York, Lucien presented *Holding Your Name Like Butter in Your Palm* (2021), a sculptural installation that transformed about 165 kilograms (365 pounds) of cocoa butter – a material associated with labours of healing and self-care – into foundation bricks and breezeblocks, which jointly memorialized Black individuals killed by the police in 2020 and individuals lost to the COVID-19 pandemic. Additional materials, such as sea salt, bronze and chicken feet, brought their own resonances of ritual and grief. For Lucien, thinking through the ways in which time allows things to set, materially and metaphorically, was a significant part of the piece.

In their work, Lucien repeatedly comes back to time, which factors into physical production – processes like mould-making – as well as the research components of their practice. 'More than any other material you'll use in the studio, time will always be the most precious and most valuable material at your resource,' says Lucien. 'When you let that sink in, it will place a whole new perspective on how to value your own professional and emotional time and labor. And importantly, that self-value will teach you how to protect your time from those who believe our labor is free.'

Abigail Lucien, Holding Your Name Like Butter in Your Palm, detail, 2021. Cocoa butter, bronze, sea salt, chicken feet, matches, soy wax, acrylic and vinyl on steel, dimensions variable.

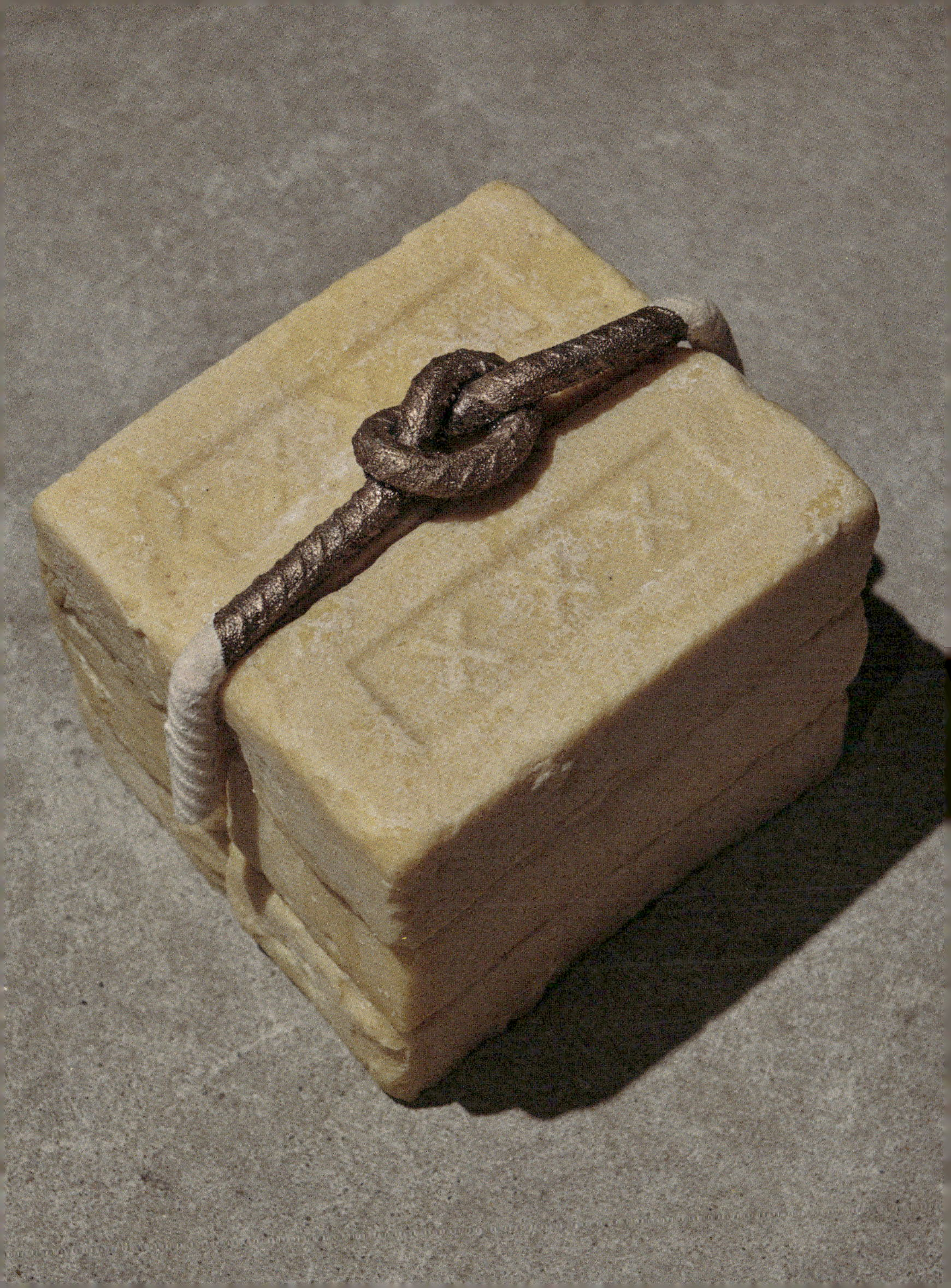

ON BEING A PROFESSIONAL ARTIST

FROM THE ARTISTS THAT CAME BEFORE YOU OR ARE CURRENTLY WORKING ALONGSIDE YOU COME THESE KERNELS OF WISDOM: ADVOCATE FOR YOURSELF, EXPERIMENT WITH ASKING, STAY FLUID AND RECEPTIVE AND HOLD OFF ON CASTING CHANGES OR CHALLENGES IN A NEGATIVE LIGHT.

SEEK OUT MENTORS

Don't be afraid to approach artists whom you admire.

In 1907, a teenaged **Egon Schiele** - a wunderkind in his class at Vienna's Academy of Fine Arts, but not yet the transgressive Expressionist and psychological portraitist that he would come to be - gathered the nerve to approach his idol, Gustav Klimt. Twenty-eight years Schiele's senior, Klimt was a well-established painter known for symbol-laden and highly embellished work often depicting women with an erotic slant. Until he resigned from the group in 1905, Klimt had stood at the helm of the Vienna Secession, a contemporary movement that espoused decoration contrary to Austria's prevailing conservative academic art scene. According to some accounts, Schiele, portfolio in tow, asked Klimt if he had talent. Klimt responded positively to the drawings the young artist offered up for evaluation, answering, 'Yes, too much!' The pair went on to trade drawings, and Klimt quickly took Schiele under his wing as a protégé.

Klimt's mentorship was indispensable for Schiele. In addition to influencing Schiele's work, particularly compositionally, the more seasoned painter facilitated his mentee's entry into the 1909 Internationale Kunstschau, a pivotal moment in the younger artist's rise. Klimt also shared his network with Schiele, introducing him to art dealers, other artists and models, most significantly Wally Neuzil, who would become not only Schiele's model but also his muse and lover. The men stayed close throughout their lives, even exhibiting together in 1916 before they both succumbed to the Spanish flu two years later.

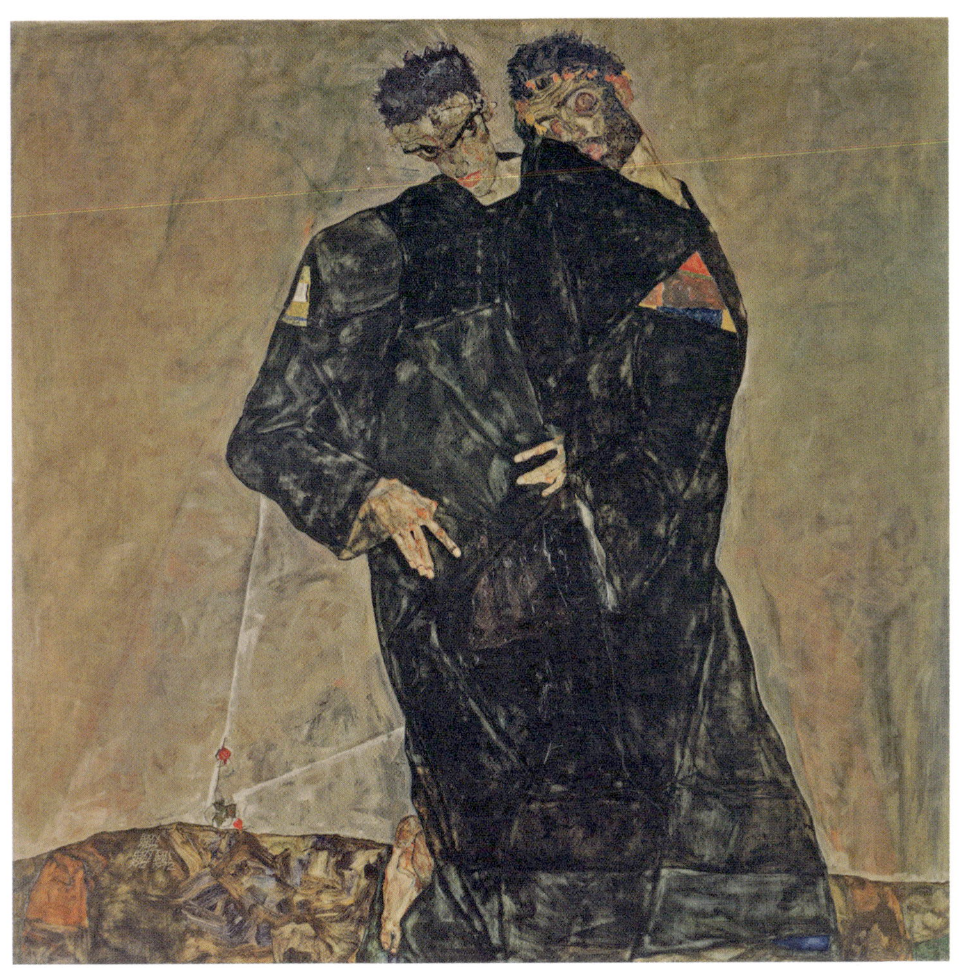

Egon Schiele, *Die Eremiten (The Hermits)*, 1912. Oil on canvas, 181 x 181 cm (71¼ x 71¼ in).

IT'S OKAY TO START LATE

Artmaking can begin at any age.

In his lifetime, French Post-Impressionist **Henri Rousseau** garnered the admiration of such avant-garde masters as Pablo Picasso and Robert Delaunay (though many of the art critics of his age were not as certain of his talent). Today, his low-relief, curiously maladroit paintings - most famously, depictions of imagined jungles concocted from visits to Paris's botanical gardens, populated by creatures inspired by illustrated books and photographs - can be found in prestigious collections throughout the world, from the National Gallery in London to the Ohara Museum of Art in Japan. Yet Rousseau didn't start painting in earnest until he was in his 40s.

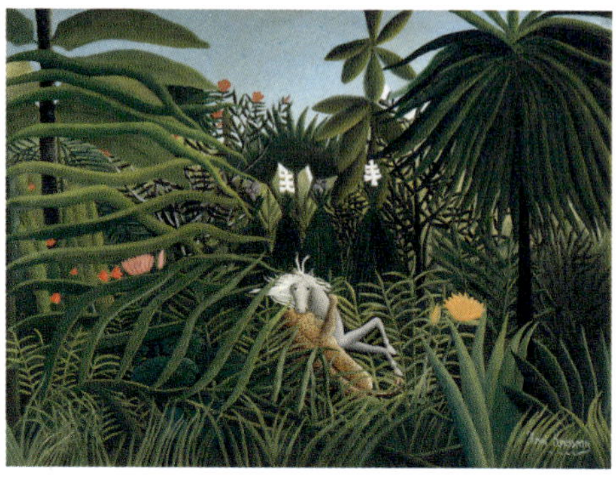

Nicknamed 'Le Douanier', or 'the customs officer', Rousseau was a toll collector in Paris. Taking advantage of the downtime that the job afforded, Rousseau taught himself to paint, with his very first works dated to 1877 - though the artist tied his entrée into painting to 1884, the year in which he obtained permission to copy art at the Louvre. Rousseau had cemented his idiosyncratic style by the time he exhibited work for the first time, at the alternative Salon des Indépendants in 1886. However, it wasn't until his retirement in 1893, when he was 49 years old, that he committed himself to painting full time.

Henri Rousseau, Jaguar Attacking a Horse, 1910. Oil on canvas, 116 x 90 cm (45⅝ x 35⅜ in).

KNOW YOUR COPYRIGHTS

Familiarize yourself with the protections available for your work – and be vocal if they fall short.

Eighteenth-century English painter and printmaker **William Hogarth** is best known for the scathing satire and moral messaging embedded in his serialized engravings. For his six-print series 'A Harlot's Progress' (1731–2), which told a moralizing story about a London sex worker, the entrepreneurial artist opted to sell the prints through a subscription model – thus cutting out unscrupulous print-sellers who would typically take a large portion of the profits, or worse, commission cheap copies that lessened the prints' artistry. However, 'A Harlot's Progress' was so well received that shoddy copies quickly proliferated.

Unlike novelists and publishers at the time, artists lacked legal protection for their work. With a group of fellow engravers, Hogarth brought the issue to parliament, arguing that the lack of copyright protections left engravers like himself vulnerable to exploitation. Because of the engravers' lobbying efforts, the Engraving Copyright Act of 1734 - also known as Hogarth's Act - broke new ground as the first UK copyright legislation dedicated to the interests of artists.

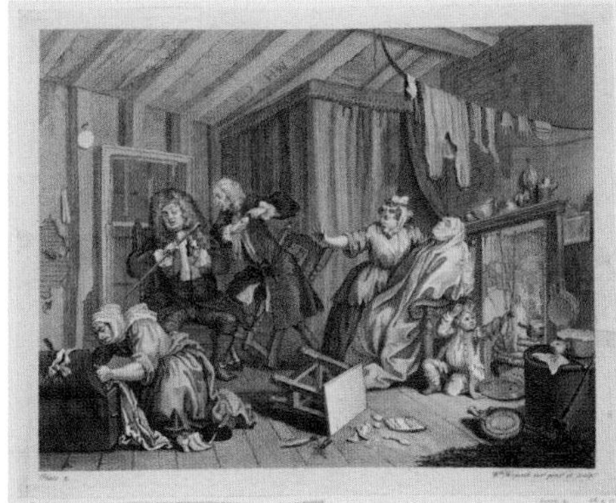

William Hogarth, A Harlot's Progress, 1732. Engraving with etching, 31.8 x 39.1 cm (12½ x 15⅜ in).

MAKE DECISIONS BASED ON HOPE, NOT FEAR

Have faith in ambitious projects so that you can realize them.

'I often remind myself to make my decisions based more on hope than fear,' says Brooklyn-born artist **Ilana Harris-Babou**, who works across sculpture, installation and video. 'As an artist, it's easy to fall into a fear of scarcity – doing things you don't have time for – or being so afraid of disappointing yourself or other people that you don't even start a piece, fearing that it won't live up to expectations. It's something I had to combat in myself – to go out there and have faith.'

Harris-Babou's work often parodies aspirational lifestyle branding, laying bare not only the phenomenon's fundamental absurdity but also its structural violences, with an eye to the people and communities whom it capitalizes upon or displaces. In the video piece 'Human Design', created for the 2019 Whitney Biennial, Harris-Babou plays the role of a high-concept home furnishings CEO in search of 'authentic design', or non-Western sculptures and carvings that could be appropriated as furniture showroom décor to lend the furnishings an aura of authenticity.

For the ambitious piece – the artist's first to riff on travel shows' narratives of self-discovery by Westerners in 'exotic' locales – Harris-Babou journeyed to Senegal, where she visited Maison des Esclaves, an African art museum and memorial to the Atlantic slave trade on Gorée Island. The decision to pursue and commit to a project of this scope and depth, perhaps particularly as an emerging artist, necessitated that fear become secondary to the desire to produce the work.

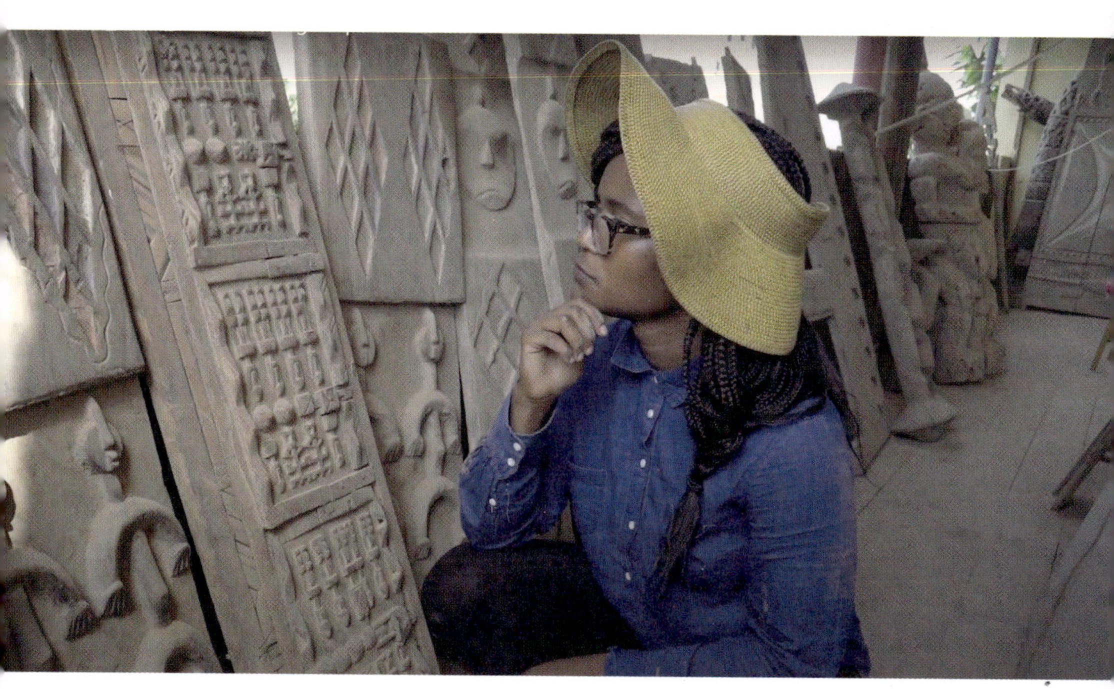

Ilana Harris-Babou, Human Design, 2019. HD Video, 40 mins.

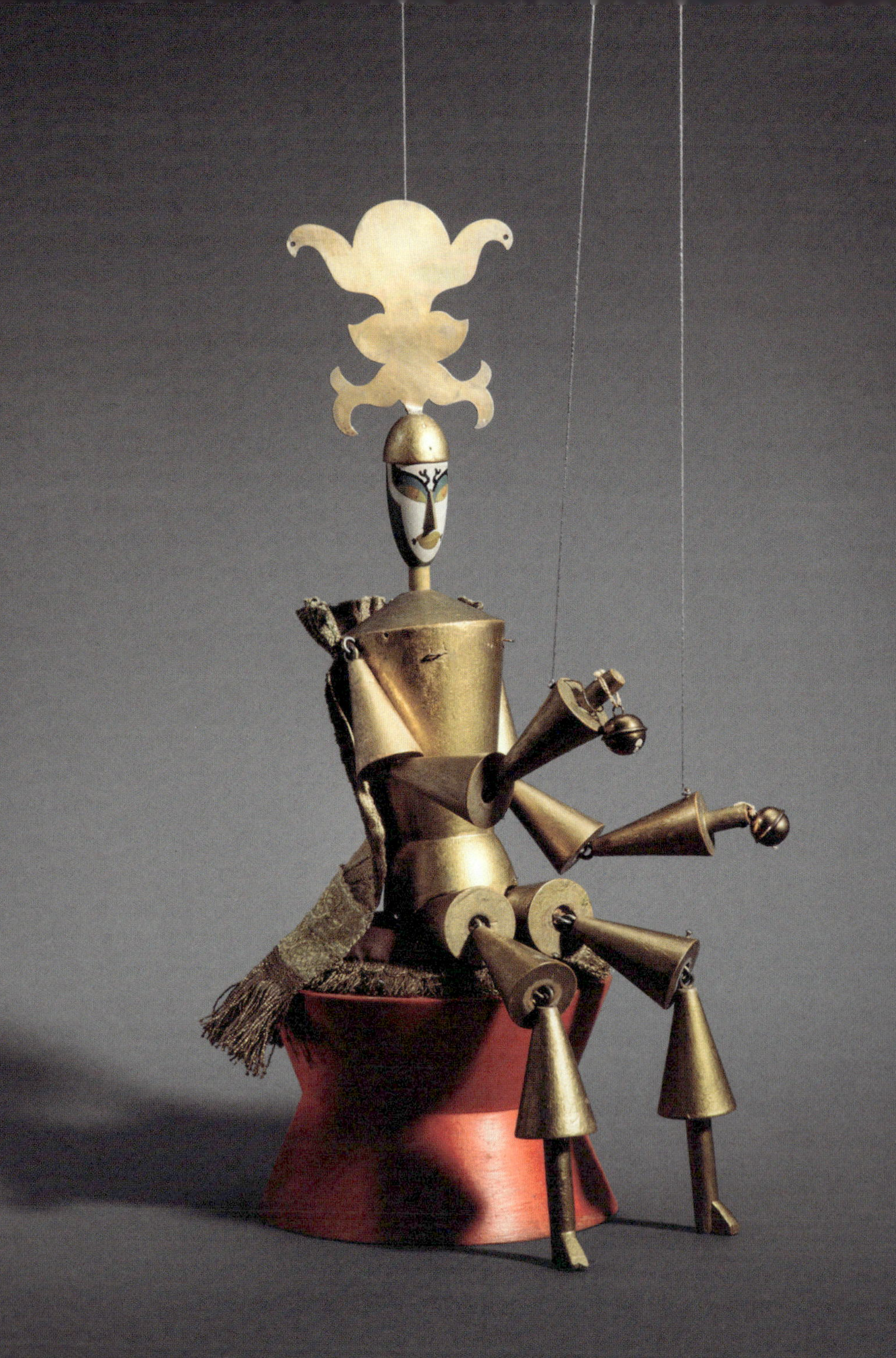

VALUE JOY

Let joy make you dauntless.

A leading exponent of Dadaism in Zurich, who later in life was associated with the Cercle et Carré and Abstraction-Création movements in Paris, **Sophie Taeuber-Arp** boldly challenged divides between the visual arts, applied arts and theatrical arts. The Swiss-born artist taught textile design at the School of Applied Arts in Zurich from 1916 to 1929 before relocating to Paris. She would remain in France until 1942, when she fled the Nazi-occupied country for Switzerland before her premature death from accidental carbon monoxide poisoning the following year.

Sensitivity to pattern, rhythm, colour and beauty, as well as the espousal of decoration and functionality, were integral to Taeuber-Arp's textile art and pedagogy; these qualities also informed her work in other media, which took forms as varied as painting, sculpture, illustration, puppetry, performance, theatrical design, fashion, architecture and interior design. Taeuber-Arp also had a humorous, absurdist streak, an underlying presence in her abstractions that was strongly evinced by her performances at the Dadaist nightclub Cabaret Voltaire and in her work on a satirical adaptation of the eighteenth-century play *King Stag*, for which she made marionettes and stage sets.

Taeuber-Arp, whom Cabaret Voltaire co-founder Hugo Ball compared to a 'a bird, a young lark, for example, lifting the sky as it took flight', combined artistic rigour with an ethos rooted in beauty, joy, fun, and the kind of freedom that comes from fearlessness. In a letter to her goddaughter, the artist wrote: 'Something to which I attribute great value... is gaiety. It allows us to have no fear before the problems of life and to find a natural solution to them.'

Sophie Taeuber-Arp, Deramo, The King (marionette for King Stag), 1918. Oil and metallic paint on wood; fabric; brass sheet; bells; metal hardware, 58.5 x 14 x 10 cm (23¹/₁₆ x 5½ x 31⁵/₁₆ in).

TRY ASKING

Asking opens possibilities.

Working across and between moving image installation, sculpture, puppetry, performance, writing and architectural intervention, New York-based artist **Sara Stern** foregrounds questions about the layered sociopolitical lives of buildings, sites and materials, casting components of the built environment as characters in experimental, speculative or synecdochal narratives. She has ambitiously orchestrated a multimedia performance with puppets sculpted from architectural materials and architectural ideologies; animated a building with facial expressions and self-reflective dialogue that addresses gentrification; and choreographed a dance by human-industrial hybrids at a stove-factory-turned-apartment-complex, exploring adaptive reuse, the mechanisms of capitalism, and the embeddedness of history in place. Many of her works, Stern says, are rooted in asking: both in a pragmatic sense, such as seeking out appropriate collaborators, requesting access to relevant archives or materials, or exhorting a building's infrastructure to operate differently, but also in a more ontological sense, wherein artmaking is a mode of posing questions, experimenting and engaging.

She recalls that a lesson in the importance of asking came early, when she serendipitously encountered an artist duo celebrated for arduous, large-scale, site-specific installations – made possible through copious asking. 'When I was younger, I saw Christo and Jeanne-Claude on the street and asked if they needed an assistant, cold,' says Stern. 'They informed me that they did not, that Jeanne-Claude was all set in the office, that Christo worked alone, etc. They started to walk away and I began to regret having asked, when Jeanne-Claude suddenly turned around with a gorgeous glint in her eye and exclaimed, "But if you don't ask, you don't get!" I was thrilled. Asking can be a great experiment.'

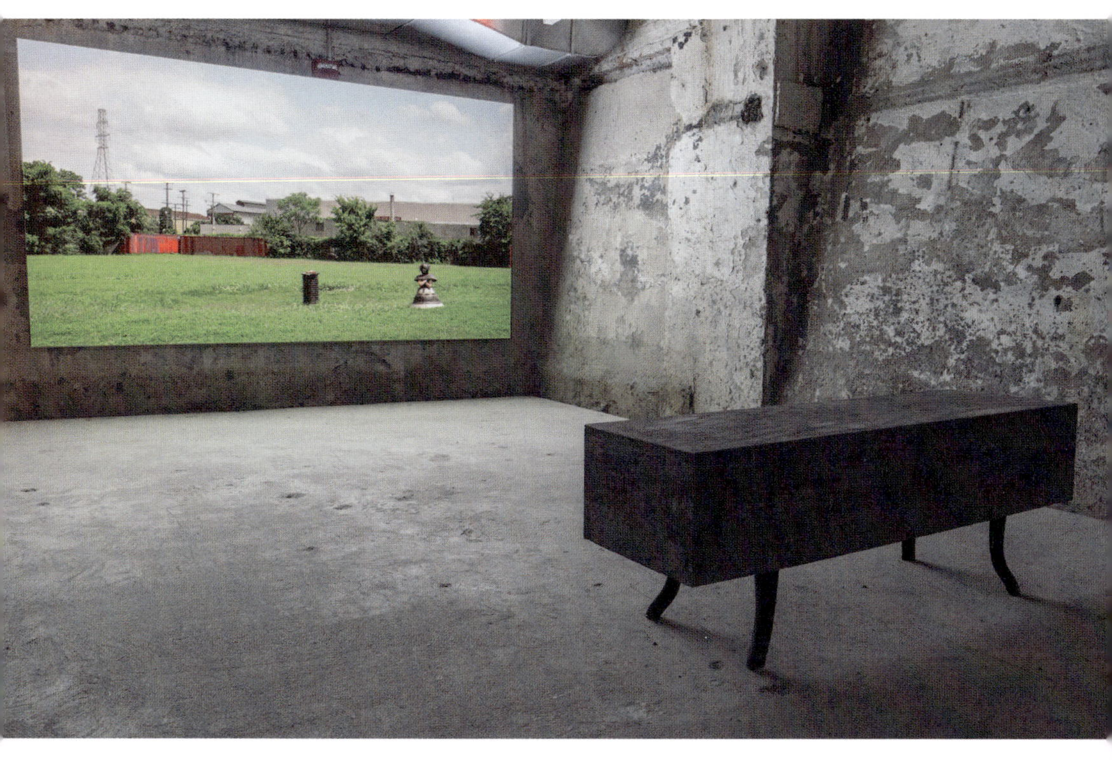

Sara Stern, Company, 2018–19. HD video, colour, sound. Concrete and cast iron stove leg seating, weathered steel walls, credits video, 13:18 min, looped. 2019 installation view at SculptureCenter, Long Island City, NY.

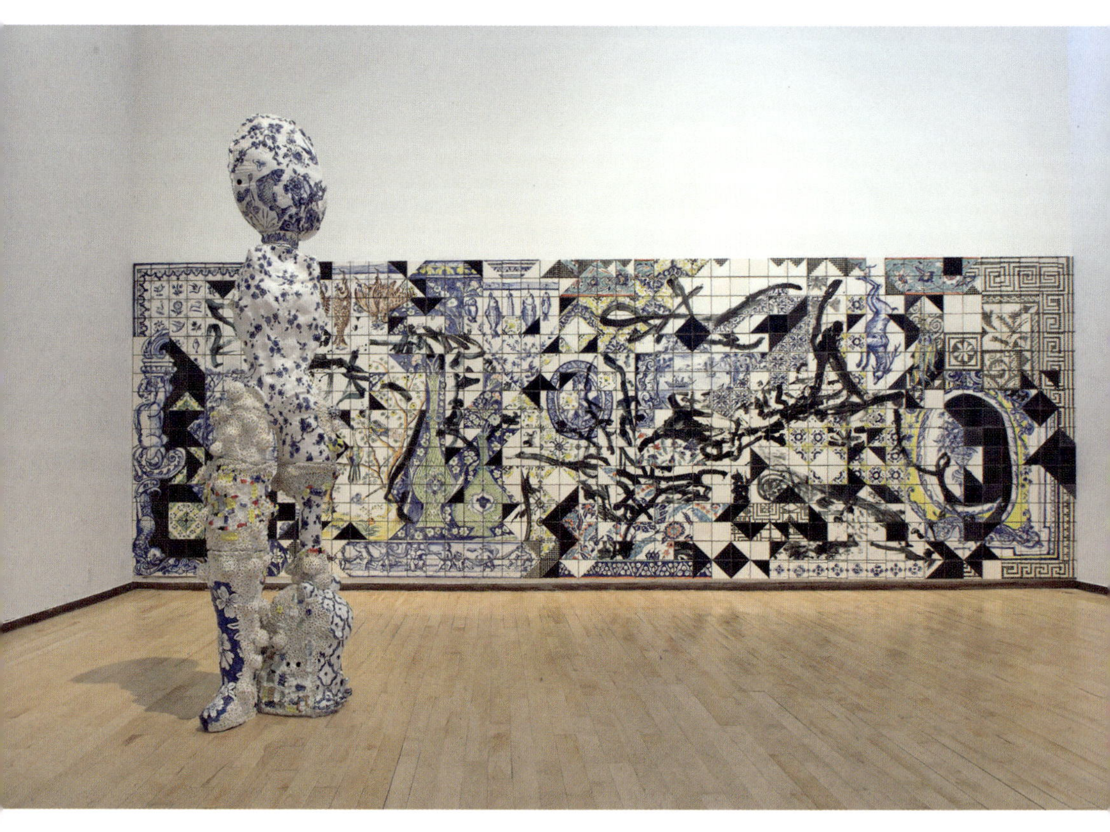

Francesca DiMattio, Installation view of Ceramics in the Expanded Field, MASS MoCA, North Adams, October 2021–April 2023.

LIMITS INSPIRE CREATIVE PROBLEM-SOLVING

Reframe hurdles as conditions for creativity.

Often executed on a sweeping scale, **Francesca DiMattio's** ceramic sculptures – variously freestanding, plinth-mounted and hanging – and tiled murals are pastiches of dissonant textures, traditions, styles and references culled from the history of art, architecture, design and pop culture. The artist's cacophonous creations non-hierarchically incorporate elements drawn from the likes of Spanish majolica, Roman tiles, Delft pottery, Wedgwood china figurines, Sèvres porcelain, Iznik tiles, Islamic fritware, mass-produced tchotchkes, and more. In their emphasis on hybridity, grotesquerie and virality, her pieces explore the complexity of the domestic, the decorative, the feminine and the maternal.

'Creativity stems from limits,' asserts DiMattio, who lives and works in New York. 'Endless possibility leads to indecision while limits narrow and inspire creative problem-solving. Recently my limitations have been created by having a baby. Instead of being frustrated that I couldn't make the large sculptures that I had been making, I tried to think of what I could do while carrying a baby.' Working with an infant strapped to her chest during New York's pandemic lockdown, DiMattio couldn't operate at her usual imposing scale, so she adapted, producing glazed tiles and dinnerware. As a result of this period, murals composed of individual tiles – like *Mosaic* (2021), which was exhibited alongside her sculptures at the Massachusetts Museum of Contemporary Art (MASS MoCA) in North Adams – became an ongoing part of DiMattio's practice, and she began to cover her large sculptures with motifs that she had worked out in dinnerware. 'Life always presents challenges... financial limitations or limitations of space come up,' says DiMattio. 'I try to see these limits as necessary conditions for creativity.'

KNOW YOUR BOUNDARIES

Be your own advocate as you navigate relationships with galleries.

In an industry where the distinction between work and play, and personal and professional, tends to get hazy, setting boundaries is particularly important. New York-based artist and writer **Eli Hill** makes figurative drawings and paintings that engage with the queer and trans community, depicting people in Hill's circle as well as historic figures with whom he becomes acquainted via archival research. Hill sensitively portrays these individuals and alludes to their rich interior lives, often with a serving of camp.

Hill advises that artists have more power than they think they do in their dealings with galleries. 'As an artist, you have agency,' says Hill. 'Galleries need your artwork just as much as you need them, if not more. In your relationships with galleries, advocate for yourself and know your boundaries ahead of time.'

In his self-portrait, *The Artist Performs Telekinesis* (2021), Hill depicts himself as Stephen King's Carrie from Brian De Palma's 1976 film, referencing the moment when years of built-up microaggressions experienced by Carrie trigger a moment of telekinesis. The painting references the transphobia and discrimination that the artist has experienced as a trans person.

'If you hold a marginalized identity, especially, look for a gallerist who has your best interest in mind for the long run,' Hill counsels. 'Galleries often "watch" artists for periods of time before approaching them – I believe artists should have a similar practice. See every show at the galleries you're interested in working with and watch how their relationships with artists evolve over time.'

Eli Hill, The Artist Performs Telekinesis, 2021. Oil on canvas, 182.9 x 121.9 cm (72 x 48 in).

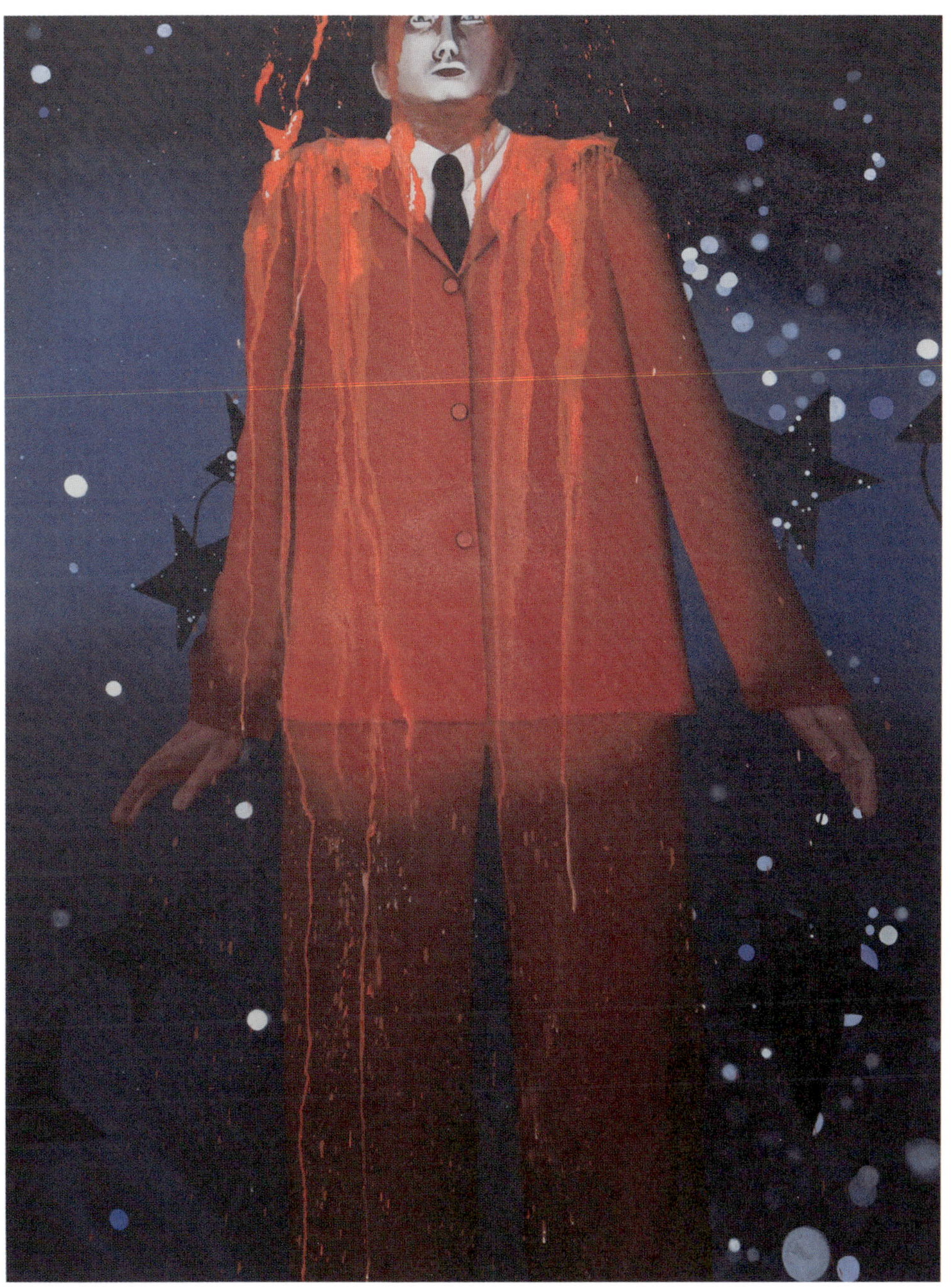

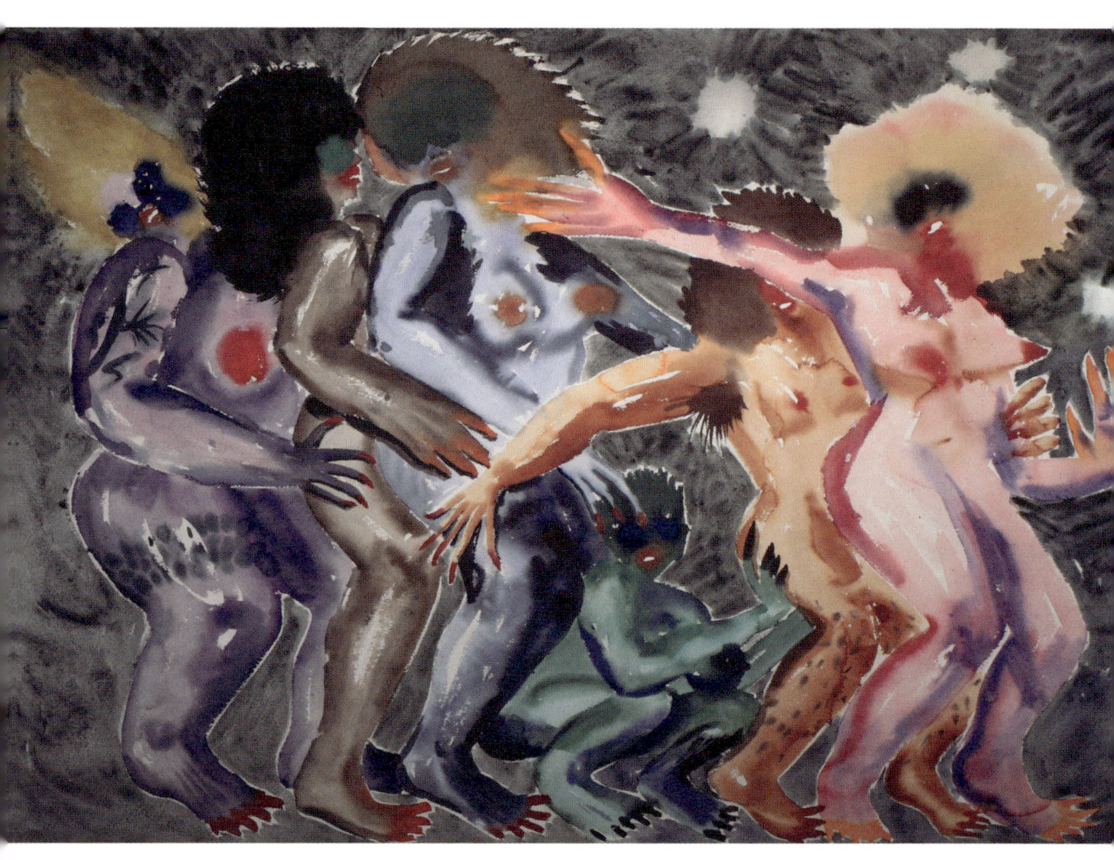

Nadine Faraj, What You Really Want Is Love's Confusing Joy, 2021. Watercolour on Arches paper, 129.5 x 180.3 (51 x 71 in).

TUNE YOUR INSTRUMENT

Cultivate the frame of mind that you want to see reflected in your work.

In the pleasure-laden watercolours of **Nadine Faraj**, bodies seep into one another in exciting and unexpected ways. As she renders ecstatic, fluid figures with porous borders, the Canadian artist celebrates queer community and furnishes female nudes in particular with the agency that art has historically denied them across many objectifying renderings, often executed by male artists.

The watercolour *What You Really Want Is Love's Confusing Joy* (2021), which takes its title from a poem by thirteenth-century Persian poet Rumi, depicts a line of six naked figures in a variety of sizes and hues, including purple, pink, green and blue; some of the figures sport tattoos or body hair. The subjects, who are in close contact with one another, simultaneously dance as independent individuals and as a single erotic unit against a dark backdrop with points of light resembling stage spotlights. The self-assured freedom and joy that the work exudes stem from qualities that the Canadian artist cultivates in herself before she even approaches the page.

'Working wet-on-wet with watercolour, I only get one chance per sheet of paper,' explains Faraj of her method and approach. 'So before starting, I tune myself, like you would an instrument before a show. By way of physical and mental practices, I relax my mind so that I can approach the void. This is where I encounter ideas and learn to trust them; this is what keeps me fluid, sensitive and receptive.'

CELEBRATE YOUR DISCOVERIES

Take pleasure in your accomplishments, big and small.

Born in Argentina and raised in Milan, **Lucio Fontana** worked at his father's funerary statuary business in Argentina, studied and honed his craft in Italy and France, and then returned to Argentina, where he established the Academia Altamira and drafted the 'White Manifesto' (1946) before resettling in Italy in 1947. The manifesto, which advocated for three-dimensional abstraction that incorporated new scientific and technological discoveries, laid the groundwork for five subsequent manifestos written by Fontana between 1947 and 1952 outlining Spatialism, a new movement devoted to transcending the confines of the picture plane through the unification of colour, sound, movement and space.

In 1949, Fontana had a breakthrough: the artist, who primarily identified as a sculptor and had not previously worked with canvas, debuted uncoloured canvases punched through with 'buchi', or 'holes', loosely arranged in circles, spirals, rows or columns. For Fontana, the empty space formed by the holes 'created an infinite dimension... corresponding to the cosmos'. As he developed this punctured series, increasingly working with bold monochromes, Fontana also began to gesturally slash his canvases, pioneering his 'Tagli', or 'Slashes', series in 1958.

Fontana celebrated the fact that he was working with exciting, groundbreaking concepts (akin to some of the new ideas being explored by Gutai in Japan). 'With the slash I invented a formula that I don't think I can perfect. I managed with this formula to give the spectator an impression of spatial calm, of cosmic rigor, of serenity in infinity,' said Fontana. In 1968, the year he died, the artist declared: 'My discovery was the hole and that's it. I am happy to go to my grave after such a discovery.'

Lucio Fontana, Concetto spaziale, Attese, 1960. Waterpaint on canvas, 41.3 x 32.8 cm (16 x 12 in).

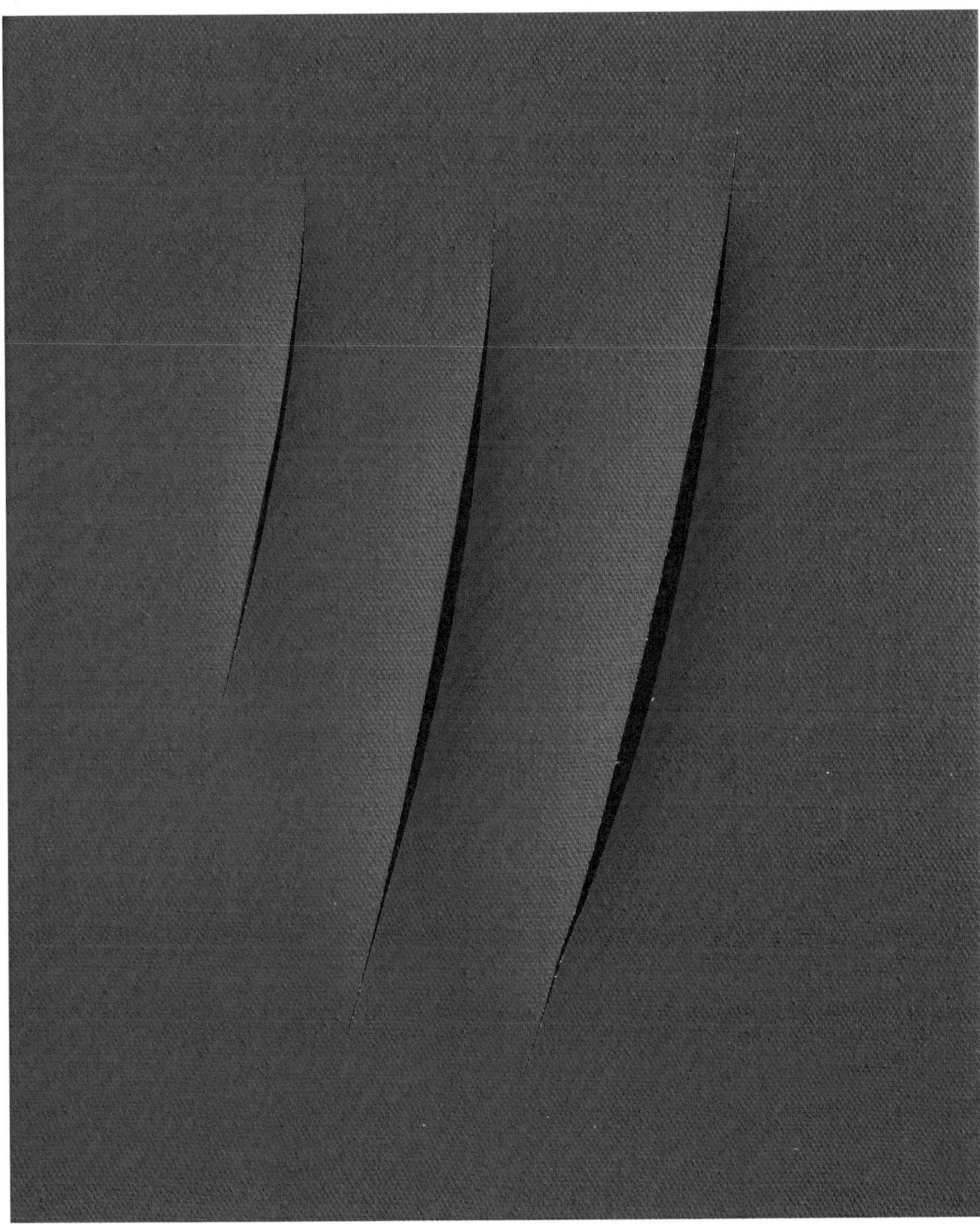

LIVE WITH YOUR WORK

Before you exhibit a piece, put it to the test by cohabiting with it.

American-born, Berlin-based trans-disciplinary artist **Evan Roth** excavates what often goes unacknowledged in our conceptions of communication technologies, from the self-portraits formed by our browser caches to the vast physical infrastructure of the web. For 'Red Lines' (2018–20), a peer-to-peer network performance, Roth shared 82 infrared videos of coastal landscapes where internet cables are located. The videos, which were stored on servers in the places that they portrayed, could be accessed by viewers on their home devices. For the artist, living with pieces from the 'Red Lines' series – as he strove to whittle down hundreds of landscape images – was particularly helpful in finalizing the work.

'This is something I just started doing in the last few years, but wish I had thought of in the beginning of my career,' Roth says. 'When possible I like to live with pieces I've made in my home for at least three months before exhibiting them publicly. In my experience, art occupies a different portion of my brain when I share space with it over an extended period of time. This really helps me understand the stronger and weaker aspects of a piece that I may not have initially seen or have tried to intellectually justify in the studio.'

'YOU'LL PROBABLY KNOW IF IT'S GOOD OR BAD AFTER WAKING UP TO IT EVERY DAY FOR ONE MONTH. IF YOU'RE STILL NOT SURE, THEN LIVE WITH IT FOR ANOTHER MONTH.'
EVAN ROTH

STRESS ASSASSINATES CREATIVITY

A sense of humour and a support network can help.

American painter **Jamian Juliano-Villani**, who in 2021 also became a gallerist when she opened an art space on Manhattan's Lower East Side, makes airbrushed paintings with repurposed imagery mined from diverse sources such as advertising graphics, memes, television and art history. These appropriated images, which run the gamut from quotidian (a neon bar sign) to bizarro (a goat in UGG boots), take on a weird and hilarious valence when compressed in the space of a single work. Juliano-Villani's paintings grapple with our present-day media overload and – particularly when they incorporate three-dimensional objects, such as a microwave or stepladder – effectively probe the ways in which 'the digital' is simultaneously a non-space and a usurper of physical space, invisible yet ever-present.

Juliano-Villani, who had a rapid rise to fame, was characteristically frank in a 2017 interview with Art21. 'Stress assassinates creativity,' she said, noting that figuring out how to work with integrity under pressure is difficult even for talented artists. She has found a sense of humour and a robust network of friends and peers to be helpful tools.

'A LOT OF WEIRD DECISIONS HAPPEN HERE BY MYSELF IN THE MIDDLE OF THE NIGHT, BUT ALSO A LOT OF IT IS TALKING WITH OTHER PEOPLE. IF YOU HAVE ALL THESE DIFFERENT VOICES COMING IN, IT'S LESS OF A ONE-PERSON LECTURE.'
JAMIAN JULIANO-VILLANI

CARE ABOUT WHAT YOU'RE DOING, EVEN IF NO ONE ELSE DOES

Let your need to create sustain you when external validation feels a way off.

Born to an opera singer mother and a sculptor father with whom she built cardboard maquettes as a child, **Kiki Smith** grew up assured of the value of self-expression. The German-born American artist and activist, who gained recognition in the 1980s in New York City's vibrant downtown scene, approaches corporeality as a common ground or meeting place. Drawing upon mythology, folklore and fairy tales, as well as religious iconography rooted in her Catholic upbringing, Smith's arresting artworks channel the intensity and complexity of embodied experience, often with a focus on pain, sex and abjection. Her body of work, which includes portrayals of individual organs, human figures and animals, manifests in sculptures made from materials as varied as porcelain, bronze, aluminium and wax, as well as in drawings, prints, textiles and photographs.

In conversation with Sarah Moroz in 2019, Smith recounted having her first solo exhibition late in her career relative to some of her peers. The artist acknowledged the benefit that she derived from the extra years spent struggling to find clarity in her work instead of chasing the external validation that is tied up with recognition and visibility. '[Artmaking] has to come from just you needing to do it,' Smith said. 'You need to find what engages you in the process to sustain yourself. Most artists' experience is of sitting at home, where nothing is going on and nobody could care less what you're doing. You have to care about it yourself.'

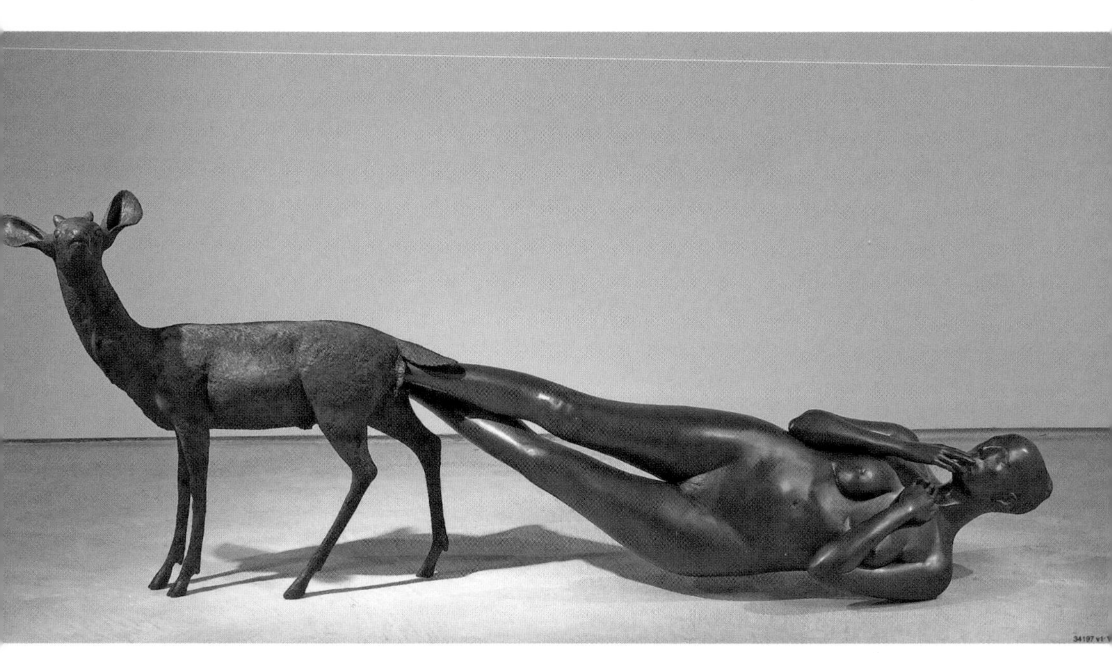

Kiki Smith, Born, 2002. Bronze, 99.1 x 256.5 x 61 cm (39 x 101 x 24 in).

'I TRY TO KEEP SOMETHING LIKE FAITH THAT
I'M MAKING MY WORK FROM A DEEP PLACE
INSIDE ME.'

KIKI SMITH

COMMUNICATE A VISION OF YOUR DESIRED WORLD

Pursue a more just world not only in your artwork but also in your engagements with institutions.

In a practice equally informed by research and his family history, Iraqi-American artist **Michael Rakowitz** critiques colonialism, interrogates the relationship between the United States and the Middle East, and advocates for a more just world. His projects include 'paraSITE' (1998–ongoing), a series of custom-built inflatable shelters for unhoused people in major US cities; *A House With A Date Palm Will Never Starve* (2018), a cookbook revolving around Iraqi date syrup, previously the country's second most prominent export; and 'The Invisible Enemy Should Not Exist' (2007–ongoing), recreations – crafted from Middle Eastern packaging and newspapers – of antiquities that were looted from Iraq, particularly the National Museum of Iraq in Baghdad, amid the US-led invasion of the country.

Rakowitz was the first artist to withdraw his work from the 2019 Whitney Biennial in protest at museum board member Warren Kanders, whose company sold military supplies including tear gas; after eight artists followed suit, demanding that their work be removed from the prestigious exhibition, Kanders stepped down from the board. Rakowitz has also refused to participate in shows funded by Israel or shows that attempt to censor him, and regularly collaborates with the galleries that represent him to ensure that the people who collect his art do not live contrary to the ethics embedded in the work. In conversation with Kelsey Ables in 2019, Rakowitz encouraged artists to convey their ethical views to the dealers and curators with whom they work, expressing a vision 'not just of the career that they want to have but of the world that they want to propose within that career'.

Michael Rakowitz, The Invisible Enemy Should Not Exist (4th Plinth), 2018. 10,500 Iraqi date syrup cans, metal frame, 4.3 m (169¼ in).

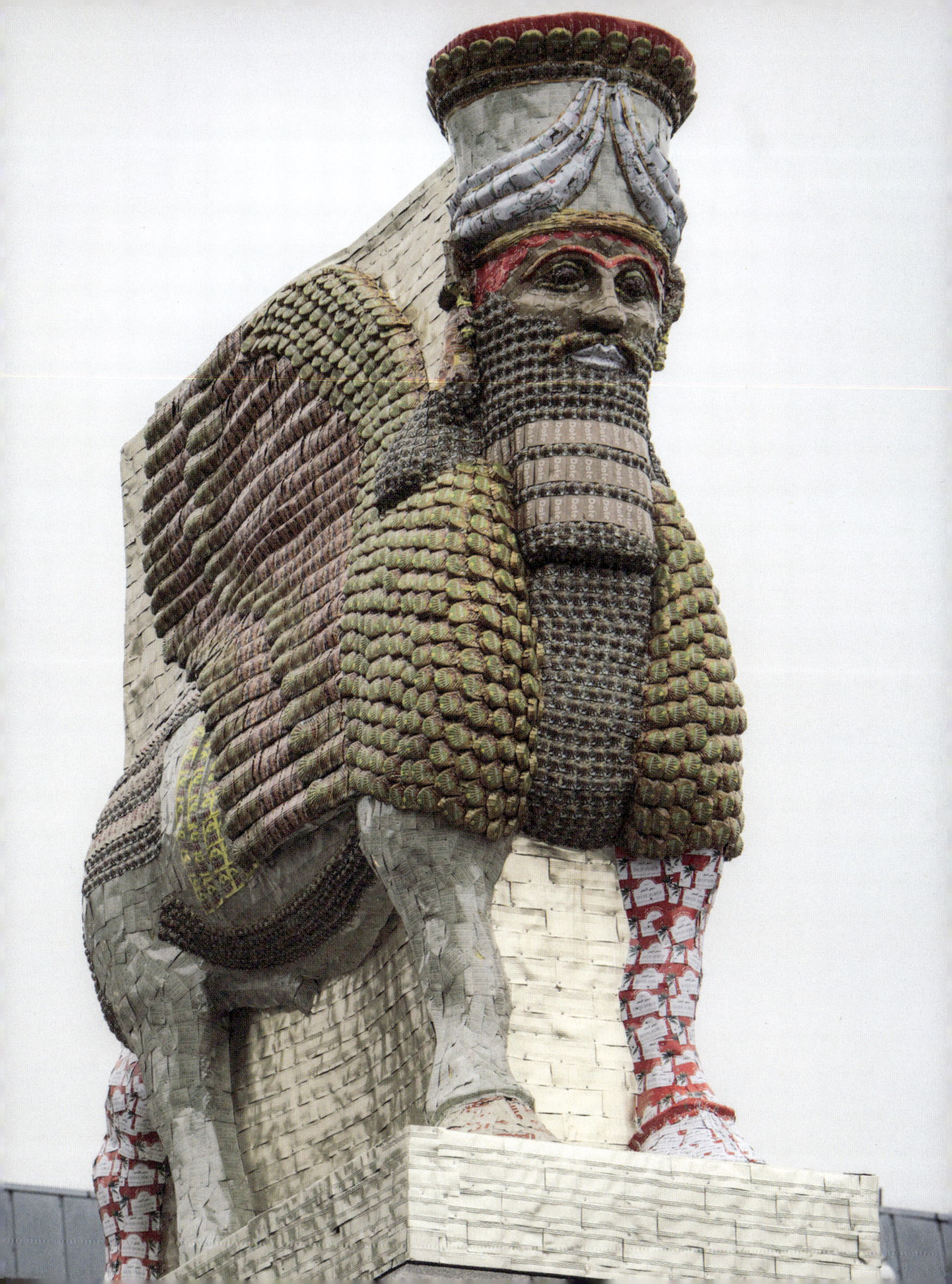

ON APPROACHING CRITICISM

CRITICISM – WHETHER POSITIVE, NEGATIVE, MIXED OR NEUTRAL – COMES WITH THE TERRITORY. SOME ARTISTS ACTIVELY SEEK OUT FEEDBACK OR CAREFULLY WEIGH WHICH CRITICISMS TO TAKE ON, WHILE OTHERS IGNORE THE CRITICS, USURP THE CRITICS OR REJECT THE IMPETUS TO MAKE WORK THAT CAN BE UNDERSTOOD.

A SCANDAL CAN BE A GOOD THING

It's par for the course in art history for exciting, radical departures to be met with vehement criticism.

In its day, French painter **Édouard Manet**'s *Le Déjeuner sur l'herbe*, or 'The Luncheon on the Grass', (1863) inspired its fair share of controversy. The grand oil painting, which debuted at Paris's Salon des Refusés after being brusquely rejected by the jury of the official Paris Salon, depicts an unconventional picnic. Set in a bucolic landscape accented with a bather in a chemise, the work portrays a starkly nude woman, her frank gaze meeting the viewer's own, accompanied by two fully clothed men. A picnic basket spilling bread and fruit lies forgotten in the corner.

Made at a time when history painting was held in high regard, Manet's painting – which he knowingly executed on a historic scale – scandalized critics for its 'vulgar' allusions to the sex work that took place in Paris's Bois de Boulogne. Also provoking criticism and confusion was the mix of contemporary dress and classical iconography (the arrangement of the figures, for example, directly referenced a drawing by Raphael) as well as the flatness of the picture plane with its almost severe contrast between light and dark.

Throughout his career, Manet's repeated, radical divergences from painterly norms and decorum regularly garnered him condemnation from the art establishment, much to his chagrin. Yet it is his flagrant rejection of convention that ultimately secured his place in the canon. Inspiring artists across media over the past 150 years, *Le Déjeuner sur l'herbe* has been reinterpreted by the likes of Paul Cézanne, Herman Braun-Vega and Mickalene Thomas, to name but a few.

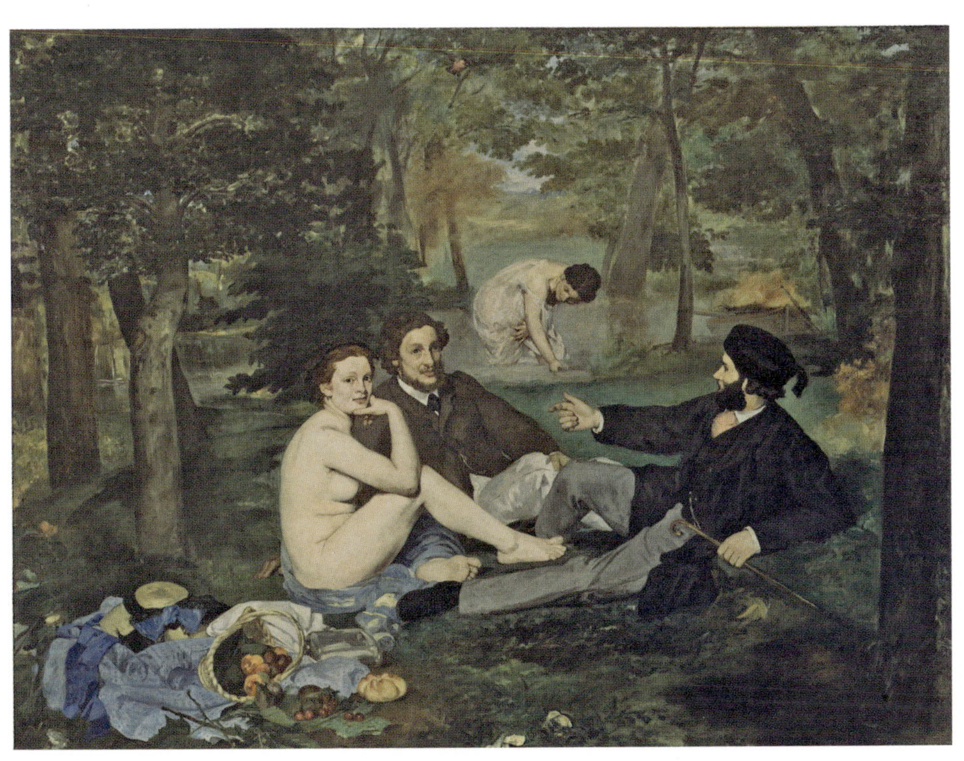

Édouard Manet, Le Déjeuner sur l'herbe, 1863. Oil on canvas, 207 x 265 cm (81½ x 104⅜ in).

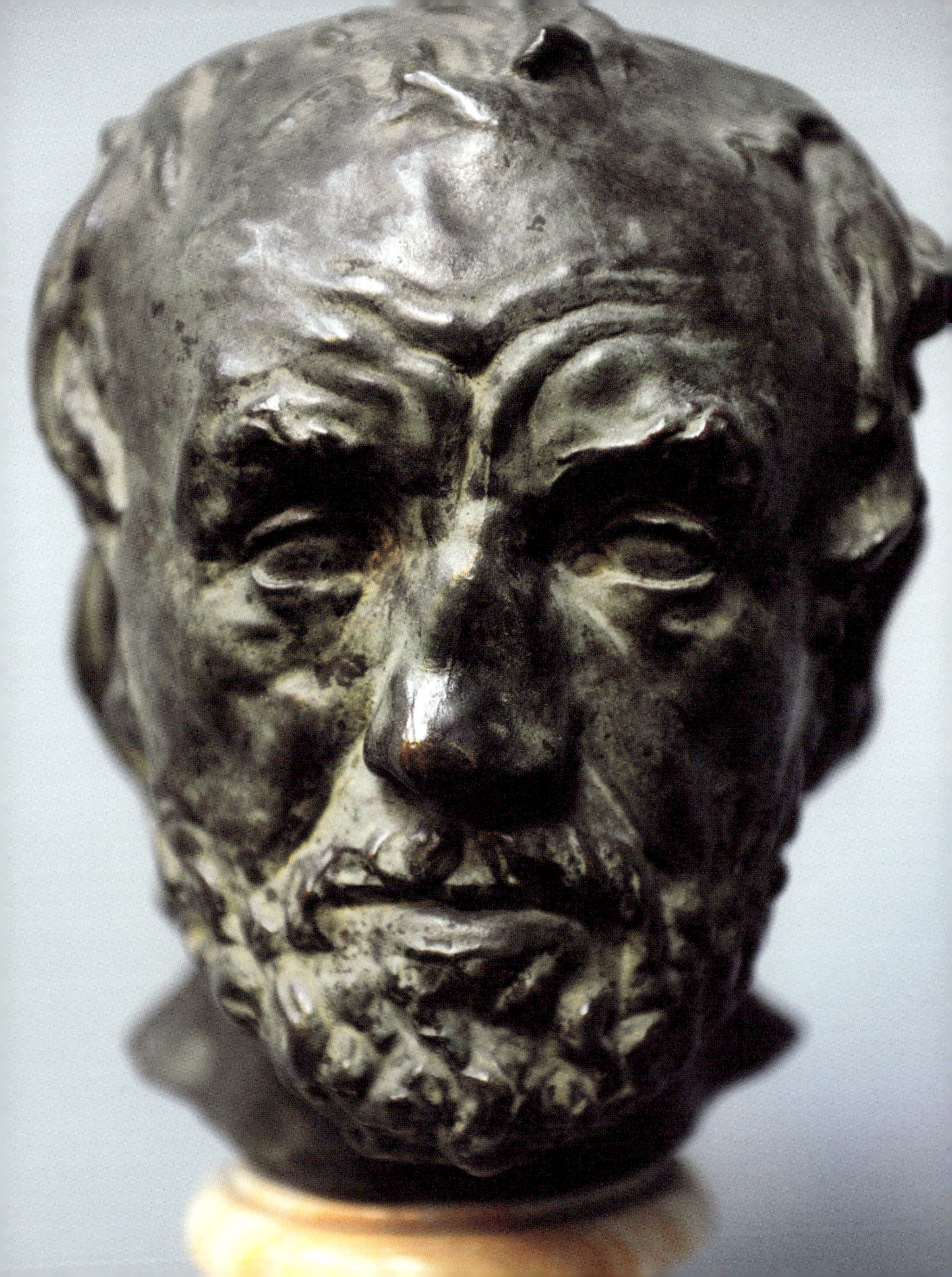

STAND BEHIND YOUR OWN VISION OF BEAUTY

Your idea of beauty may not align with popular opinion.

After early training in decorative arts at the École Spéciale de Dessin et de Mathématiques, **Auguste Rodin** decided to attend the École des Beaux-Arts with the aim of becoming a sculptor – but was rejected on each of the three occasions he applied. Prior to achieving recognition and public commissions, Rodin spent two decades assisting other artists' studios with decorative stonework or plaster modelling, making his own work on the side.

Around the time that he began assisting the sculptor Albert-Ernest Carrier-Belleuse, Rodin rented a studio of his own for the first time, a stable in Paris. Because he couldn't afford to pay a model, Rodin asked the stable's handyman, an older man who was not conventionally attractive and had a broken nose, to sit for a portrait bust. In the 18 months that the artist spent naturalistically rendering the sitter's lined face and misshapen nose in contrast to idealizing and decorative tendencies in sculpture of the time, Rodin began to see the beauty of the man. When the back of the clay mould of the head broke off, the artist decided that he liked the unfinished appearance and cast the mould in bronze, giving rise to *Mask of the Man with the Broken Nose* (1863-4).

Though the work's reception was initially icy – its radically unvarnished realism led it to be rejected from the Salon in 1864, and a contemporaneous sculptor declared that it should be thrown in the trash – Rodin asserted: 'The mask determined all my future work.' Ruminating on beauty in conversation with Paul Gsell in 1910, the artist said: 'The vulgar readily imagine that what they consider ugly in existence is not fit subject for the artist. They would like to forbid us to represent what displeases and offends them in nature. It is a great error on their part... There is nothing ugly in art except that which is without character.

**Auguste Rodin, Mask of the Man with the Broken Nose, 1863-4.
Bronze, 31.8 x 18.4 x 15.6 cm (12½ x 7¼ x 6⅛ in).**

LEARN TO WRITE ABOUT YOUR WORK

Cultivate the writing skills and the language to communicate around your practice.

Mike Kelley, who was born in a suburb of Detroit but spent the bulk of his career at the heart of the Los Angeles art scene, blended high and low culture in subversive and sometimes challenging explorations of abjection, repression, trauma, religion, education and the psyche of American youth. The interdisciplinary artist found himself frustrated with the critical reception of his art when he began to be noticed for his found object assemblages of blankets and soft toys in the 1980s. As reviews accrued, Kelley saw critics radically mispresenting his work and the work of other artists with whom he was associated, erroneously ascribing meaning and intent as they purported to speak for him and his peers.

'I was so unhappy when I was younger with what critics wrote about my work, I was forced into a position of writing about it myself,' said Kelley in a conversation with Isabelle Graw published in 1999. (Five years earlier, he likewise told Robert Storr: 'I really developed my writing skills. I didn't want to. I'm not a natural writer. I did it on purpose and it was not a pleasant task.')

'Those who possess language have an advantage over those who do not,' Kelley wrote in 2002. Beyond the personal empowerment afforded by finding words for – and communicating around – his vision of his work and practice, Kelley established himself as a skilled art writer, covering not only his own oeuvre but also the work of other artists in texts that he published in alternative art publications.

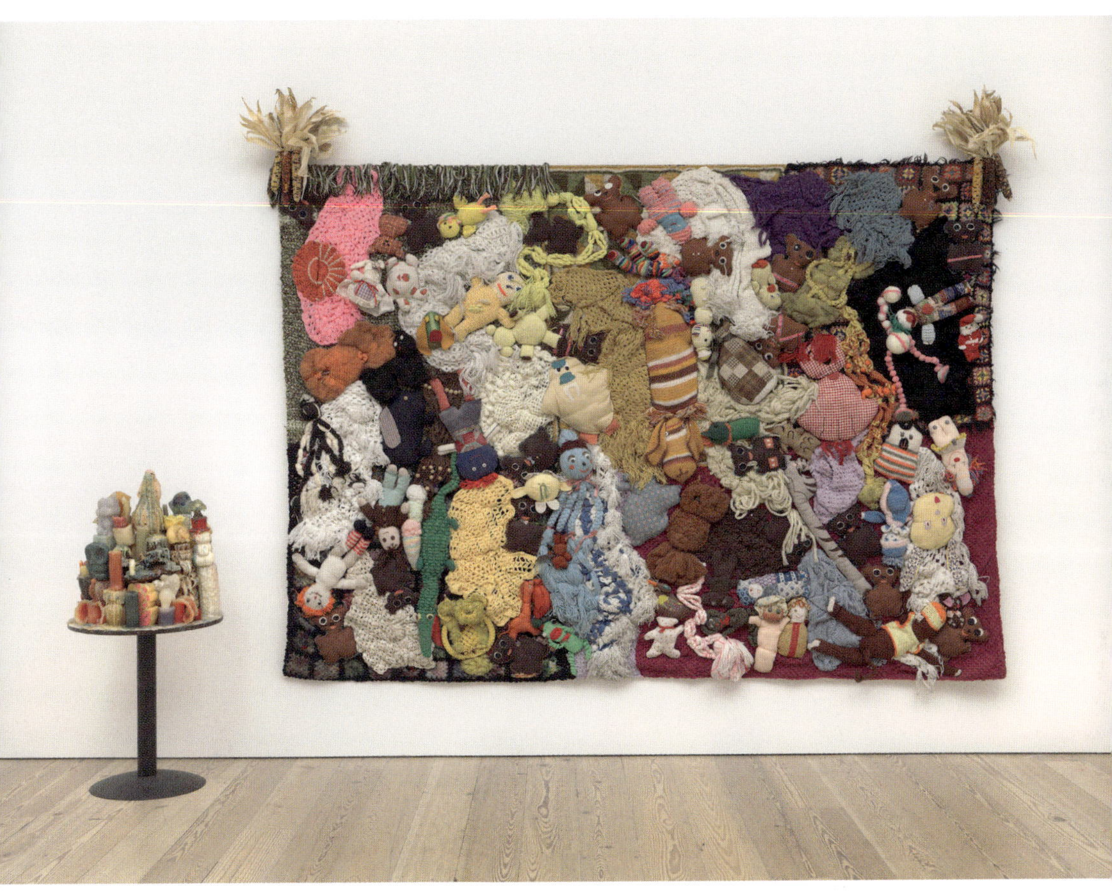

Mike Kelley, More Love Hours Than Can Ever Be Repaid and The Wages of Sin, 1987. Stuffed fabric toys and afghans on canvas with dried corn, wax candles on wood and metal base. Overall: 306.7 x 385.4 x 80.6 cm (120¾ x 151¾ x 31¾ in).

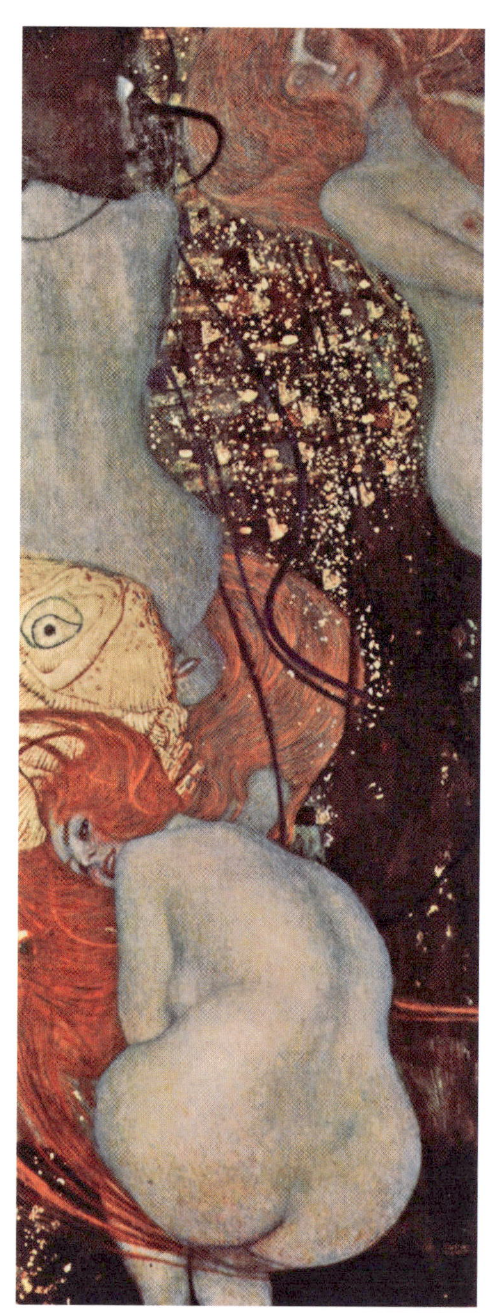

Gustav Klimt,
Goldfish, 1901-2.
Oil on canvas,
181 x 66.5 cm
(71¼ x 26⅛ in).

MAKE SOMETHING OUT OF CRITICISM

Are the critics carping? Use their disapproval to fuel new work.

In 1894, three years before he cofounded the pro-decorative, anti-nationalist Vienna Secession in reaction against the Viennese Academy and conservative salons, Austrian Symbolist painter **Gustav Klimt** received an official commission from the Ministry of Education. Along with the artist Franz Matsch, Klimt was asked to design allegorical paintings for the ceiling of the University of Vienna's Great Hall - specifically, on the themes of Philosophy, Medicine and Jurisprudence.

The first of the sweeping 'Faculty Paintings', *Philosophy* depicted a twisting tower of nudes – an image of human turmoil – and a sphinx, a mythical symbol of knowledge's impenetrability. Members of the public, seeing the painting at the 1900 Vienna Secession exhibition, were scandalized by the work's 'pornographic' nature; university faculty were additionally offended by the implication that reason was powerless against chaos. The subsequent paintings, in which nudes abounded, likewise infuriated viewers, sparking protests from scores of university professors and officials: *Medicine* depicted medicine and science yielding to death and destiny, while *Jurisprudence*, which featured an octopus, suggested that the world was bereft of justice. In 1905, Klimt withdrew from the commission - the last public commission that he would ever have - and repaid his fee with the help of a patron.

During the 'Faculty Paintings' scandal, Klimt created the lustrous painting *Goldfish* (1901-2), originally titled *To My Critics*. An iconic rejoinder, the underwater scene features the titular goldfish as well as four seductive naked water nymphs with diamanté skin, an embodiment of the psychosexual turmoil that so rankled viewers of the 'Faculty Paintings'. One of the naiads turns her rear to the spectator, a clear message to those who would criticize Klimt's creations.

TAKE CONTROL OF THE NARRATIVE

Meet criticism head-on to challenge misrepresentations of your work or assert how you want to be understood.

Proto-Expressionist painter and printmaker **Edvard Munch** channelled his feelings of anxiety, depression and alienation into his work, seeking to exorcize a traumatic childhood rife with death and illness. His iconic painting *The Scream*, the first iteration of which he made in 1893, depicts an agonized, shrieking figure on a bridge under a striated red and orange sky; the work was partly inspired by an onslaught of panic and horror that the artist experienced on a sunset walk with two companions in Oslo. Exhibited in Munch's native Norway at a time when Naturalism was the country's prevailing painterly genre, *The Scream* was met with criticism, much of which questioned or attacked the artist's mental health. In 1895, shortly after the painting was first shown, Munch was publicly called a 'madman', a disparagement that stung.

In 2021, researchers at the National Museum in Oslo determined that a mysterious statement pencilled in tiny letters in the upper left corner of Munch's canvas – 'Could only have been painted by a madman' – was not an act of vandalism. Rather, the words were written by Munch himself two years after making the work, as a means to challenge and take ownership of the painful criticism levied at him. The Oslo museum's curator of old masters and modern paintings, Mai Britt Guleng, explained: 'By writing this inscription in the clouds, he took possession, in a way, or he took control of how he was to be perceived and understood.'

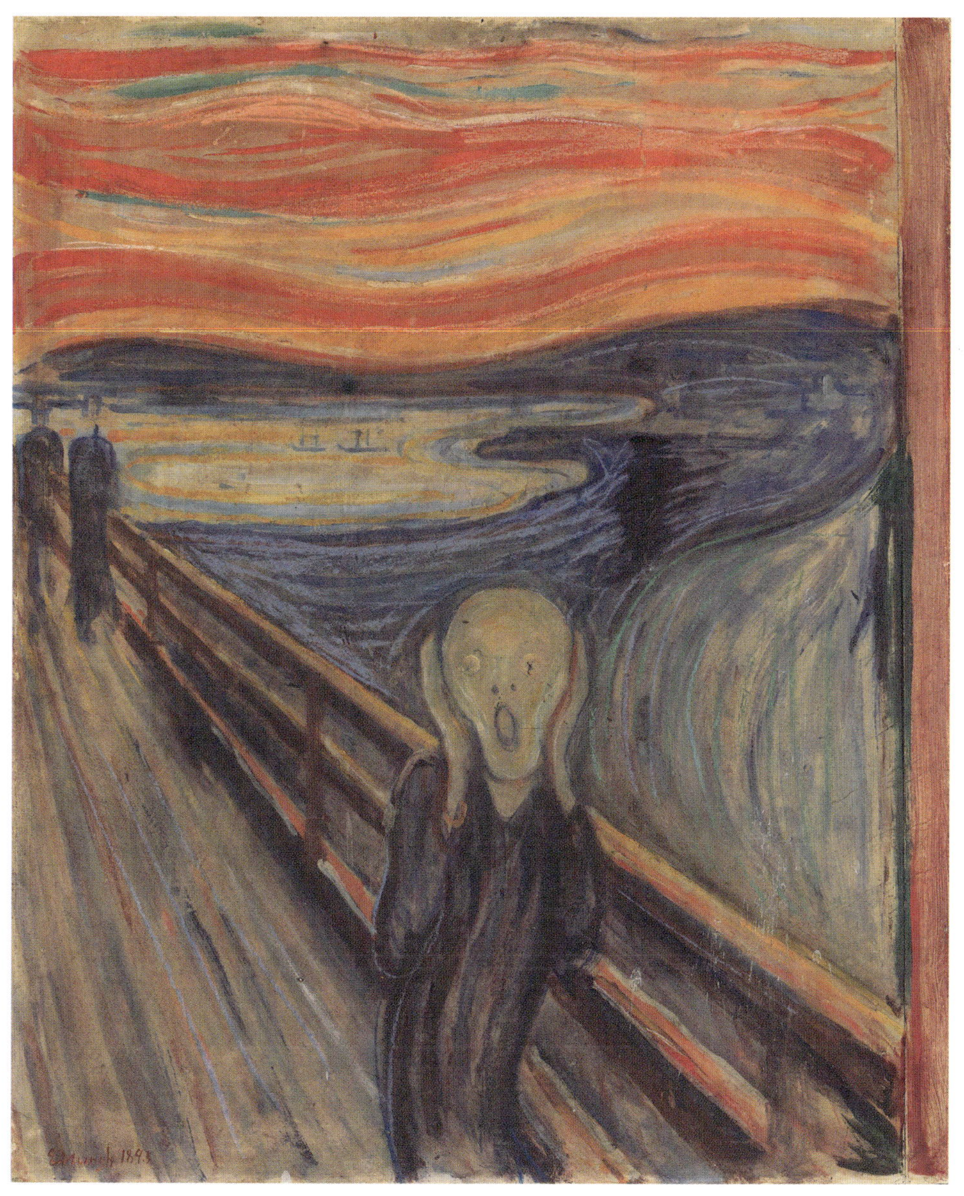

Edvard Munch, The Scream, 1893. Oil, tempera, pastel and crayon on cardboard, 91 x 73.5 cm (36 x 28^{9}⁄$_{10}$ in).

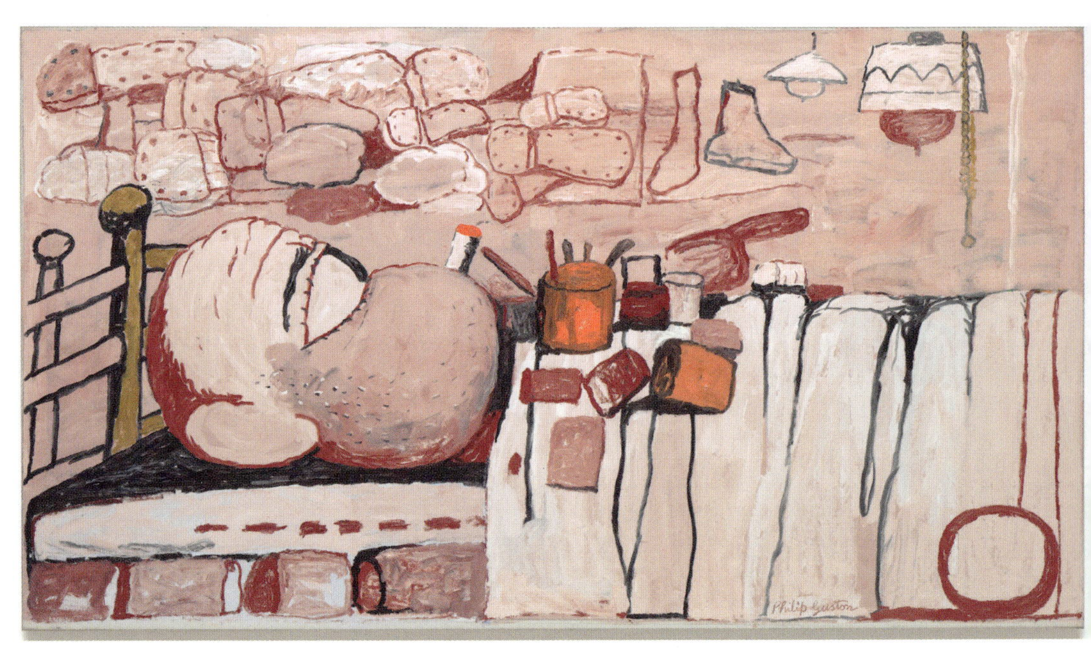

Philip Guston, Painter in Bed, 1973. Oil on canvas, 151.4 x 264.8 cm (59⅝ in x 8 ft 8¼ in).

PAINT EVERYBODY OUT OF THE STUDIO

As you work, try to distance yourself from external voices and influences – including yourself.

In October of 1970, Canadian-American artist **Philip Guston**, whose success as an Abstract Impressionist painter was firmly cemented at the time, debuted a collection of new figurative paintings at Marlborough Gallery in New York City. Prompted by a renewed desire to 'tell stories', Guston's caricatural scenes were a far cry from the elegant and airy - though increasingly concretized - abstractions for which he was known. The new works were characterized by bold graphic lines, clunky forms and a fleshy palette, as well as an idiosyncratic personal iconography of shoes, pointing fingers, books, lightbulbs and hooded Klansmen-style figures who drove cars and smoked cigarettes. The critical response to Guston's pronounced aesthetic shift was largely negative, with art writers deeming the works clumsy, embarrassing or artificial.

Guston, who was thrown by this condemnation, sought a reset after the show. He headed to Italy for a residency at the American Academy in Rome, where he spent seven months immersed in the viewing and making of art; resiliently, he put the critical voices aside and kept on with his impulse to create the cartoonish paintings (sometimes incorporating classical Italian motifs) for which he is most celebrated today. 'You go in your studio and everybody is in the studio - your friends, art writers and museums - they're all in the studio... and one by one they leave until you're really alone and that's what painting is,' the artist told avant-garde composer John Cage. 'You prepare yourself and then ideally you leave.'

GET DISTANCE FROM CRITICISM, THEN DECIDE IF IT'S USEFUL

Give yourself time and space to process negative feedback.

For more than five decades, artist **Howardena Pindell** - who was also the first Black woman to hold a curatorial position at the Museum of Modern Art in New York - has made paintings, drawings and videos that address issues of racism and sexism: both her personal experiences of discrimination as well as the broader societal structures that produce, sustain and propagate bigotry and violence. In her work she has also explored topics such as homelessness, war and genocide. While thematically linked, Pindell's pieces are aesthetically varied, ranging from unstretched canvases full of hole-punched or stencilled dots (a reference to the circles that demarcated mugs from which non-whites could drink in Kentucky) to videos laying out a lifetime of microaggressions or the history of lynching in the United States.

In July/August 2005, *Art on Paper* published a special issue containing letters of advice from 12 established artists addressed to a fictional 'young artist', inspired by Rainer Maria Rilke's correspondence with a 19-year-old seeking feedback on his poetry. In Pindell's letter, which offers a wealth of wisdom acquired over the course of a hard-fought career, the artist counselled that when she receives negative criticism, she writes it down or records it on a tape. 'I find that that gets it off my mind and out of my worrying about it, as I do not need to bother to remember it because it is captured somewhere for me in writing or on tape including my reactions to it,' Pindell wrote. 'Once you have distance from it, you can decide what is useful.' Pindell relinquished misguided criticisms declaring her art to be either insufficiently or overly political, or chiding her to work exclusively figuratively or exclusively abstractly.

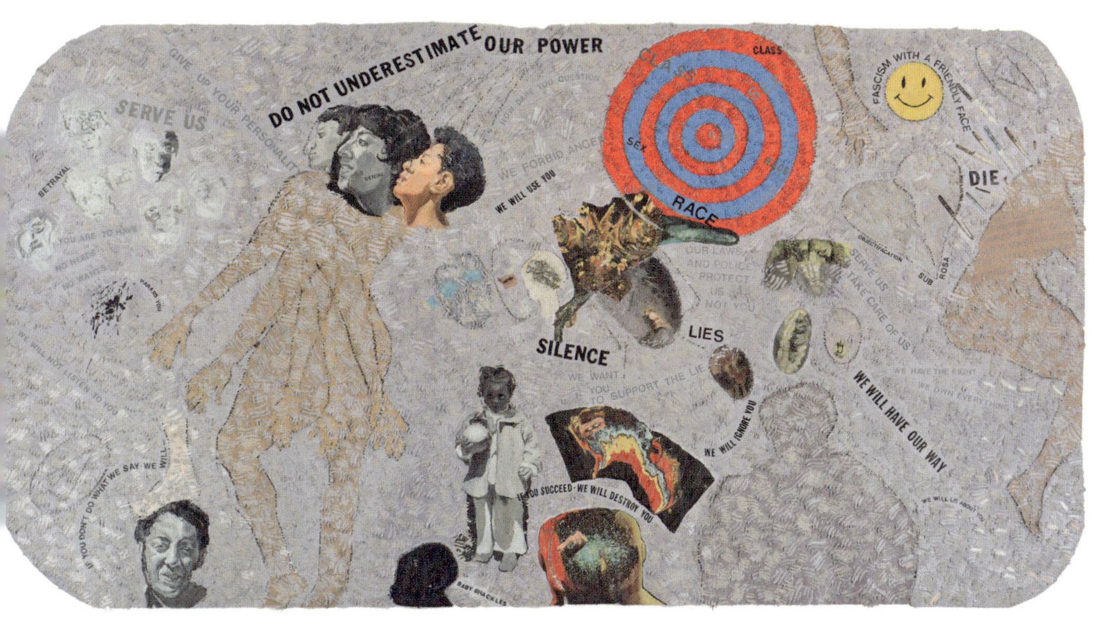

Howardena Pindell, Autobiography: Scapegoat, 1990. Mixed media on canvas, 182.9 x 358.1 cm (72 x 141 in).

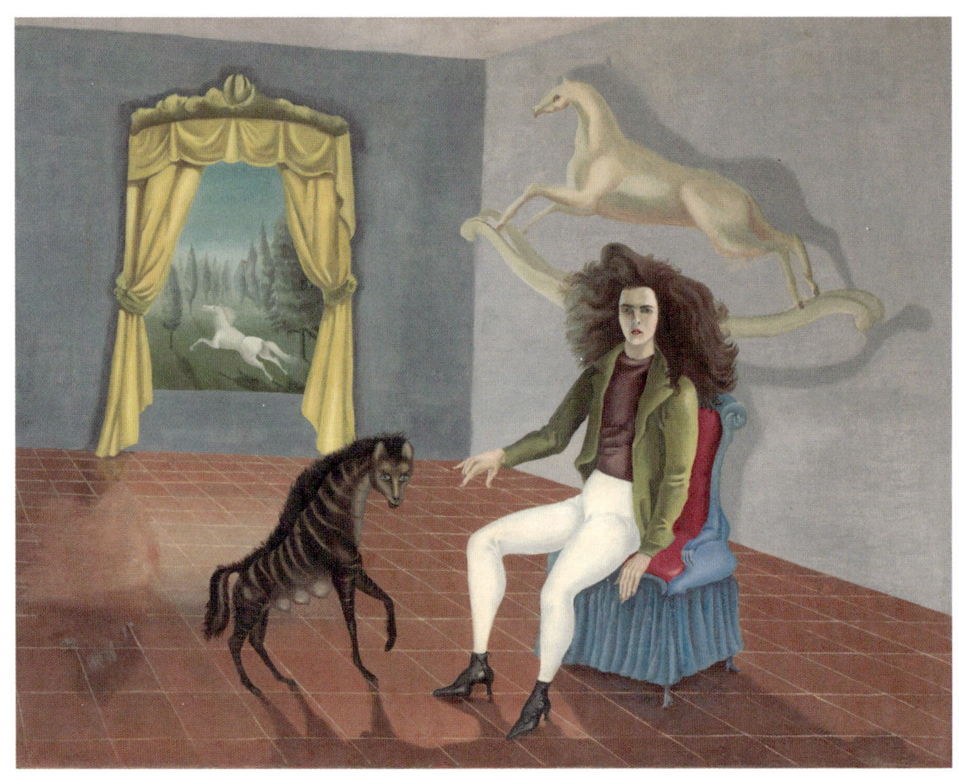

Leonora Carrington, Self-Portrait, 1937–8. Oil on canvas, 65 x 81.3 cm (25⅝ x 32 in).

YOU DON'T OWE ANYONE AN EXPLANATION

Artists are constantly under pressure to explain their work – especially in simple, digestible terms. You can decline to do so.

In a conversation with Silvia Cherem, the Surrealist **Leonora Carrington** offered a word of warning: 'Do not psychoanalyze my paintings,' Carrington cautioned. 'If you continue I will go on strike.'

The British-born artist and writer, who spent time in France, the United States and Spain before permanently relocating to Mexico, was smitten with the fantastical and the occult. Populated by a recurring cast of animal characters, including hyenas and horses, her works across media - most famously paintings, but also drawings, sculptures, textiles and murals - are characterized by a distinctive iconography informed by the artist's deep knowledge of folklore, alchemy, witchcraft, kabbalah, tarot and mythology, with repeated nods to Robert Graves's 1948 book *The White Goddess*, about a matriarchal society.

Encountering Carrington's singular creations can feel like stumbling into a dream with its own impenetrable and shifting logic. With a no-nonsense taste for the absurd, metamorphic and magical, the artist depicted humans and real and mythical creatures of all stripes - and on all scales - holding court in various liminal or otherworldly meeting places: perspectively unsettling rooms, frozen tundras, strangely manicured gardens, empty plazas, outer space.

In interviews, the artist protected the inscrutability of her symbology and declined to expound upon the meaning of her works, being well aware that such elaboration might dilute their powers. Deflecting eager interviewers' theories and queries with retorts including 'I don't discuss that', 'Well, that's what I did', 'There are things that are not sayable; that's why we have art' or 'You're trying to intellectualize something, desperately, and you're wasting your time', Carrington protected the sanctity and mystery of the worlds she created.

ON DEFINING SUCCESS

BY A LOT OF METRICS, SUCCESS IN THE ARTS IS PROFOUNDLY NEBULOUS AND DEEPLY SUBJECTIVE. ARTISTS COUNSEL COURAGE AND PATIENCE AND ADVISE THAT SUCCESS HAS MORE TO DO WITH YOUR ART AND YOUR EXPERIENCE OF MAKING IT THAN WITH YOUR ART CAREER.

IDENTIFY FLUFF

Your relationship with the work you make, and your experience of making it, are the most important things.

American abstract painter **Louise Fishman** approached her medium with the muscled dexterity of an athlete. The artist, who worked intuitively, was not one for preparatory drawing or otherwise pre-planning her gestural compositions. Using not only paintbrushes but also trowels, squeegees, palette knives, scrapers, rags and even wire netting, she would vigorously apply, scrape off and reapply paint to the canvas, letting the picture evolve through continuous reworkings and undoings.

For Fishman, painting was a process of discovery - and the energy of that approach courses through her work like a current of electricity. From her early gridded pieces, emerging from 1960s Minimalism; to her scrawled 'Angry Women' series from 1973, made after she became involved with feminist consciousness-raising and lesbian activism; to paintings that incorporated ashes from a 1988 trip to Auschwitz; to more recent compositions of shuddering, textured blocks of blue and green paint, she led with a whole-bodied belief in her art, regardless of the art world's attitudes towards women and lesbians.

In conversation with painter and art critic Sharon Butler in 2012, Fishman said, 'The painting, and my experience in the studio - and I think most painters would say this - is really all there is. The rest of it is fluff.' After warning against the seductions of art world success, and reliance upon a fickle audience for validation, Fishman added: 'I just want to be able to be in that studio, listen to music that I love, and continue to change, so that there's a flow somehow to the work. I want to be alive, to have a really alive experience of working.'

Louise Fishman, Iron Sharpens Iron, 1993.
Oil on linen, 279.4 x 177.8 cm (110 x 70 in).

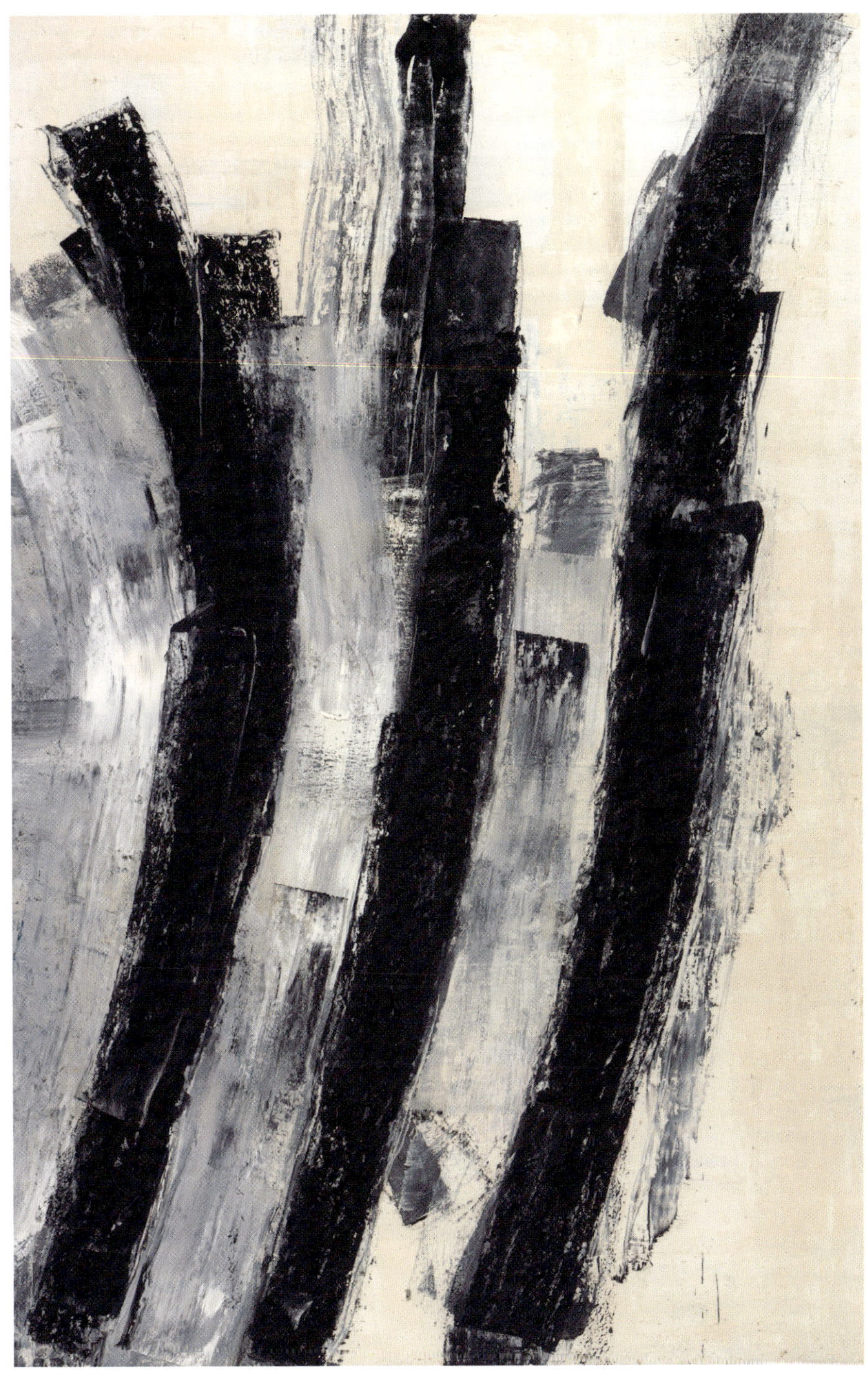

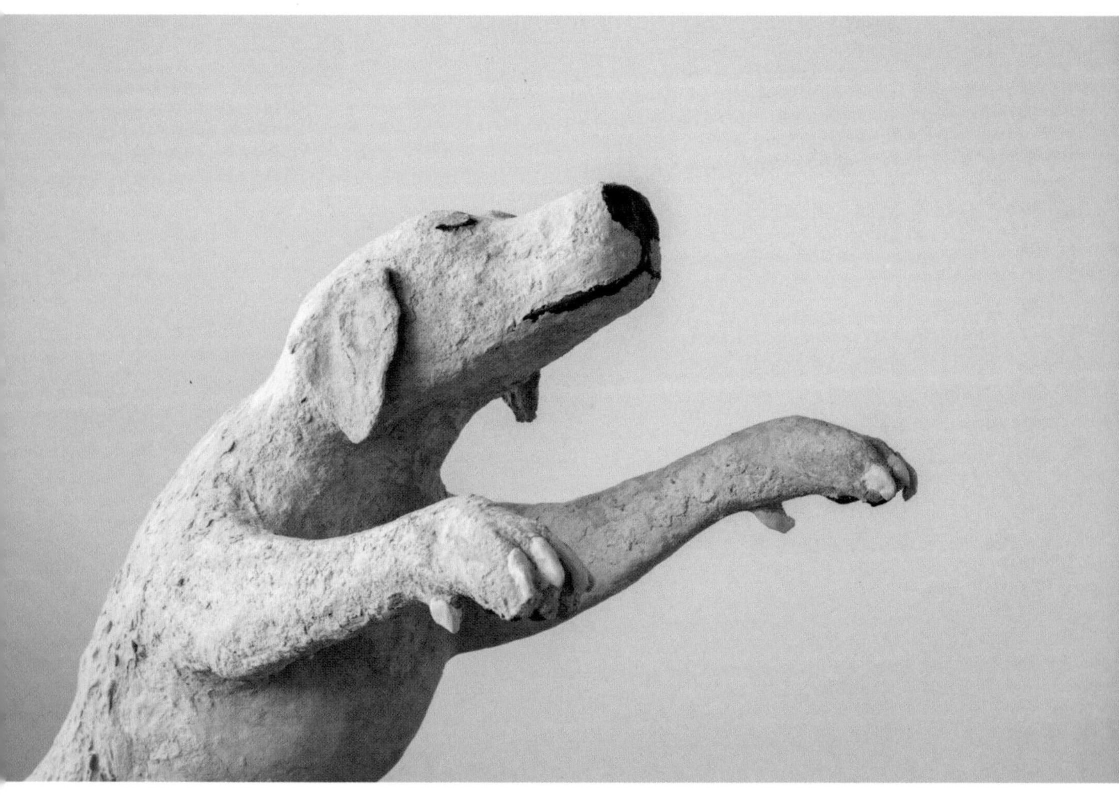

Emilie Louise Gossiaux, Detail of Dancing with London, 2018. Sculptural installation, dimensions variable.

SUCCESS MEANS MAKING ART YOU LOVE

Create work as a monument to the love and care in your life.

'For me, success means being able to make art that I love,' says **Emilie Louise Gossiaux**, an American artist working across sculpture and drawing. 'Make work for yourself and the people you love and care about – whether your family, friends or community.'

Gossiaux's sculptural installation *Dancing with London* (2018) is one such labour of love, made with an important figure in the artist's life in mind. Slathering carved polyurethane foam with layers of papier-mâché, Gossiaux fabricated two larger-than-life canines. The matching dogs stand on their hind legs with their front paws outstretched, their eyes serenely closed as half-smiles hover around their lips. The artist, who lost her vision in 2010, made the installation as a monument to her guide dog, London, an integral and beloved part of her daily life since 2013.

Gossiaux began making *Dancing with London* after London was diagnosed with a tumour. Though the tumour proved to be benign, the experience provoked Gossiaux to contemplate her profound relationship with the dog, whom she views interchangeably as a 'sister, daughter, mother, collaborator and protector'. Recreating an intimate, loving experience that she had with London, who sometimes dances on her hind legs, Gossiaux invites visitors to grasp the sculpted dogs' paws in a dance of mutual affection and interspecies family. London has continued to be a significant subject in Gossiaux's work, as the artist has sculpted human–dog hybrids as well as objects that are important to the canine, including leads, harnesses and chew toys.

BEING AN ARTIST IS A VERY VERY LONG GAME

No matter where you are, there is everything to do yet.

Mumbai-born, London-based sculptor **Anish Kapoor** meticulously engineers optical enigmas that dissolve distinctions between inside and outside, or sculpture and environment. Constructed from materials as varied as pigment, sandstone, resin, plastic, stainless steel, concrete and aluminium, Kapoor's geometric and curvilinear sculptures are typically monochromatic or reflective and characterized by convex and concave surfaces, as well as recesses and voids, that introduce uncertainty into the viewer's perceptions.

Kapoor creates these elegant abstractions on a grand scale for public commissions, the most famous examples of which include 'Cloud Gate' (2004) in Chicago and the 'Sky Mirror' series, iterations of which can be found in the United States, Europe and Asia. While Kapoor - who received a Turner Prize in 1991, was named a Commander of the Order of the British Empire in 2003 and garnered a Knighthood in 2013 - is most widely associated with static if incorporeal sculptures, in the past decade he has declined to rest on his laurels and has instead continued to innovate with installations in which kinetic sculptures move large amounts of red wax.

In an interview with Kapoor broadcast on BBC radio in 2003, John Tusa asked the well-established artist whether he was at a stage in his career - 'stage three' - in which he was asking himself, 'What am I going to do next?' Kapoor responded: 'Being an artist is a very very long game. It is not a ten-year game... I think the idea that somehow one has done what one has to do and therefore you can kind of steadily carry on - well it's not something I recognize. I feel there's everything to do yet.'

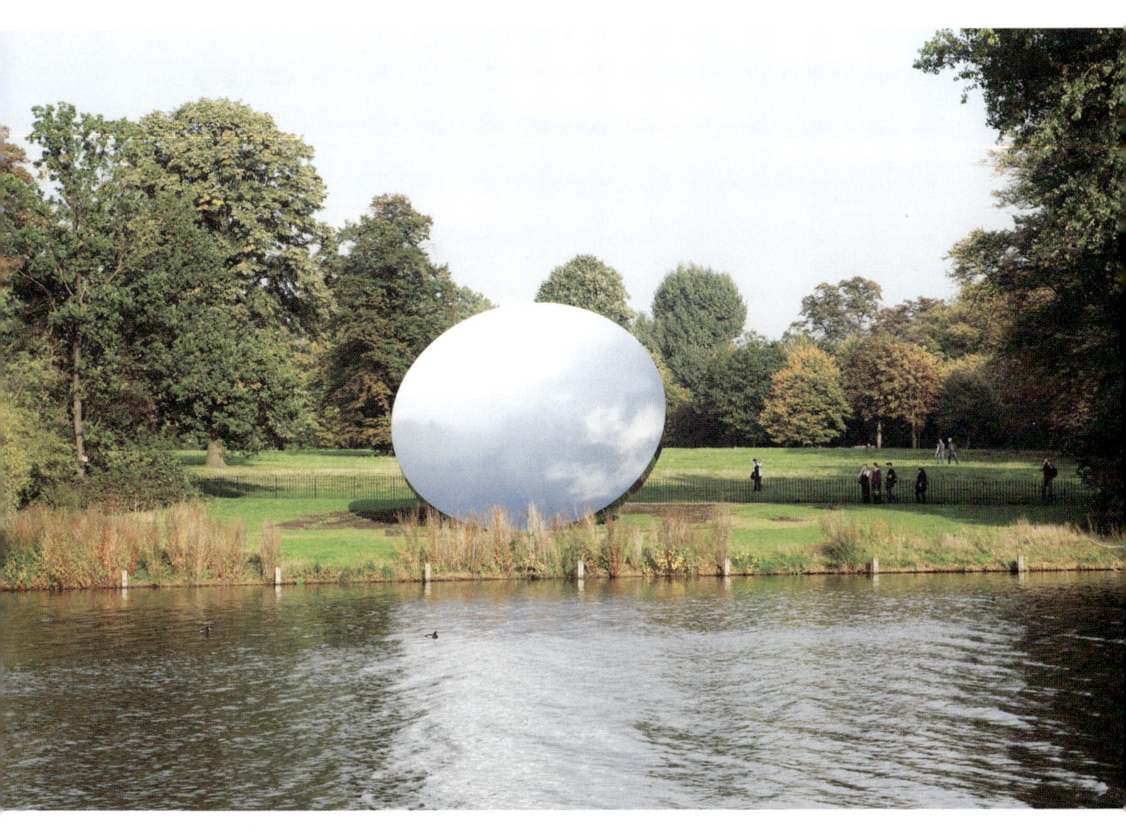

Anish Kapoor, Sky Mirror, 2006. Stainless steel, diameter 10m (32ft).

PUT YOUR ART OVER YOUR CAREER

Sometimes, what is best for your art and what is best for your career are not the same thing.

In her 2016 commencement address at the School of the Art Institute of Chicago, Cuban artist **Tania Bruguera** spoke about a subject commonly referenced at these celebratory speaking engagements: success. After noting what success is *not* – material, monetary, contagious, external – Bruguera offered up an expansive vision of what success *is*, or can be: 'Success is doing your work under any circumstance and to be inspired by every circumstance. It is to be true to yourself. Success is doing what is good for your art even when it is not good for your career.'

In her socially situated practice, Bruguera choreographs interactive performances that directly engage the public. Investigating how power and oppression operate, and either taking to task or intervening with those operations, her projects have included opening an activist art school, embedding herself in an immigrant community in Queens, New York, and forging a temporary public space for free speech in Havana. Bruguera puts her art and the values that drive it over market success, easy accolades, and even personal safety: she has been arrested for her work on multiple occasions.

'SUCCESS SHOULD BE ON YOUR OWN TERMS AND IT SHOULD BE WHATEVER IT MEANS TO YOU, REMEMBER TO BE THE BEST YOU CAN AT WHAT YOU DO BUT NEVER FORGET TO BE A GOOD PERSON BECAUSE WE DO NOT NEED MORE ASSHOLE ARTISTS, SORRY.'

TANIA BRUGUERA

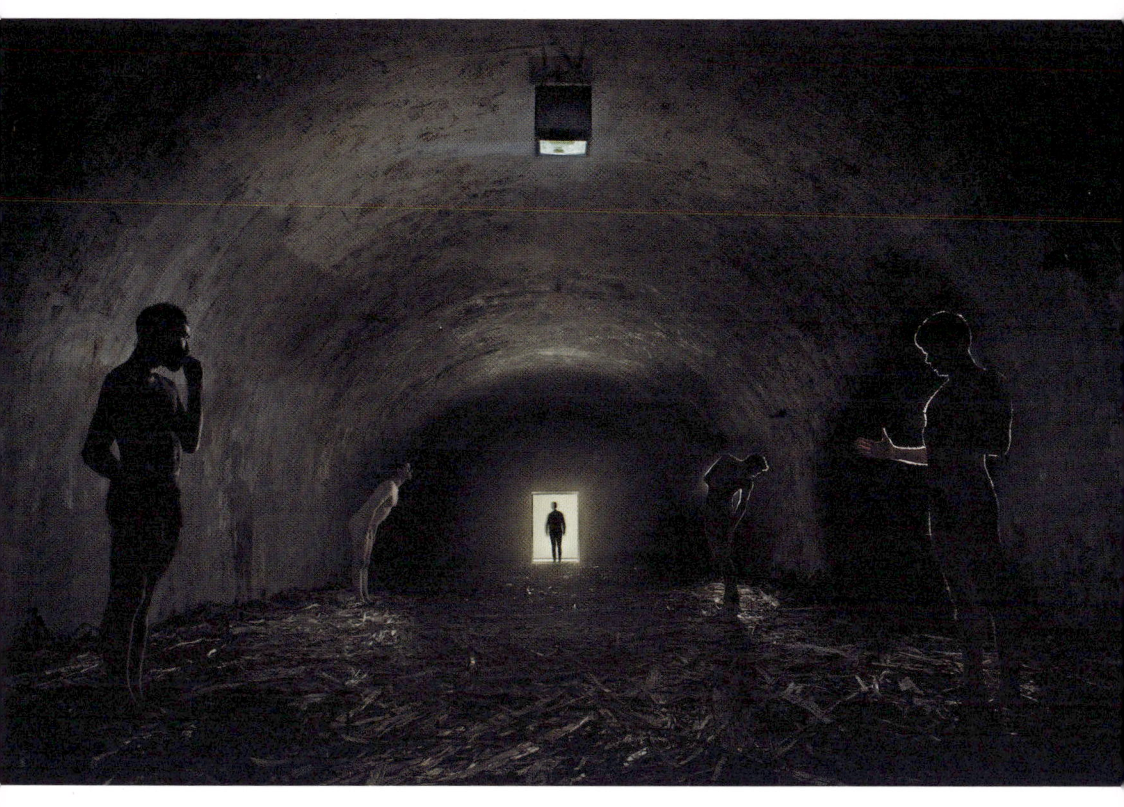

Installation view of the exhibition 'Tania Bruguera: Untitled (Havana, 2000)'. MoMA, NY, 3 February 2018–11 March, 2018.

YOU OWE IT TO YOUR DREAM

Remember that your real obligation is to your artistic vision.

Friends of the Italian sculptor and painter **Amedeo Modigliani**, who is celebrated today for his distinctive, highly stylized portraits and nudes, nicknamed the artist 'Modì', a play on the French word for 'cursed'. Modigliani, who died from tuberculosis at the tender age of 35 after several near-death experiences in his teenage years, had only one solo show in his lifetime – an exhibition of nudes, which was promptly shut down for obscenity – and struggled to sell his work.

An artist from a young age, Modigliani departed Italy for Paris in 1906, seeking an avant-garde milieu that would nurture his artistic growth. Soon, he renounced his bourgeois upbringing and became a full-blown bohemian, with a life marked by, on one hand, poverty and substance abuse, and on the other, frenetic artmaking and a robust artistic community. While Modigliani may have had an overblown belief in the value of suffering, his commitment to his art in spite of hardship was profound. Writing to his friend, the Italian painter Oscar Ghiglia, in 1901, Modigliani advised: 'It is our duty never to be consumed by the sacrificial fire. Your *real* duty is to save your dream. Beauty too has some painful duties: these produce, however, the noblest achievements of the soul.'

Amedeo Modigliani, Female Nude, c.1916. Oil on canvas, 92.4 x 58.9 cm (36⅜ x 23¼ in).

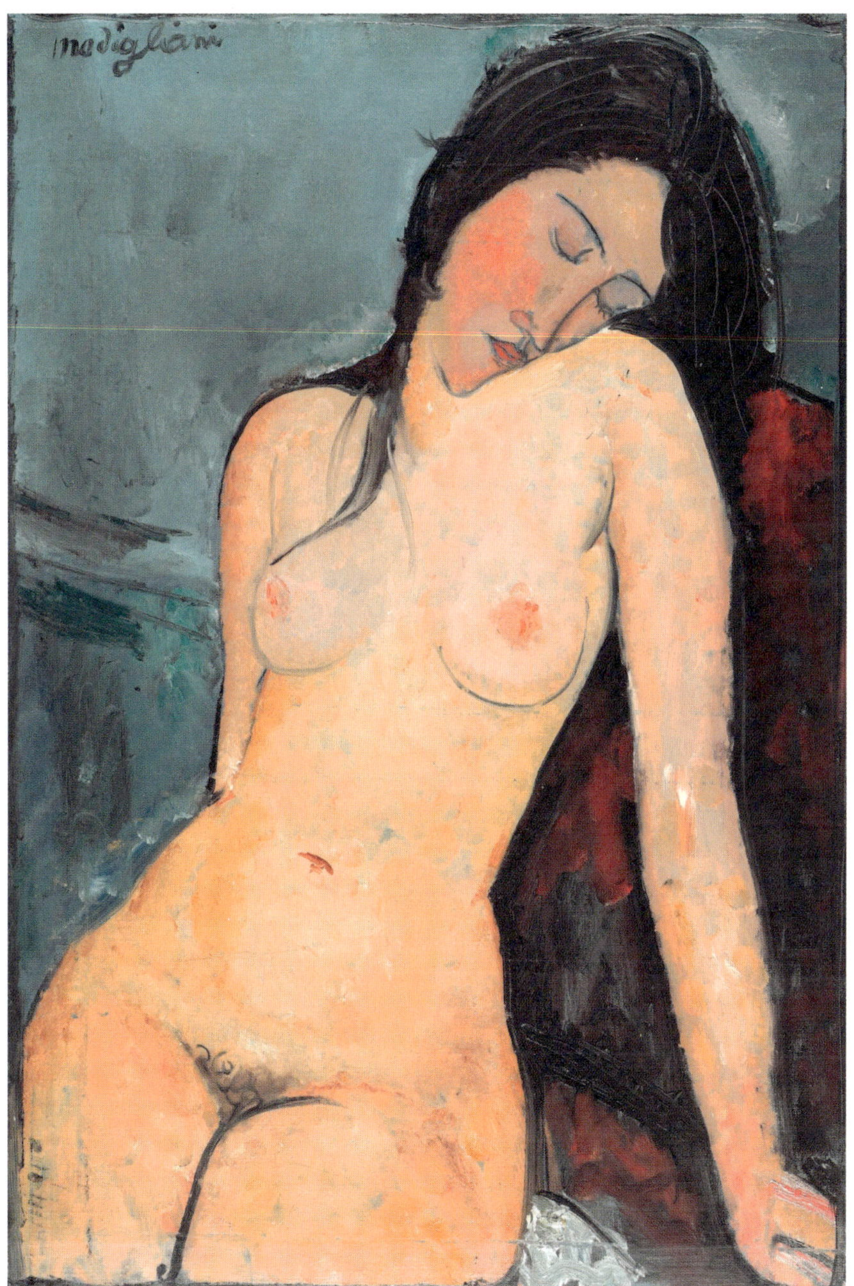
modigliani

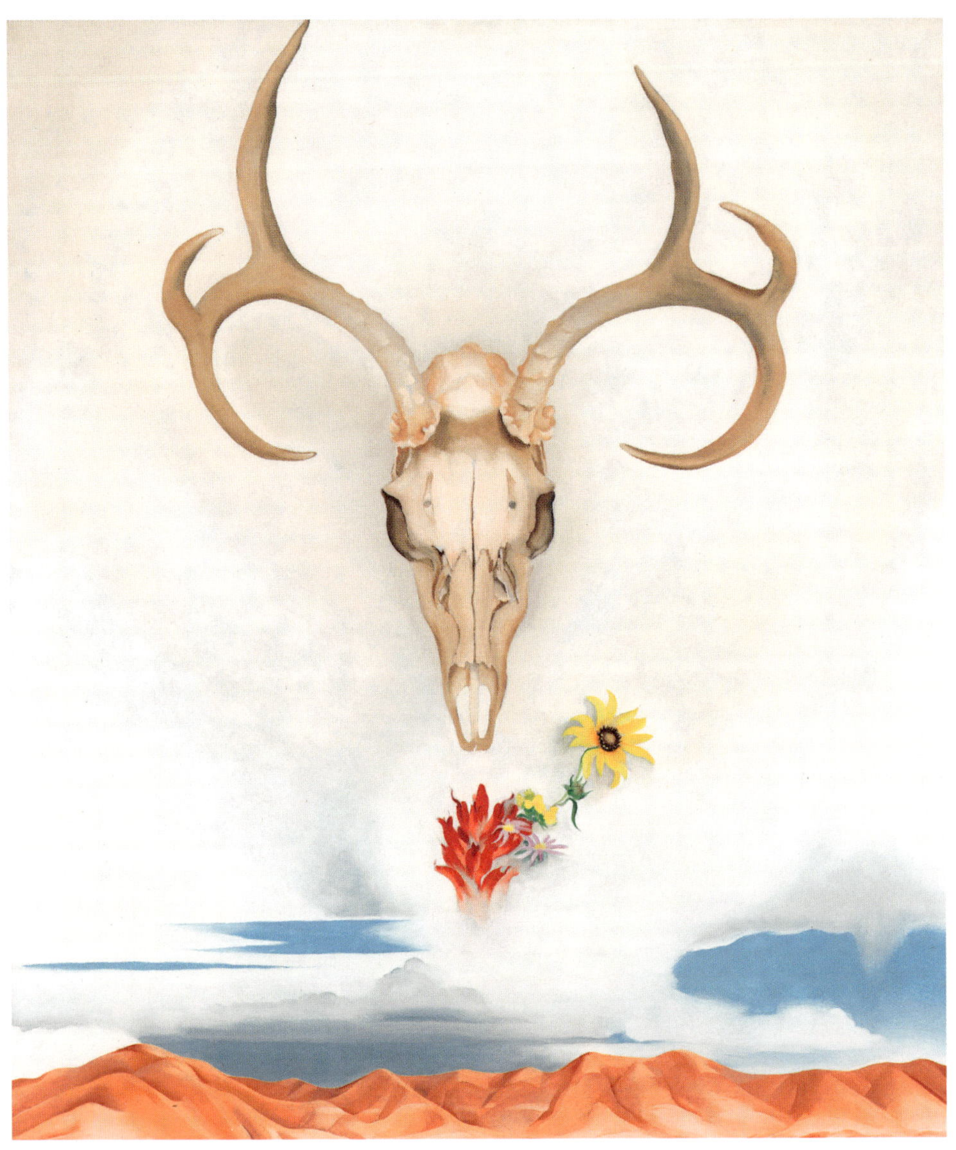

Georgia O'Keeffe, *Summer Days*, 1936. Oil on canvas, 91.8 x 76.5 cm (36⅛ x 30⅛ in).

MAKING YOUR UNKNOWN KNOWN IS THE IMPORTANT THING

Don't chase success; chase the unknown.

Working in watercolour, oil paint, pastel and charcoal, **Georgia O'Keeffe** made self-assured drawings and paintings that were representational yet abstract, observational yet surreal. Throughout her life, she turned to her surroundings for inspiration, depicting skyscrapers and bird's-eye views of the city when she was in Manhattan; lakes, mountains, plants and flowers during regular visits to an upstate New York holiday home that belonged to her lover, and then husband, the photographer Alfred Stieglitz; and churches, deserts, mesas, canyons, flowers, sun-bleached animal bones and sky in New Mexico, which she first visited in 1929. For O'Keeffe, the Southwestern landscape and its forms were inexhaustible: after paying regular extended visits - and bringing bones back to New York with her - for two decades, she relocated to New Mexico for good in 1949.

In O'Keeffe's correspondence with a friend, the writer Sherwood Anderson, in the autumn of 1923, the artist asserted that the presence of a 'real living form' in a work of art resulted from an individual's drive to distill, understand and internalize profound spiritual experiences. Problems of form, O'Keeffe suggested, will take care of themselves if the artist keeps her vision clear and continues to reach for that understanding. 'If I stop to think of what others - authorities or the public - or anyone - would say of my form I'd not be able to do anything,' she wrote, adding: 'Whether you succeed or not is irrelevant - There is no such thing - Making your unknown known is the important thing - and keeping the unknown always behind you - catching, crystallizing your simpler clearer version of life - only to see it turn stale compared to what you vaguely feel ahead - that you must always keep working to grasp.'

SUCCESS COMES FROM FAILURE

Approach failure as part of the process.

Today, **Vincent van Gogh**'s impassioned impasto, skewed perspectives and wildly colourful palette – perhaps especially his inimitable yellow – are indelibly imprinted on the minds of art lovers worldwide, but until the last two years of his life, he had relatively little professional success, and commercial triumphs only arrived posthumously. (Perhaps the situation would have shifted had van Gogh lived longer; the artist, who only began painting in earnest around 1881, died in 1890 at the age of 37.) In his correspondence with his supportive younger brother, the art dealer Theo van Gogh, the Dutch Post-Impressionist often wrote of failure – at times, despairingly, but at other moments, with the acknowledgement that failure, multiple attempts and trial-and-error were all integral to making successful work.

In an 1882 letter to his brother, Vincent described an in-progress watercolour that depicted a group of worshippers in a church pew located in a working-class district in The Hague. He enclosed a rough sketch of the image he wished to render. 'Things like this are difficult, though, and won't come off in one go,' he explained to his brother. 'Success is sometimes the outcome of a whole string of failures.' In another letter sent to Theo several weeks later, the artist added, 'One mustn't begin by despairing; even if one loses here and there, and even if one sometimes feels a sort of decline, the point is nevertheless to revive and have courage.'

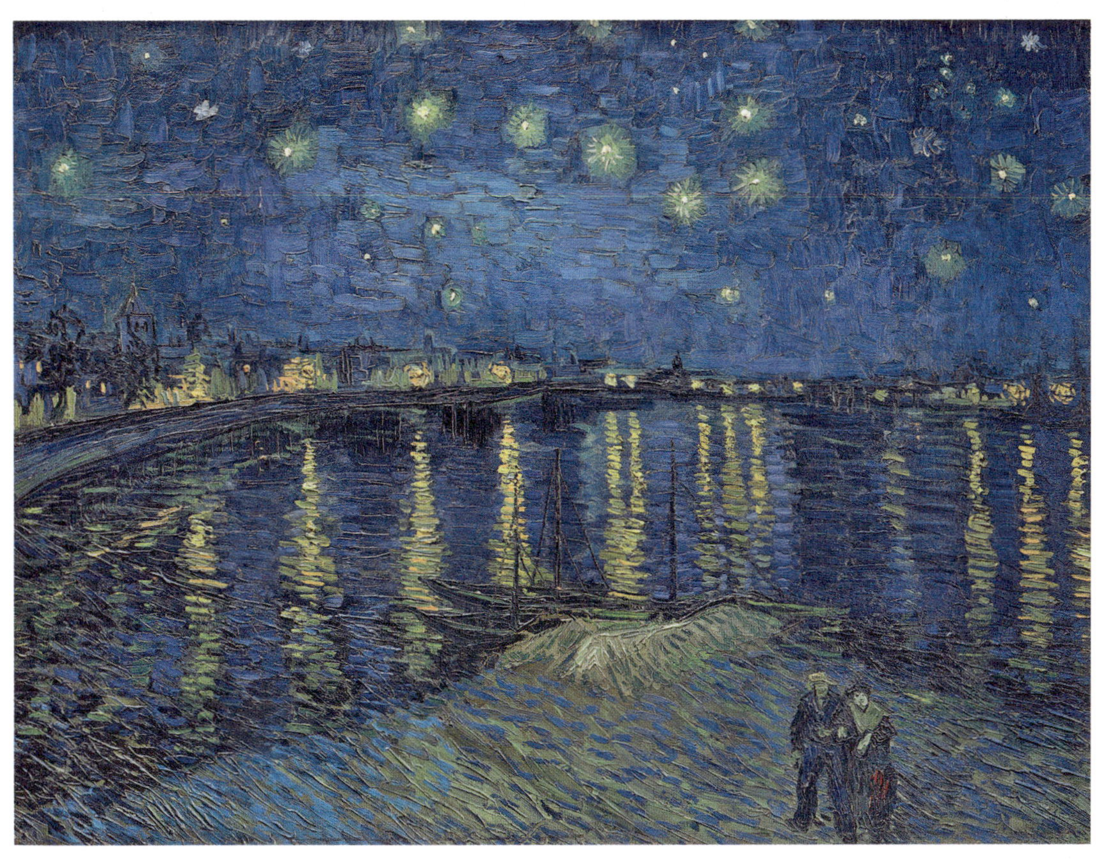

Vincent van Gogh, Starry Night Over the Rhône, 1888. Oil on canvas, 72.5 x 92 cm (28½ x 36⅕ in).

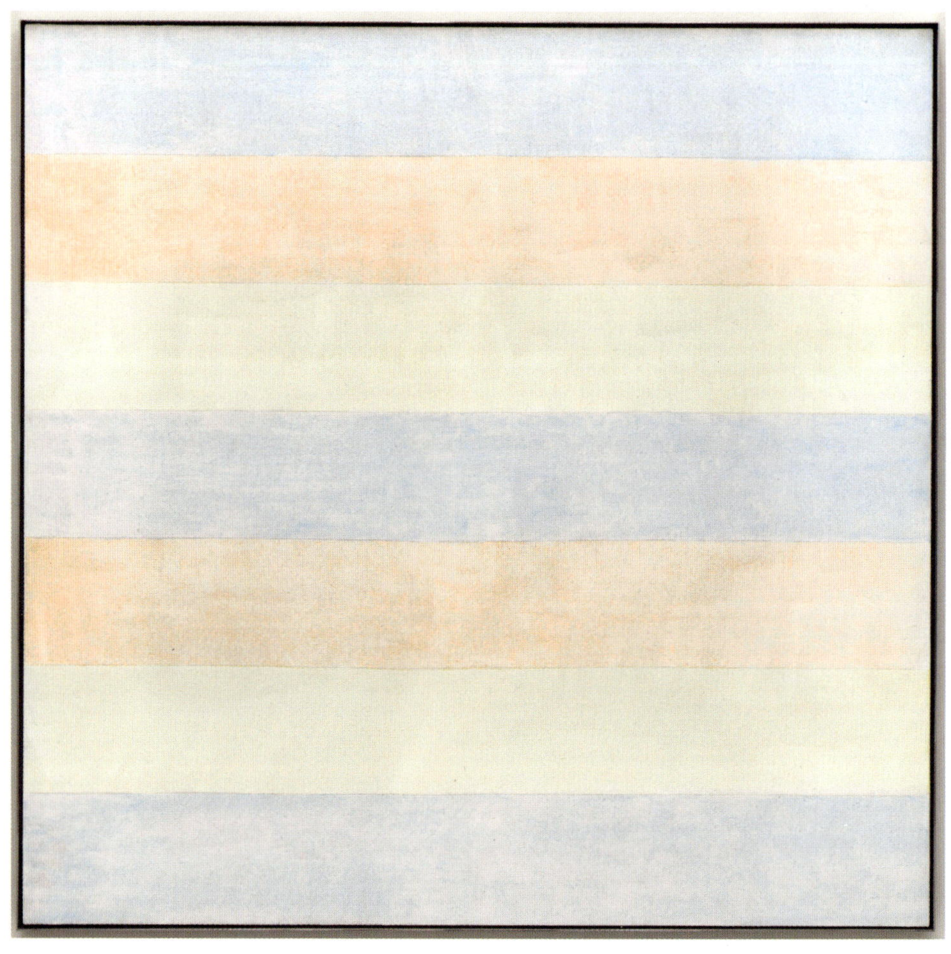

Agnes Martin, Untitled #5, 1998. Acrylic paint and graphite on canvas, 152.4 x 152.4 cm (60 x 60 in).

YOUR PATH IS AT YOUR FEET, WHETHER YOU REALIZE IT OR NOT

You're already on your way.

Agnes Martin's path was an unconventional one. Born in rural Canada, Martin studied art education in New York before relocating to New Mexico, where she shifted her emphasis from teaching art to making it, producing biomorphic paintings in muted hues. At the urging of a gallerist, she returned to New York in 1957, joining an artist community that included Lenore Tawney, Ellsworth Kelly and Ad Reinhardt. Executed in her hallmark subtle palette, Martin's sublime, spare works became increasingly geometric, characterized by delicately pencilled grids on square gessoed canvases.

In 1967, amid mounting struggles with her mental health and the planned demolition of her studio, Martin departed New York. After travelling throughout Canada and the American West in an Airstream, she resettled in New Mexico, where she focused on writing and meditation for several years before returning to her painting practice. The Southwestern landscape permeated her work, as urban grids were supplanted by horizontal stripes.

In her notes for a lecture delivered at Cornell University in 1972, Martin, who was informed by Zen Buddhist and Taoist ideas, described enlightenment and inspiration as phenomena that were available to anyone who was receptive to them and able to access, even for a short time, an untroubled state of mind. 'Do not think [inspiration] is reserved for a few or anything like that,' she advised. 'Your path is at your feet whether you realize it or not. That is the most important thing that I will say but I will not enlarge upon it.'

Further Reading

Ashby, Chloë, *Colours of Art: The Story of Art in 80 Palettes* (Frances Lincoln, 2022).

Battenfield, Jackie, *The Artist's Guide: How to Make a Living Doing What You Love* (Da Capo Press, 2009).

Bhandari, Heather Darcy and Melber, Jonathan, *ART/WORK: Everything You Need to Know (and Do) As You Pursue Your Art Career (Second Edition)* (Free Press, 2017).

Chipp, Herschel B. (ed.), *Theories of Modern Art: A Source Book by Artists and Critics* (University of California Press, 1968).

The Creative Independent (thecreativeindependent.com, 2016- ongoing).

Jacob, Mary Jane and Grabner, Michelle, *The Studio Reader: On the Space of Artists* (University of Chicago Press, 2010).

Morrill, Rebecca (ed.), *Akademie X: Lessons in Art + Life* (Phaidon, 2015).

Obrist, Hans Ulrich, *Hans Ulrich Obrist: Interviews,* Vols. 1 & 2 (Charta/Fondazione Pitti Immagine Discovery, 2003/2010).

Paper Monument (ed.), *Draw It with Your Eyes Closed: The Art of the Art Assignment* (n+1 Foundation, 2012).

Pickens, Beth, *Make Your Art No Matter What* (Chronicle Books, 2021).

Resch, Magnus, *How to Become a Successful Artist* (Phaidon, 2021).

Salle, David, *How to See: Looking, Talking, and Thinking about Art* (W. W. Norton & Co., 2016).

Stiles, Kristine and Selz, Peter, *Theories and Documents of Contemporary Art: A Sourcebook of Artists' Writings (Second Edition)* (University of California Press, 2012).

Storr, Robert, *Interviews on Art* (HENI Publishing, 2017).

Further Viewing

Art21 - Art in the Twenty-First Century (PBS, 2001- ongoing).

BOMB Magazine (New Arts Publications, Inc., 1981- ongoing).

HENI Talks (HENI, 2018- ongoing).

Louisiana Channel (Louisiana Museum of Modern Art, 2013- ongoing).

Acknowledgements

It takes a village to make an art writer, and a book, so I've got some thanking to do!

I'd like to express my gratitude to the team at Quarto, especially Bella, Alice and Joe, for realizing this project with me. This book was a puzzle, and I appreciate the care and diligence with which you nudged the pieces into place.

I want to recognize the magazine editors over the years who have made me a stronger writer and a sharper thinker, more considered in my word choices and more sceptical of my assumptions. What you do is invaluable, and I count myself lucky to have had your keen eyes on my work. I'd also like to thank the research department at Hauser & Wirth, where I learned about due diligence and deep dives.

To artists: I am perpetually floored by your creativity and vision. This book could not exist without you. The art world could not exist without you. Thank you.

A big thank you to my mother, a culture lover and perpetual Queen Bee who took me to museums from a young age and kindly looked the other way when I stayed up late reading. You and Jamie are my staunchest supporters, and I am profoundly grateful to both of you. Lauren, Sam, Charlie and Claire, you're part of this too.

Sara, thank you for everything. On top of the rest, it is a joy to bat around ideas with someone so singularly brilliant.

Thank you, Elyse and Jack, for giving me a home away from home.

I would be remiss not to acknowledge my unflagging live-in editorial assistant, Beckett the Pug.

Dad and Gramma, who both told me I would be a writer one day, I wish you could see this! Maybe you can. I carry you in my heart.

About the Author

Cassie Packard is a Brooklyn-based writer and cultural critic with bylines at publications including *Art in America*, *Artforum*, *ArtReview*, *BOMB*, *frieze*, *Hyperallergic* and *Los Angeles Review of Books*, among others. She has contributed to art books and catalogues and is the recipient of several fellowships.

Quarto

First published in 2023 by Frances Lincoln,
an imprint of The Quarto Group.
1 Triptych Place,
London, SE1 9SH,
United Kingdom
T (0)20 7700 6700
www.Quarto.com

A catalogue record for this book is available from
the British Library.

ISBN 978-0-7112-7029-9
Ebook ISBN 978-0-7112-7030-5

10 9 8 7 6 5 4 3 2 1

Design by Eleanor Ridsdale Colussi
Printed in China

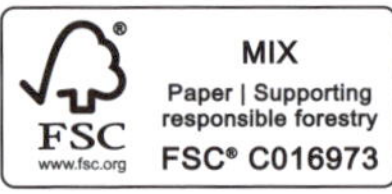